CLANLANDS

CLANLANDS

Whisky, Warfare, and a
Scottish Adventure Like No Other

SAM HEUGHAN
AND GRAHAM MCTAVISH

with Charlotte Reather

HODDER &
STOUGHTON

First published in Great Britain in 2020 by Hodder & Stoughton
An Hachette UK company

I

A CIP catalogue record for this title is available from the British Library

Hardback ISBN 9781529342000
Trade Paperback ISBN 9781529351309
eBook ISBN 9781529342024

Typeset in Dante MT by Hewer Text UK Ltd, Edinburgh
Illustration by Owain Kirby (owainkirby.co.uk)
Maps & diagrams by Rosie Collins (rosiecollins.co.uk)
Lyrics to 'Scotland the Brave' written by Cliff Hanley
'Massacre of Glencoe', words and music by Jim McLean
'Porridge' by Spike Milligan, reproduced with permission
from Spike Milligan Productions LTD
'Spean Bridge' by Barbara McPhail, 2003. Reproduced with
permission from the Estate of Barbara McPhail
Extract from *Homes & Properties* magazine, © James
Mowbray / The Evening Standard
Printed and bound in Great Britain by Clays Ltd, Elcograf S.p.A.

Hodder & Stoughton policy is to use papers that are natural, renewable
and recyclable products and made from wood grown in sustainable
forests. The logging and manufacturing processes are expected to
conform to the environmental regulations of the country of origin.

Hodder & Stoughton Ltd
Carmelite House
50 Victoria Embankment
London EC4Y 0DZ

www.hodder.co.uk

This book is for my Mum and Dad who showed me the power of dreams, and for my children, Honor and Hope, who have given me more than I could ever have dreamed of.

– Graham

To our fans. For coming on this journey and always supporting me.

To Scotland and its people for remaining welcoming and progressive. I hope we always embrace newcomers to experience the mountains, glens . . . and midges.

'Alba' has constantly inspired me and filled my heart.

– Sam

CLANLANDS ROUTE

NORTH ATLANTIC OCEAN

THE MINCH

NORTH SEA

HIGHLANDS

Outer Hebrides

Prickly Thistle

INVERNESS
Castle Leod
Cawdor Castle
Lochardil Hotel
Clava Cairns
Eden Court Theatre
Urquhart Castle · Loch Ness
GREAT GLEN
Drumossie Moor/
Culloden Experience
Museum

Inner
Hebrides

Glencoe Folk
Museum
Achnacarry Castle
Clachaig Inn
Kingshouse Hotel
Glencoe Mountain Resort
GLENCOE
OBAN
Finlarig Castle
Kilchurn Castle
Taychreggan Inn
Balquhidder
· Loch Awe
Monachyle Mhor Hotel

ATLANTIC OCEAN

LOWLANDS

IRISH SEA

ENGLAND

N
W — E
S

0 kilometres   50
0 miles   20   40

Foreword

Well, in The Beginning . . . there was a man in a kilt.

I've always figured that if there's something you want to do, you should start doing it, and if it's the right thing, the universe kind of comes out to meet you. So, I started writing a novel about a man in a kilt, and the universe brought me a television show.

I've been indirectly responsible for a lot of strange things since I wrote *Outlander* – from:

. . . five seasons (so far) of a hit TV series

. . . the names of dozens of purebred dogs, racehorses and housing developments

. . . thousands of babies named Brianna or Jamie (no one has ever, to my knowledge, named a child 'Murtagh', which is puzzling . . .)

. . . Lord John Grey's Tea

. . . symphonic band compositions

. . . a musical

. . . a Scottish woolen mill specialising in tartan

. . . a marvelous pair of cookbooks

. . . three million knitted cowls

. . . dozens of female fans who lower their trousers at book signings to show me 'Da mi basia mille' tattooed on their tailbones (as my husband remarked to me, 'Well, how many people can say, "Kiss my ass" in classical Latin?')

. . . a 72% increase in Scottish tourism (as VisitScotland was kind enough to tell me), and

. . . an excellent whisky called 'Sassenach'

But this book may be one of the strangest, and definitely one of the best!

I'm deeply honoured that Sam and Graham have asked me to write the foreword to one of the most interesting, unusual (to put it mildly . . .) and hilarious books I've read in a long time. I'm not quite sure what you'd call it, but then I'm used to not being able to describe my own books in twenty-five words or less, so this is probably not a problem.

To start with, it's a buddy book. Two good friends banter (and bicker) their way across the Scottish Highlands, risking life and limb in that casual way that makes men attractive. Why? Well, because they're both Scottish and they have both been a large part of *Outlander* (not just the television show, but the whole weird phenomenon), have realised that they *are* Scottish (wearing a kilt every day for two years will do that to you), and want to find out where their heritage came from and what being Scottish actually means (aside from being born liking whisky).

It's also a road book. (Think Jack Kerouac, but with fewer drugs, more paragraphs and no sex. Well, almost no sex . . .).

Our two friends are in fact making a television series about several historical locations in the Highlands. Accompanied by a small film crew – including a talented makeup artist and a drone operator – they visit spectacular historical locations in the Scottish Highlands to learn the true history of some of the best-known massacres, fights, betrayals, beheadings, and other typically Scottish recreational activities. This is the story of that journey, accomplished via an aged Fiat campervan, tandem bike, kayak and any number of other improbable modes of transport that only make sense to people suffering from testosterone poisoning.

And on their way, they talk. Not only to each other, but to themselves. In some of its phases, the book is a twin memoir. Each man recalls his life as an actor – in bits – because every actor (like every writer) pretty much makes it up as they go along. Which means a lot of the stories are of the kind that are only funny to the protagonists with twenty years' perspective, but are endlessly entertaining to the spectators.

These reminiscences include a good many stories from the *Outlander* set, as well. I'm only on set myself intermittently, but I do recall the day in Season Two when Sam's horse – which he was preparing to mount – decided to take its mother's advice and relieve itself before setting out (there's a reason why most costumes are made in multiples). And another occasion during Season Two wherein Graham was required to ride a mechanical horse (as the director said to me, 'It looks like shit, but you won't be able to actually see it on film').

The mechanical horse was carried on the back of a truck, followed by another truck with a camera, and Graham was supposed to leap into the mechanical horse's saddle while moving (supposedly jumping from another horse). This being television, they filmed the scene many, many times to ensure enough footage to get the effect they were after. When they finally stopped, Graham staggered downhill from the road where they'd been doing this, pausing by me and Anne Kenney (brilliant writer of the other episode in that block of filming) to say, 'I've just been having a conversation with my balls. They said, "We'd really rather you didn't do *that* again"'. And staggered on, muttering, 'I knew I should have worn a cup this morning . . .'.

And finally, there's the actual history of the 'clan lands', woven through this tale of a journey. The travelers reach the most interesting/famous/relevant Highland locations, where they *do* learn what their history and heritage are, assisted by some of the most colorful inhabitants of those places.

So, you're actually getting four books in one! (A real bargain . . .).

But the most important part of this book is the friendship between its authors, that colours and illuminates every page.

I was both intrigued and immensely entertained by the story, but also touched on a personal level. One of the most unexpected aspects of the whole 'Outlander phenomenon' is the amazing way in which it seems to draw people together. People read the books and watch the show – and they want to talk about it. So, they form fan groups and book clubs and Facebook forums, and deep, lasting friendships, all because of a shared love of a story.

I will always recall one woman who brought me a book at a signing, who told me that she lived alone, had been alone for many years, seldom got out and had no family – but that she'd become attracted to the story, found others who felt likewise, and who invited her to go with them to book-signings, premieres and conventions. 'Now I have friends!', she said. She cried, and so did I.

I hope you'll feel that sense of friendship in these pages.

A final word, since this book is all about returning to one's roots:

Some years ago, one of my novels won the Corine International Prize for Fiction, and I was invited to go to Germany to accept the award. This was rather a Big Deal for the German publisher, and they took advantage of my presence to have me interviewed by the entire German press corps; newspapers, magazines, radio, television, literary journals, you name it. By the end of the week I was sleep deprived and a bit glazed over when I met a nice gentleman from one of the literary journals.

Delightful man, he went on at great (and flattering) length about the books. He loved my narrative drive, my characters were tremendous, my imagery transcendent!

So I'm sitting there in a pleasant daze, thinking, 'Yes, yes, go on . . .', when he suddenly said, 'There is just one thing I wonder: can you explain to me, what is the appeal of a man in a kilt?'.

Well, had I been totally conscious, I *might* not have said it (then again . . .). Anyway, I looked at him for a moment and said, 'Well . . . I suppose it's the idea that you could be up against a wall with him in a moment.'

<ahem>

A few weeks later, home again in Arizona, I get a packet of interview clippings from the German publisher, and on the top is the interview from *that* journal. The publisher had attached a Post-it note, saying, 'I don't know what you said to this man, but I think he is in love with you!'.

A man in a kilt. A very powerful and compelling image, yes . . .

And now you have *two* of them . . .
Pour yourself a good dram, open the covers and enjoy yourself!

Slàinte mhath!
Diana Gabaldon
Scottsdale, Arizona
August, 2020

CHAPTER ONE

Taken for a Ride

'The story of two men who know nothing.'
Sam and Graham

'It's a dangerous business, Graham, going out your door. You step onto the road, and if you don't keep your feet, there's no knowing where you might be swept off to.'
Sam Heughan on behalf of
J.R.R. Tolkien, *The Lord of the Rings*

INT./EXT. CAMPER VAN. CAR PARK. GLENCOE VALLEY.
SCOTTISH HIGHLANDS – DAY (September 2019)

GRAHAM
AS I BUCKLE up in the passenger seat of the Fiat Auto-Roller Camper a creeping sense of dread begins to form in my stomach – I have never been driven by Sam before. Ever. We all know our own

abilities. I'm a very good driver. I have a fast mid-life-crisis car; however, I do not exceed the speed limit. (Okay, maybe I've exceeded the speed limit a *couple* of times) and in forty years I've never had an accident. Sam, on the other hand, has a litany of prangs and scrapes to his name.

Whilst in Los Angeles he locked his keys in the boot, reversed a Mustang into a post (which apparently 'came out of nowhere') and scratched a brand-new electric car down the entire passenger side, allegedly the fault of the City of Angels as it was 'a bad place to put a pipe'.

I look at his boyish grin as he jiggles the gearstick, barely able to stifle sniggers, and realise this is a man capable of *anything*. Perhaps he'll drive us off a cliff, just to see what it's like. Perhaps he'll jump out as we are moving, leaving me to wrestle control of a runaway RV. All these thoughts swirl around my hung-over brain as Sam engages 'reverse' on the gearstick.

Ka-chunk wheeeeeeeeeeeeerrrrrrrrrt ka-chunk

I assume he's engaged the clutch but the screeching of the gearbox tells me otherwise. He manhandles the gears some more, looking at me with the smile of a psychopath and, in that moment, *Clanlands* is born – with no plan, no script, just our true selves: a man masquerading as a tough guy about to be driven by a *total maniac*.

I know with certainty Sam is going to find new and awful ways to risk my life.

Sam: As if I would . . .

He casually tells me he hasn't driven a manual for five or six years and never anything as big as a large camper van. Marvellous.

Sam: I've no idea which pedal to use?

Graham: You *are* joking?

Sam: No. Er, ABC.

Graham: Yes, but which order? Does it start from the left?

Sam: It starts from the left.

Graham: No. It's from the right. Accelerator, Brake, Clutch.

In modern driving parlance it also means Antecedent, Behaviour, and Consequence, but this is a man who thinks he can bluff his way through, act the part of a competent driver and that consequences are just exciting events that haven't happened *yet*.

SAM

Sam: You all right there, Graham?

If he had a handbag, McTavish would be clutching it tightly now and we hadn't even left the car park. Yes, there is a gear crunch or two but in my defence I've not driven a manual (stick shift) for years, maybe five or six . . . and never a vehicle as big as this, not that I am going to tell Graham . . . yet. I finally find reverse, take a breath and back out at speed.

Graham: *Jesus!*

As Graham holds onto the handrail, squirming in his seat, I get a surge of adrenalin – this is going to be fun, even if we don't make it out of the car park. Just seeing him squeak and squawk is deeply satisfying. He gives me a withering look as I crash the gearstick into first and we start gaining speed, missing the Kingshouse Hotel sign by inches.

'Well, here we go!' I say with great confidence. 'Clanlands, the story of two men who . . .'

'. . . know nothing!' Graham finishes.

And he is right. We are setting off on a journey together – a journey of discovery to find the real Scotland and what it means to be Scottish, but we only have a rough plan. We know we want to discover more about six of the main Highland clans and meet as many interesting people as possible, from clan chiefs (still bickering) to musicians, historians, chefs (Graham needs feeding) and, of course, master distillers (well, why not?). But with only a week to pack everything in, it's going to be a full-on adventure fuelled by whisky, adrenalin and caffeine.

HuuuuhhhhhuurrruH-GUNKKKK

Graham: That's second, not fourth.

GRAHAM

We are starting in, arguably the heart of the Highlands – Glencoe – a steep-sided glen (valley) formed by an ice-age glacier which the

River Coe runs through. It's an area of Scotland I know well having
visited and holidayed here many times and it's also the site of the
1692 Glencoe Massacre, which piqued my interest in Scottish history
over twenty years ago.

Well, in 1992 to be exact.

I was the ripe old age of thirty-one. It shocks me to think that
Sam was probably only getting ready to start secondary school and
was possibily still in short trousers. Perhaps wetting the bed? I'm
going to take a moment to absorb this painful realisation.

I was at Pitlochry Festival Theatre, doing the season there,
immersed in the Highlands for nine months performing six different plays a week. It was fantastic. I've always been fascinated by the
Highlands and felt a deep connection to the area. My father couldn't
wait to get away from Scotland. Born and raised in Glasgow, as a
pilot he had travelled the world. Whenever he flew over Scotland he
always used to say it was cloudy! So whatever caused me to become
so interested in the Highlands and their history came from within;
almost like some kind of 'race memory', a notion which says experiences that have happened to a group of people or 'tribe' over
hundreds of years can be passed on.

Whilst at Pitlochry I'd become fascinated with the infamous
massacre at Glencoe and had previously done exhaustive research at
the British Library. My plan was to write something for the 300th
anniversary of Glencoe so I wrote a treatment called *Clanlands* and
tried to get people interested in making it into a TV programme
with me, but as a thirty-year-old Scottish theatre actor that was
never going to happen.

Years later I'd talked to Sam many times about my love of Scottish
history on the set of *Outlander*, as one of the things I immediately
liked about him was his enthusiasm for such a lot of things. Sam
loves to jump in but little did I know when I met him again, six years
later, he'd be behind me on a tandem bike in Argyll. But I'm getting
ahead of myself . . .

In March 2019, I was standing in my kitchen in New Zealand
when Sam called. He knew I'd been thinking about doing a documentary about Scottish history, and wondered if we could do
something together as a podcast. It was instantly appealing to

imagine sitting and bantering with him over whisky in a pub. However, it wasn't long before the idea of a podcast had turned into us planning to use GoPros to film ourselves while we walked and talked.

Great, I thought, even though I had no idea how this would actually work. My grasp of technology is tenuous at the best of times, so I was imagining Sam recording excellent footage of me, while I still hadn't managed to even press 'play' on my device.

Then, Sam suggested an actual TV camera, with actual people, actually knowing what they were doing. Okay – this was getting bigger. We decided our way into Scottish history was through its clans, looking at one clan per episode. I already had my favourites, based on my slight obsession with feuding. There is a saying, 'Scotland was born fighting', and feuding is something that the Highland clans have turned into an art form. Venetians have their glass, Persians have their rugs and the Scots have their feuds. I sent over my suggestions and we decided upon the clans we would feature based on geography and accessibility, as we were on a ridiculously tight schedule with no weather cover against a Scottish September (fools!), no script, no real prep, just a 'turn up and shoot' idea.

One camera became two and then three . . . with a drone.

And, after taking various planes, trains and automobiles – me from New Zealand, Sam from the set of *Outlander* – we finally arrived at the Kingshouse Hotel, on the southern edge of the Glencoe mountain range, to meet Michelle Methven, our wonderful line producer, and the rest of the *Clanlands* crew.

SAM

Let me introduce you to the team. We have:

Michelle Methven – our line producer, who is the hardest working person in Scotland, with a great collection of wellies. She is a schedule guru, expert 4x4 driver and you want her on your team because she can play every position.

Alex Norouzi – a producer and director, who was a whisky virgin until I met him. A creative genius with a funny accent.

John Duncan – director of photography and drone genius.

Jonnie Lewis – second assistant camera. Enthusiastic, with great hair.

Tim Askew – third assistant camera for our last weekend. Caught a great amount of cutaways and 'B' roll (i.e. cutaway shots, close-ups of thistles, mountains, Graham's angry beard), some of which I'll deny ever happened!

Merlin Bonning – sound wizard who travelled in the back of the Fiat camper.

Wendy Kemp Forbes – make-up artist/groomer/chief morale officer. Big laugh and even bigger heart. Gave extra attention to Graham's bald head. *[Graham: I got five minutes in the make-up chair, Sam was barely out of it. Constantly being primped like something from Best In Show.] [Sam: It's because I have hair, Graham.]*

Laura Strong and Linzi Thompson – the stylist team who set up camp in Glen Etive.

Davie 'Hollywood' Stewart – my *Outlander* driver for six years, who took over the controls whenever we were too drunk to drive. Most days. *[Graham: Thank God he did!]*

Paul/Stewart/Daniel – PAs/drivers and all-day multitaskers. Coffee-making, whisky-pouring, light-holding, Graham's latte and snack suppliers.

Peter Sandground – our photographer, who managed to get some terrific images in seconds and shared in my enthusiasm to place Graham in precarious situations. *[Graham: Note to self – beat Peter Sandground to within an inch of his life.]*

Michelle Methven is a machine – a hands-on, proper grafter type of person. I think we all are on *Clanlands* and we all clicked because no one was looking for the perks or trappings of fame (apart from maybe Graham, with his insatiable appetite for fine wine, fine dining and high-end hotels). What sets Michelle apart is that she's not only emotionally invested in a project but always maintains a cheery disposition, even when faced with a soggy pair of actors and crew that are hungry, hung-over and slightly dazed. She thinks of everything.

I first met Michelle working on a commercial shoot a few years ago. She was driving a rusty old Land Rover, wearing a pair of her iconic green Barbour wellies and a beaten-up wax jacket. She beamed at me and told me to hop in. 'Do you want a go?' she asked, seeing I was itching to try my hand at off-roading. This was highly irregular, but she knew I'd be okay as I jumped into the driver's seat and stared down the steep hill. I put my foot on the accelerator and set off down hill. 'Oh God!' came a cry from make-up artist Wendy in the back seat, covering her eyes and giggling manically. 'It'll be fine,' said Michelle, never one to panic and always ready with a backup plan. As we hurtled down the hill I could see her trying to work out what to do if we found ourselves in a ditch. We made it safely down the steep incline, and rolled to a halt next to a group of bemused commercial clients. I jumped out of the driver's side and quickly hid myself behind Wendy, a difficult task given she's half a foot smaller than me! But before the executives had a chance to express concern, the ever-ready Michelle stepped in with her charming smile. 'Cup of tea? Or too early for a hot toddy?' The suits relaxed and agreed it was never, ever too early and I realised in that moment, Michelle was a woman you *always* want by your side.

And, Wendy is another incredible crew member I couldn't be without. We've worked together on *Outlander* since the beginning in 2013. She applies all my make-up in record time, usually around forty-five minutes to an hour for mud, blood, ageing, wig and any extras appropriate for the day's shoot. Not only in charge of the continuity of my character Jamie Fraser – who gets beaten up a lot – Wendy also applies the back scars I wear when topless on the show. [*Graham: which is a lot. Can't keep his bloody clothes on. He is almost certainly writing this passage naked.*] In the beginning it used to take a three-person team three hours, but Wendy has perfected the technique and can give me full scar coverage in only ninety minutes. Whether it is raining, cold, late at night or we are covered in a cloud of midges, she always has a smile and a joke for me. In fact, we laugh *a lot* and our bond has become very close.

And, if you don't know *Outlander*, where have you been? No, it's not that one with Sean Connery as a Spaniard and a Frenchman as a Highlander. Although that film did have an awesome soundtrack (Queen – 'Who Wants to Live Forever') and a scene where they discuss the contents of haggis in a rowing boat (actually, sounds like an episode of *Men In Kilts*).

Outlander is the multi-award-winning Starz show (streamed on Amazon Prime in the UK and Starz in the US) about a 1940s nurse, Claire Beauchamp Randall (played by Caitriona Balfe, my long-suffering and utterly brilliant co-star), who is transported back to eighteenth-century Scotland, one year before the Jacobite Rising of 1745, and meets the love of her life, the flame-haired Jamie Fraser, played by me. My character's full name is: James Alexander Malcolm MacKenzie Fraser – try saying that name fifty times in front of a group of adolescent-behaving, overheating actors in fake wigs and beards and see how you do!

Caitriona and I have been on this terrific journey together for almost seven years now. Both rather green at first and thrown together to play soul-mates Jamie and Claire, in Caitriona I have not only had a brilliant and sensitive co-star but a loyal friend. Cait and I are like brother and sister, we know how each other works. There's an ease and comfort when working together and of course we have our disagreements but ultimately always we have each other's backs. I insisted during Season One negotiations that our fees/contracts were the same and that we were always in it together. Now as producers on the show, we have an added responsibility to the rest of the cast and crew, plus Diana and the fans, to get it right. We confide in each other and I consider her one of my closest friends. It's hard not to have fun on set and we laugh a lot, both sharing a rather childish sense of humour. We know each other's 'tells' and many a time Cait has given me a shoulder to lean on or offered some good advice. I'm so lucky to share this journey with her. And I guess the 'chemistry' takes care of itself.

The TV show *Outlander* is based on a series of books written twenty years earlier by the uber-talented Diana Gabaldon. Diana was actually inspired by *Doctor Who*: in one episode there was a man in a kilt called Jamie, who was played by the actor Frazer Hines, who appeared in Season Three of *Outlander* as Sir Fletcher Gordon, the governor of Wentworth. A unique mix of historical fact, action, romance, spirituality, darkness, medicinal information, and humour [*Graham: and more close-ups of Heughan's arse than is strictly necessary; the show is best described as 'tartan and soft porn']* [*Sam: Harsh*]*,* her work has gained a loyal and voracious readership. Thankfully, the fans have embraced us and we love to present them with our version of Diana's books and I consider myself the guardian of her character, Jamie Fraser. However, there is a small, hardcore group of fans who believe that with me measuring an inch shorter than Jamie, I am an ill-fitting choice to play the 'King of Men'.

I'm not a ginger *[Graham: You kind of are]* or a virgin, either!

GRAHAM

After having a conflab with Michelle and meeting the crew, Sam and I are both excited and slightly daunted about going to so many places and meeting so many people on such a tight schedule, it almost defies the laws of physics. So it is of vital importance to be fresh in the morning for our first day of filming. With that in mind we have a bite to eat together and a little nightcap in the bar and all is well with the world until . . . ENTER Duncan Lacroix (Murtagh in *Outlander*) stage right, with his dipsomaniacal sidekick 'The Irishman' already half-cut and in the mood for carnage. We had asked Duncan – *Outlander's* resident Oliver Reed – to do a comic turn on our *Clanlands* adventure and he willingly signed up. But now I realise this could have been a dreadful mistake . . .

It starts with whisky, then wine and then whisky. *Lots* of whisky, my alcoholic fate sealed until 3am. Sam sneaks off, well oiled, at one; damn him for remembering to go to bed. My experience has always been: the more important the next day's task, the later I go to bed. Not ideal, I know.

My alarm goes off louder than it should. Urgh. It's 7am. I pull apart my eyelids and feel wretched. Downstairs at breakfast I am astonished to see Duncan up and moving – perhaps he's not even been to bed? However, on closer inspection he looks like he may die at any moment, or like a warmed corpse still wearing the clothes he was buried in. His Irish friend is nowhere to be seen – presumably in bed, possibly alive, possibly not.

Sam is his annoying perky self, bounding with energy like some kind of muscular springer spaniel. After forcing down a breakfast of porridge, a full Scottish fry-up, toast, jam, the works (well, I did), Sam and I are finally off in our motorhome, careering in third gear along the Glencoe road to a location where Duncan is pretending to hitchhike. In his state, holding his thumb upright will be a miracle. Sam has spotted him up ahead. He asks me what we're meant to be doing. I tell him I haven't got the faintest idea – *he* organised this road trip! He speeds towards Duncan. 'Slow down,' I say. He obliges and we both affect complete astonishment at seeing our mate Duncan in the middle of the Highlands.

Graham: Shall we pick him up?

Sam: Nah.

I wind up the window, shutting out Duncan's expectant, haggard and severely over-refreshed face as we accelerate off, Sam trying his best to make the wheels spin on this plastic leviathan. John, the director of photography, suggests we talk about Duncan as we drive away – perhaps feeling bad about leaving him – but I say it's much funnier if we don't reference it. We simply drive on, with no concern at all.

As we continue on the road I open my window again, feeling queasy. I drank a vat of coffee at breakfast but already the caffeine is wearing off. The sun warms my face (in September) and suddenly I begin to notice our incredible surroundings. Sam and I both crane our heads forward to get a better look through the windscreen to absorb the arresting, heart-poundingly beautiful, majestic, but in reality harsh and inhospitable, glen. On a day like today there is no beating the Scottish landscape. The layers of blood, feud, romance, myth and passion are like the rock of the mountains themselves, grand in scale, ancient, and sometimes overwhelming.

Life is hard in these hills. The rock in the Highlands is so hard that it's a barrier to drainage. Topography alert! The rain collects in valleys with no subterranean chambers so moisture lingers on the surface, making the land marshy, sodden, and treacherous. The Highlands, up to the eighteenth century, were virtually an island, cut off by the Firth of Forth and the Firth of Clyde with the only route being through Stirling. Hence, Robert the Bruce was able to drown scores of English knights at Bannockburn in 1314 with the odds against him. The marshy land around Stirling was only drained in the late 1700s and most movement in the Highlands until the late eighteenth century was by sea.

SAM

You may have gleaned already that Graham is a bit of a history buff because, let's face it, he's from another time (and planet!). I think he was born in the 1940s . . . *[Graham: 1961, thank you]*. Anyway, he really does know a lot about the clans and his Highland ancestry; although I have a keen interest in my Scottish heritage, I'm yet to fill in the gaps of my own lineage. I'm hungry to learn more, which is why I decided to produce *Men In Kilts* as a TV show because, for me, there's no better way to learn than by 'getting amongst it'. I'm a 'let's get sh*t done' type of guy and organising a road trip around the Highlands with a mate, meeting a variety of Scottish characters and drinking cask-strength whisky is my sort of history field trip. So if Big G's the fusty, bushy-eyebrowed professor of this adventure, I must be Steven Spielberg! Baldilocks has got twenty years on me and comes with the elderly's pedantry for detail such as battle dates, numbers killed, injuries sustained and what the weather was like – a strange and unexpected benefit of our cross-generational friendship!

And, before us lies an epic journey starting in the resplendent valley of Glencoe. The dramatic Buachaille Etive Mor (Scottish Gaelic for 'the herdsman of Etive') mountain guarding the glen looks unreal in the early morning sunshine. To the right is the jagged and precarious Aonach Eagach ridge, which runs the length of the glen. It can only be traversed in one direction using rope and harness, and is something I have always wanted to climb. *[Sam: Graham, fancy it?] [Graham: Not today, thank you.]* It's crossed by the aptly named Devil's Staircase, an old military road and a steep climb for even the most adventurous. I used to come to Glencoe as a kid; I even learned to ski here when I was a teenager. However, unlike Graham, who spent his youth in Glasgow, I spent my early years in the Lowland countryside. I was born in a stone cottage near the town of Balmaclellan in Galloway, south-west Scotland, in 1980 . . .

Graham: I felt a disturbance in the balance of the world in 1980, I seem to recall.

Sam: You'll like this bit, Graham. I was actually called 'Samwise' at times by my parents and my brother, Cirdan, after the characters in J.R.R. Tolkien's *Lord of the Rings*. Graham was Dwalin, the grumpy/angry Scottish dwarf in *The Hobbit Trilogy*. Typecast again.

Graham: Really? I didn't know that, mate. I knew there was a reason why I liked you. Although, having said that, I always found Samwise to be the most annoying of hobbits in *Lord of the Rings* – the one I secretly hoped Sauron would put in some kind of Mordor chokehold.

Sam: Nice touch.

Raised by my mum, Chrissie, we moved to New Galloway (the smallest royal borough in Scotland) to a converted block of stables, called the Steadings [*Graham: You literally grew up in an animal outhouse, like some Scottish baby Jesus*], in the grounds of Kenmure Castle, a thirteenth-century ruin on the shores of Loch Ken. Things were tight back then but it didn't matter because my brother and I had the ancient walled garden, banked meadows (archery range in my imagination) and dense Forestry Commission woods as our playground. I now realise how idyllic this was and how lucky we were. History was always around us. The gloomy presence of Kenmure Castle looked down with the open windows and door like the face of a ghoulish monster ready to swallow a young child. I would occasionally build the courage to sneak inside the crumbling castle and find evidence of past inhabitants, an ancient fireplace, walls and flooring exposed. I'd imagine warriors creeping up the spiral staircase, just as I did in *Outlander*. It's in this land that I began to play and develop my imagination. I was obsessed with Merlin, Excalibur, King Arthur and Robert the Bruce; all have links to ancient British history and that part of Scotland claims to have originated many of those myths.

Bang!

We hit a bump at speed.

Graham: Slow down! God, it's like a crap remake of *Speed*.

Sam: And you're Sandra Bullock?

Graham: Sandra Bullock did the driving! (PAUSE) And what exactly is *this?*

Graham's beard bristles as he pokes the miniature Highland 'coo', dangling from the rear-view mirror, with his long index finger. 'What *is* it?' he says, his tone even more suspicious than usual, like he's expecting it to moo, or blow up in his face. I've decked out the camper van with as much Scottish memorabilia as I could find in my house and the local charity shop. Old maps of Scotland, a broken set of bagpipes, a basket-hilted sword, a shinty stick, a Scottish flag, a couple of rusty bicycles tied to the back and any other 'shortbread tin' rubbish I could find, just to make the hairless-headed one feel more at home. 'It's all research material with a few surprises,' I smirk, keeping him on his toes and making sure he doesn't feel comfortable enough to fall asleep. I imagine him with the tartan blanket over his knees, handbag on top.

Sam: I've got a single malt hidden under the sink. *(And shortbread, which he mustn't find.)* And, I did actually bring you a cigar . . .

Graham: Nice thought. I've never smoked so I would probably just choke and die.

Sam: That was the idea.

Graham's eyebrows rise up to the roof and his mouth opens.

Graham: Why is the engine making that *whirr whirr* sound?

Sam: Sh*t, wrong gear.

Graham: I've got a mouth like the bottom of a parrot cage – I *need* a latte.

Graham always *needs* a latte. On the set of *Outlander*, Graham's catchphrase was 'I'll have a latte,' and he swiftly became known as Lady McTavish for being so high-maintenance, the polar opposite of his hard-core warlord character in *Outlander*, Dougal MacKenzie. And, if Graham has low blood sugar, we are doomed. Honestly, the man runs on his stomach. It's necessary to keep him grazing constantly. I normally sink a couple of black coffees to jog my brain out of its slumber in the morning and perhaps eat a bowl of steaming porridge. But Graham will have porridge, a full cooked breakfast, toast, yoghurt . . . Always one to order a starter, main and possibly cheeseboard, he also is the first to ask for the accompanying wine list. I usually go straight to the whisky collection.

GRAHAM

In my defence, I am not high-maintenance, I am just a person who needs coffee at all times of the day and, when I arrive on set, or anywhere such as a hotel, I like to know some simple information: where I can put my belongings, where I can sit down, where the coffee is and what time breakfast is served . . .

Sam: . . . And lunch and tea and dinner, all organised whilst you're still eating breakfast.

Graham: I just like to know when my next meal is.

Sam: There's fruit and protein bars in the glovebox.

SAM

I glance over and realise His Ladyship is already surrounded by empty wrappers, covertly munching. FFS, Graham.

He smiles at me. When did I first meet this man? Had it been love at first sight? I can't remember. I cast my mind back . . . We were in a small, hot studio in Soho, London. I sat with some of the executive producers and the casting team of *Outlander*. I was 'reading in' for several actors auditioning for the parts of Dougal MacKenzie and Colum MacKenzie, brothers and fearsome clan leaders. Dougal was a hot-headed war chief and Colum was a crippled politician and arch-manipulator. Jamie had mixed loyalties to both men and, even though they were his uncles, there was a great deal of mistrust.

First up was Tim McInnerny (Captain Darling in *Blackadder*) to audition for both characters. He actually went on to play Father Bain, a priest who accuses Claire of being a witch and had a rather sticky moment during shooting with a pack of overzealous wild dogs; still has all his fingers, though. Then came Graham McTavish; sporting a salmon-pink or maroon sweater, he was charming and confident. We played a couple of scenes and I remember trying to intimidate him as Jamie, getting in his face. He was taller than I expected and didn't back down, his white beard [*Graham: It wasn't white then. That only happened on this trip.*] bristling in my face as he threatened me. Who knew that years later I would be sharing a smelly camper van and riding a rickety tandem bicycle with him along the shores of Loch Awe on our own TV show.

GRAHAM

I met Sam for the first time in August 2013. I'd just finished *The Hobbit* trilogy – two and a half years of running all over New Zealand dressed as a dwarf. A life experience like no other. Prosthetics, a seventy-pound costume, lifelong friendships forged amidst a 750-million-dollar budget. It had been amazing and I was ready for something new. Something without prosthetics. I remember the producer telling me they'd expected to find it very difficult to cast Jamie Fraser but they'd found him straight away. His name was Sam Heughan. I googled him, of course. Handsome, almost to the point of annoying, and very little in the way of credits, he'd just landed the lead in a major multimillion-dollar TV show based on an incredibly popular series of books (seven at that point) – so a 'multi-season option'. *That lucky bastard*, I thought, and immediately hated him.

I arrived and, yes, was first greeted by Sam. Firstly, he was tall; for a moment I thought, *Is this swine taller than me? [Sam: Yes!]* I'm used to being the tallest person on set and it's a source of great pride that Richard Armitage had to have lifts in his shoes to get him to my height in *The Hobbit*, even though we were both dwarves!

Sam seems to believe I was wearing a salmon-pink or maroon jumper. Firstly, it was *boiling*. I wouldn't have worn a jumper, unless I wanted Dougal MacKenzie to be sweating like a footballer in a spelling test. Secondly, I would never wear salmon pink. Maroon – possibly. It was more likely a T-shirt, or a shirt. Something fitted, to hopefully make me look muscular! Of course, Sam *always* looks muscular. He is getting more muscular on a daily basis. I suspect in the time I've taken to write this paragraph Sam's muscles have grown – noticeably. He was big in Season One; by Season Eight no horse will be able to carry his sheer bulk of muscularity. Every close-up will have to be done on a wide lens. But I digress. Sam was, I think, wearing a T-shirt. Tighter than mine.

I do remember being impressed he had a firm handshake. I place great store by someone's handshake. Jamie Fraser cannot have a limp handshake. Talking of Jamie, I gather he's described in the books as being as tall as the hearth of a particularly spacious fireplace. By those standards, Sam is somewhat vertically challenged. But I do remember being won over by his sheer openness and honesty. He put me instantly at my ease. Sam was destined to play Jamie Fraser because he is exactly as you imagine – a thoroughly kind-hearted bloke, with a streak of insanity.

Seven years on, here we are on the road in a margarine tub on wheels. Roads in this part of Scotland are blissfully uninterrupted by turn-offs. General George Wade was the British officer who came up with the idea that troops would benefit from actual roads (some would describe this is as patently obvious, given that the Romans seemed to have managed to grasp this concept 2,000 years earlier) and when he built his roads into the Highlands in the eighteenth century as a way of 'civilising' the Highlanders and bringing them to heel, he wasn't much bothered about byways and lay-bys. Our turning was going to be on the right, probably the only one for twenty miles . . . and Sam missed it.

'We've gone too far,' I say.

Sam: Really?

Graham: Yes. We just passed it.

There followed a terrifying turnaround to go back the way we came. I think sheep stopped mid-chew to look on in wonder at the mangling of the gearbox and the revving of the Fiat Fallacious. Highland cows hung their shaggy heads in shame. Fortunately, the road was deserted of traffic.

As we *finally* take the turn we had missed, we judder onto the single-track road and soon Sam is gathering pace. I gird my loins. There is another car coming in the opposite direction. 'Car! Car!' I say like an injured crow. We come to an abrupt standstill and stare at the driver of the black Audi. He looks at us with palpable contempt. We encourage him to go backwards with hand gestures. He replies with a jabbing finger – it is *we* who must go back. 'You have to reverse, you've done it before,' I tell Sam. 'I can't! There's no way,' he replies. We shake our heads and point back at the Audi driver, who is looking menacing.

[Sam: It was a BMW driver. Only gentlemen drive Audis.]

[Graham: You would say that with your free Q59 Sporty Turbo E-schlong or whatever.] (More on his free stuff later . . .)

SAM

Finally the BMW driver *[Graham: Audi – I have the footage]* gets the message and, realising we are not moving, he reverses to a spot where we can pass. We wave, thanking him; he sneers at our battered motorhome. Not initially a fan either, I am getting quite a crush on the camper. A little further down the way there is a man with a long shaggy beard and hair walking determinedly down the centre of the road. He refuses to let us pass for a good fifteen minutes – he looks like Duncan Lacroix. Maybe it *is* Duncan? He sits down by the side of the road, staring up at the sky, a mad look in his eye. Yup, definitely could be him.

Graham: Where are we actually going?

Sam: Whisky tasting.

Graham: What? It's nine in the morning.

Sam: Hair of the dog, you auld dog.

Graham: Bring it on, Young Pretender.

CHAPTER TWO

Freedom and Whisky Gang Thegither

'Scotch Drink' by Robert Burns (1785)
O thou, my muse! guid auld Scotch drink!
Whether thro' wimplin worms thou jink,
Or, richly brown, ream owre the brink,
In glorious faem,
Inspire me, till I lisp an' wink,
To sing thy name!

GRAHAM

We enter the sixteenth-century Clachaig Inn, which until recently bore the sign, 'No Hawkers or Campbells!' – meaning neither were allowed inside. It's strange to be in a pub at nine in the morning. It reminds me of parties I woke up at in my early twenties. The place reeks of stale booze. The only thing missing are people passed out on the floor, however. The place is empty, save for the band: four men in a corner surrounded by their instruments, looking strangely incongruous.

Sam introduces me to Richard Goslan from the Scotch Malt Whisky Society (SMWS) who has several bottles of whisky and tasting glasses arranged on a table in front of him. My liver stiffens. As a young man it was always beer. It was the very first thing I drank at fifteen in my local pub – the One Oak in Frimley, Surrey. I started with lager. Then I moved on to ale. I used to love Deuchars IPA (a fine Scots brew), and I have tried many in Scotland. Another favourite was Traquair ale (brewed at Traquair House in the Borders). For a long time Scottish beer was rubbish. Nothing could rival their English counterparts with their bewildering number of brews: Abbots, Sam Smiths, Greene King, Fuller's London Pride, even Boddingtons. The list is long. Scotland had Tennent's (flavoured lavatory water).

SAM

Having been the face of Tennent's for three years or more, I felt this attack was coming. I played Hugh Tennent and I love the stuff! It's Scotland's unofficial 'other' national drink, besides whisky, water, Irn Bru, Buckfast, gin . . . etc. I played the creator of the marvellous brew, who journeyed to Germany and brought back a Pilsner yeast, which is still used today. Not only did I get to drink a ton of the stuff, play with monkeys and get VIP passes to Scotland's largest music festival, T in the Park, sponsored by Tennent's, I also had a butler in the commercials, played by Tim Downie. We became great friends, travelling to Prague by tour bus, filled with lager, and also South Africa, where I first climbed Table Mountain. Tim now plays Governor Tryon in Season Five of *Outlander* and is excellent as the power hungry 'Gov'. He also happens to be one of the funniest men I know and I'll be inviting him to be my next travelling companion if you don't shut yer gob, McTavish.

GRAHAM

As I said, Tennent's is like water from a clatty shitter. (Heughan will promote anything – he's one job away from haemorrhoid cream.) And McEwan's has the aromatic taste of swamp water, with a dead wildebeest in it. But things have improved. Now Scotland boasts a bewildering choice of excellent craft breweries such as Stewart Brewing and Fallen Brewery, as well as some of the best gin I've ever tasted, including Isle of Harris gin infused with sugar kelp. However, these days – and I am loath to admit it – given the choice I'd rather go for a chilled New Zealand Sauvignon, or a Pinot Noir from Central Otago any day. *[Sam: Blasphemy! String him up!]*

I wish I was the whisky-drinker Sam is. I stand in admiration as he chooses a whisky, casting his eye appreciatively over the selection, murmuring with surprise at a particular bottle he's not tried before. Ordering with confidence, tasting with élan. You can see the barman realises this is a man who knows his shit. I just stand there nodding impressively, once again managing to look like I know what I'm doing without actually having a clue. And Sam and I have sampled some good ones. We both went to an Italian fan convention where our green room was furnished with a 1939 Laphroiag (listed at an eye watering $40,000 per bottle), a 1953 Mortlach and a 1970 Glenfarclas. Incredible.

And now, Richard and Sam are waiting for me to choose which whisky to sample and it's not that I don't like whisky, please don't get me wrong, it's just I don't know what I like at nine in the morning nursing a hangover, after a bowel-loosening drive with Heughan. I point randomly at one. Richard hands me a glass. Sam has his nostrils all over it, breathing in the notes of Scotland like a professional 'nose' – a real job in the perfume industry. (Some 'noses' have their snouts insured for millions.)

And, he of the rusty roof has his own whisky, don't you know. Of course, he does. The aftershave's in the pipeline. No, it really is.

SAM

You need a splash of 'Hero by Heughan' cos you smell like an old soak. And, you've brought your breakfast in yer beard, I see. I expected better.

The concentration of driving a boat on wheels has made me parched; as we say in these parts, my thrapple is dry. Richard hands us a glass of twenty-six-year-old cask-strength whisky distilled in the Black Isle in the northern Highlands at a gentle 46.9% proof.

All: Slainte!

Graham looks at me sheepishly as he takes a sip. He struggles to swallow. Richard explains it's cask-strength, meaning it's not watered down. I love the stronger stuff – it's heavier on the tongue and feels special. If you're a fan of Scotch, even just 'nosing' a whisky and smelling the sugars or flavours can be very enjoyable. The clear liquid takes on the colour and flavours of each barrel, such as French oak, as many are aged in barrels that previously held bourbon or sweet wine. As they age, the whisky deepens, becoming more balanced and less fiery, with notes of butterscotch, cinnamon, honey, leather, citrus and tobacco. The smell can transport you . . .

Graham: You remind me of Jilly Goolden.

Sam: Who?

Graham: Never mind, before your time. Similar hairstyle.

Richard recommends a wee splash of water with cask-strength whisky, which breaks up the oils and releases more flavour. Scotch. No other drink is named after a country, which is why whisky is more than just a drink for me. When I'm feeling homesick, I'll have a dram. It brings me great comfort: the smell brings back memories of Scotland; the taste takes me home. It's a huge part of Scottish culture and has been produced all over the world for hundreds of years. Back in the day, before the licensing act of 1780, many Highlanders distilled their own fire-water, particularly in north-eastern Scotland, due to their proximity to grain-producing farms. As whisky's popularity grew over the centuries, five distilling regions emerged: the Lowlands, Campbeltown, Highland, Isles and Speyside. It's believed the 'terroir' – water, climate, soil, topography and surrounding plants – influence each batch, giving it a unique flavour.

Many crofters supported themselves by generating income from the sale of their whisky. The earliest written record of Uisge-beatha, 'Water of Life', is in the Scottish Exchequer Rolls for 1494, where there is an entry of 'eight bolls of malt to Friar John Cor wherewith to make aquavitae'. A boll was an old Scottish measure of not more than six bushels. (One bushel is equivalent to 25.4 kilograms). Shared around the hearth, it would 'bond' men together as they exchanged stories and banter, just as it does today, even with Graham's stinky chat. Oops, he's slumping. 'Sit up, Graham.' Honestly, it's like going out with yer granddad. Next he'll be telling stories from the war . . .

GRAHAM

By 9.15am I am already drunk . . . again. More alarmingly, so is Sam. We soldier on through whiskies drawn from all of the whisky-making regions. We begin with the 'lighter' malt, which feels like I'm gargling lighter fuel, but with every dram the whisky becomes more delicious and different in flavour to the last. My palette is happy; however, my liver is back working like a pit pony to keep this show on the road. After five or six (I honestly can't remember) I am officially 'aff ma heid'. I can't remember my favourite but we both agreed upon the same one. Which one was it again?

Sam: The Speyside.

Graham: Oh yes.

Sam gets up and disappears, probably to refill his hip flask(s) with the cask-strength Scotch. (He drinks in secret.) However, I find out he's actually gone to get changed into yet another outfit and is being primped by his personal make-up artist – the wonderful Wendy from *Outlander*. Oh yes, he travels with his make-up artist so she can work her contouring magic and draw on a six-pack if he suddenly needs one. Wendy did my make-up in the car park earlier, but I couldn't help thinking compared to Golden Balls she was polishing a turd. Sam's make-up is lovingly and extensively applied.

Sam: Right to reply.

Graham: Denied.

Sam returns more youthful and glowing, like Odysseus after the goddess Athena has worked her magic, and in the time-honoured tradition of television we pretend to meet the band (Fras) who just 'happen' to be in the pub, preparing for a rousing evening with the locals. The fact that the bar is bereft of locals, and only has a motley collection of film crew in it, is one of the magical wonders of film-making. But having been loosened up by the whisky we are ready for a good old sing-song. The musicians – Murdo, Angus and Cailean – are amazing as they play a local tune called 'Three Crowns'. I've always envied the effortlessness of someone who is a master of their craft and these boys are masters. We stomp our feet and I forget for one blissful moment that I am in an empty bar with a film crew.

There are Jacobite connections to many famous Scottish tunes such as the nineteenth-century 'Skye Boat Song', used over the opening credits of *Outlander*. The song recalls the journey Bonnie Prince Charlie made from Benbecula in the Outer Hebrides to Skye, after evading capture at the Battle of Culloden in 1746, which put paid to the dream of a restoration of the Stuarts to the throne. *[Sam: The Bonnie Prince escapes dressed as a woman – he was a very forward-thinking man!]*

Recently experts at Durham University even claim 'O Come All Ye Faithful' is a coded Jacobite ode to Charles Edward Stuart. And, of course, there's 'The Bonnie Banks O' Loch Lomond' . . .

By yon bonnie banks and by yon bonnie braes,
Where the sun shines bright on Loch Lomond,
Where me and my true love were ever wont to gae,
On the bonnie, bonnie banks o' Loch Lomond.

Chorus:
O ye'll tak' the high road, and I'll tak' the low road,
And I'll be in Scotland a'fore ye,
But me and my true love will never meet again,
On the bonnie, bonnie banks o' Loch Lomond.

SAM

He's away. With the fairies. It doesn't feel like ten in the morning and it doesn't feel like we are filming. I am enjoying myself so I have another nip of the Speyside with Richard and start to tell him all about how I've been approached by whisky distilleries asking me to 'white-label' (put my name to a bottle) before realising I actually wanted to make my own.

[Graham: Ah, here we go.]

'Richard, I know single malt is traditional and steeped in heritage but I've found myself drinking more of the Asian blends. *[Graham: You treacherous bastard.]* Smooth, rich and delicious . . . Sooo, I thought there's a gap in the market for a good blended Scotch and over the past couple of years my business partner, Alex the German, and I have travelled around Scotland, visiting distilleries from the Lowlands, all the way up to and including Inverness and the Highlands *[Graham: all freebies]*, meeting the people who work hard, pouring their passion into every cask. It was a gruelling trip, many days spent on the road whilst liaising with our international partners and of course, sampling multiple expressions upon each stop. Someone's gotta do it.'

[Graham: Get ready for THE ADVERT.]

'We wanted to create something unique, something that takes you home to the Highlands of Scotland: a roaring fire, the wind and rain outside the window. Our logo is the unicorn – Scotland's national animal, the strongest of all animals. The unicorn is the only beast that can defeat the lion. The unicorn can only be tamed by a virgin. The individual spirit of the unicorn captures my pride and passion for Scotland.'

[Graham: Hate to break it to you, mate – a unicorn isn't a real animal.]

'And, in the dead of night I awoke with a revelation. Behold! Sassenach Whisky was born.'

[Graham: Sounds more like an aftershave.]

'Richard? Can I call you Rich? The Sassenach is a nonconformist, an outsider, and anyone who doesn't just want to fit in. It's inspired by the Highland landscape: the ancient peaks, hidden glens, rising morning mist, fresh water and firm oak run deep in its veins.'

[Graham: Oh dear God.]

'We mature it in Madeira casks so that the underlying rich fruit character is at the forefront of the blend. The nose is packed with citrus fruits, almonds and vanilla. And I'm really proud to say, Rich, it won Double Gold in a blind taste test at the 2020 San Francisco World Spirits Competition, yah, I know, amazing right? We then won another double gold for the bottle design and packaging. That's a lot of Gold, Richy! But listen, I promise when you taste it, it caresses your palate with peach, apricot, honey and butterscotch and the sweet unmistakable finish of cinnamon and nutmeg . . .

GRAHAM

As your fictional uncle and real friend I advise you to stop with the 'rising morning mist' and 'caressing your palate' shite! Honestly, he's always at it, flogging products. The amount of free stuff he gets I imagine his room looks like an outlet store. He's probably got an Audi in his bathroom.

Believe me, I would love to talk at length about Sam's whisky (he certainly does), but this would require me to have properly sampled it. Like Richard.

I remember seeing him at the *Outlander* Season Five premiere. Coincidentally, he appeared to be carrying a bottle of his whisky. I spy him on the carpet. We hug. Normal length. (Gary Lewis, Colum in the show, wouldn't have approved. He thinks a good hug can't be rushed and should take at least an hour.)

'I'd love to try your whisky,' I say over the noise of fans and interviewers.

'I'll get you a bottle,' he assures me.

I had an image of a bottle arriving perhaps at my hotel. Or maybe a couple of days later at my house. Me opening it excitedly, savouring several samplings, before calling him up to gush about its woody finish. That was February 2020. It is now nearly Christmas. Perhaps it's been held up in the post?

[Sam: I actually gave a bottle to every cast member staying at the cast hotel. Graham was holed up in some LA mansion and likely wouldn't give me his address for fear Lacroix and I might turn up, unannounced.]

I was finally able to sample the nectar at a dinner party in LA at the home of Karen Bailey, the Starz executive in charge of *Outlander*. It was a small sample (Lacroix was there, I think he'd been busy), but nevertheless it was really very good. I repressed the beginnings of a jealous twinge and concentrated on what I was tasting. Sam had spent a lot of time and energy perfecting this and it had paid off. I can't rival Sam's own description of the whisky but I will do my best:

It blends the throaty power of a Formula 1 racing car with the nimble meanderings of a Highland sheep, but this is no ordinary sheep. This sheep has drunk from the ambrosial springs of a misty glen, its slopes shrouded in tender dew. If wolves still roamed in Scotland you would feel their fangs as this whisky slid across your palate, like a hungry ballerina. I tasted heather, I tasted wild mountain thyme, I tasted tweed. As I let it glide down my throat and settle in my eager stomach I could have sworn I heard the sound of Bonnie Prince Charlie's voice whispering in my ear, and the distant rumble of cannon fire. I wept.

Sam: Shut yer gob, old man. There'll be no bottle of Sassenach for thee now.

SAM

Anyway, some time later we are behind the bar pulling pints for the landlord and his family, battered. And that's when *she* enters, dressed in a T-shirt with 'These Puppies Love Outlander' on. We nickname her Delilah. But the real danger is the woman behind her – The Mother, known as Glenn (after Glenn Close in *Fatal Attraction*). Glenn is a woman of intimidating proportions. I'd seen her before in Prague. And Glasgow. And Edinburgh. And now she is here, offering her daughter.

'I think you know why we are here, Jamie Fraser,' she barks in a deep Glasgee burr. She prods her daughter who looks at me and flutters her fake eyelashes. Last time, I ended up hiding from Glenn in a stairwell in Prague as security wrestled her out of the hotel.

Graham is still pulling pints and talking bollocks as I sidle off to the gents and make a break for it to the car park. I am dazzled by blazing sunlight at 10.30 in the morning. I look at the camper, take out the keys from my pocket but there's no way I can drive. Fuck.

Michelle is behind me. She has anticipated our incapacity and tells us to get into the back of the camper. 'John will drive,' she says. I tell her we need to get away – there are super fans on site and they mean to have me illegally, like Captain Jack Randall.

Michelle understands. She goes into the pub and returns with Graham who, like me, is blinded by the sun like a balding Icarus. He can't see and is running in the wrong direction. Michelle pulls at his olive-green desert shirt and redirects him to the safety of the camper. Michelle goes back for Richard, who rushes to the vehicle as if through a battlefield of invisible bullets. Richard jumps in. 'You're going on ahead to the illicit still,' says Michelle. John, now in the driver's seat, starts the engine. Glenn and Delilah rush out of the pub as we disappear in a cloud of dust. That was close. Too close.

Without getting into too much detail, most *Outlander* fans are lovely and very normal but there are one or two who believe I am

actually Jamie Fraser and that they are my true love or that I should
be married to Claire (Caitriona Balfe). I know Graham would give a
kidney to have this kind of attention but sometimes it's a bit much.
He claims to have been mobbed by super fans after the Tartan
Parade in New York 2015, but that's all in his mind!

As we head to our next destination, slumped on sofas in the back
of the camper, we see a man walking along the road, the image of
Lacroix. Is that Duncan? It can't be. 'Duncan said he was going
hiking,' says Graham. I honestly can't imagine him or the Irishman
getting to the end of the drive, let alone up a mountain. I pull out a
flask and offer it to McTavish.

Graham: No, I can't. I mustn't. (Beat.) Oh, go on then.

He has a swig and I take one and we recall the night Duncan
Lacroix fell through Graham's plate glass table.

We were filming Season One of *Outlander* (2014) when we were
summoned from Glasgow to Edinburgh by Lady McTavish. It was a
Sunday before read-through day, and he had organised a whisky-
tasting online so fans could participate via social media and basically
get drunk alongside cast members.

Graham emailed me:

> *To: Sam Heughan*
> *Hey mate*
> *Went to a very good whisky shop for five Speyside*
> *recommendations:*
> *Mortlach 21yr*
> *Ben Riach 15yr*
> *Ben Rinnes 15yr*
> *Glenfarclas 105*
> *Craigellachie 18yr*
> *I am getting the Mortlach and Craigellachie. I've asked Maril to*
> *get the Ben Rinnes – perhaps you could grab the Glenfarclas? I*
> *will get Lacroix to get the other one.*
> *Or perhaps I could get them all here and you could sort me out then?*
> *See you at 7pm at the restaurant tomorrow!*
> *G*

Most of us had been working every day, still on twelve-day fort-nights. Tired but happy, we had wrapped a block (two episodes shot together) and the next morning would start a new double-episode shoot, complete with a new director and director of photography. Bundled into several black cabs from Glasgow, the cast and a couple of producers arrived at Graham's chosen restaurant: a Japanese sushi bar. We eagerly got involved in the saké and Sapporo beer chasers. Duncan led the charge and by the time we made it back to Graham's palace, we were all steaming.

His Majesty was residing in a large apartment in Edinburgh, next to the castle (though they didn't seem to realise he was there, as there was no flag flying from the battlements). Carrying a Glenfarclas 105, a fire-monster of a bottle, robust, like a Highland warrior's kick to the face, we rang the doorbell of the Monarch's residence. It all started rather socially but by the end of five or six drams we were frazzled. I recall towards the end finding myself upside down, my feet against the ornate palace walls, staring at the ceiling. Tobias was tweaking someone's nipples (maybe mine?). *[Graham: Definitely yours.]* Duncan and Caitriona were in a pile on the sofa.

GRAHAM'S DIARY ENTRY
Great party with Tobias, Sam, Cait, Grant, Duncan, Maril and Matt. Lovely evening. Grant, me and Duncan finished up at 3am (I don't even remember Grant being there!). Duncan collapsed through my table smashing glasses and plates.
I had to carry him to bed.

GRAHAM
I blame the saké. We drank it like water. It is worth noting Caitriona's prodigious capacity for booze. By the time we got to my flat, my kids were asleep and my (then) wife joined us for a couple before wisely retreating to bed. We were trying (and failing) to speak lucidly about the various flavours in the different whiskies on camera. Matt Roberts valiantly tried to post about what we were doing. He might as well have just written 'Getting pished. #hammered #booze-hounds #renalfailure #Icannotspeakcoherentlymylipsarenumb'

I was somewhat shocked to see that of the five bottles only two had *any* whisky left at the end of the night. I think Sam took one, leaving the other. Duncan took care of that. After he fell through my glass coffee table (and I think had a fight with the soundman?) I carried him to bed. I managed to get his shoes off and left him snoring like a billy goat.

I set my alarm.

Four hours later I got Duncan up. The car was outside to take him to the set. The driver thought he was joking around as he staggered towards the vehicle. He wasn't. I retired to my soft king-sized bed and enjoyed a day off. I had carefully organised the evening to coincide with my free time.

SAM

The next morning I found myself strapped in and being driven by Cait's driver to work. Cait was upside down in the back, her feet the wrong way up. She had slept in and was still blind drunk as we raced to the studio for the read-through. I was chugging water and couldn't see straight as I listened to her laughter and giggles coming from the back seat. We fell into the studio and found our seats.

I wasn't sure if Caitriona could speak. She glazed over and her head began to fall forward. As the stage directions were being read out I gave her a nudge. Maybe because I was watching out for her, I didn't notice my hangover as much, but I was sweating hard and clinging onto each word hoping they'd reveal some meaning. Constructing a sentence or following the story was beyond my grasp, we were definitely still 'aff our heids' drunk.

Grant, normally the jolly and pun-cracking Rupert in the show, was pale and quiet, gripped by a panic attack and ready to walk out. Duncan, to my left, his eyebrows even darker and more furrowed than I had ever seen before, growled, then spat his lines out. *Was it Gaelic?* I thought. I couldn't understand a word. Maybe he was making it up.

Moments earlier, he had walked into the main producer David Brown's office and thrown a copy of *Dragonfly in Amber* at him, exclaiming: 'I suppose you expect me to read this!' I could tell the director and producers were angry and beginning to suspect we were not at our best. Or was it my paranoia? Were they looking at me? What if I started drooling or throwing up on Cait?

And who was to blame?

One man. Nay, king. The only member of cast not required and still comfortably sleeping off his hangover, wrapped up in his king-size bed, snoring delightfully in Edinburgh.

***

Graham: Oh look, we're stopping. Is there more drinking?

Sam: Come on you, lightweight.

I had found a hidden spot in the heather, next to a tributary of the River Coe, as the location for our chat about illicit stills and whisky-making. I knew a thing or two about illicit liquor as my character, Jamie, becomes a wine importer in Season Two and distils his own whisky in Season Five.

My trusty grey companion stumbles behind me like a pigeon-toed alpaca as we make our way down a narrow track to the water's edge. Richard follows too, carrying the beautiful copper still I had found online and constructed myself, ignoring all the instructions. My proud wee still, albeit slightly rickety, was a beauty, its copper shining bright. For the rest of our epic Scottish quest it took pride of place perched on the camper van toilet seat, the safest place for it as we drove along those windy Highland roads.

What if we could distil whisky in our camper van? I imagine driving through the Highlands in our trusty wagon, creating some real road whisky in the back. Completely illegal. I wonder what the police would say and immediately think better of the idea.

Graham, still in the booze bubble, thinks it's a tremendous idea. 'It will be like Scottish *Breaking Bad*. Cooking it in the back, selling it out the front!'

Eventually, the rest of the film crew arrive having finally thrown the voracious fans Glenn and Delilah off their tail. Richard sets up the portable still and guides us through the process of making illicit whisky. Ever since the first taxes on whisky were introduced in 1644, illicit whisky distilling and smuggling became normal in Scotland for nearly 200 years. 'We're in a remote location away from the prying eyes, close to running water,' he says conspiratorially. 'The bootleggers were quite sophisticated because there was so much illegal distilling going on. They were playing a cat-and-mouse game with the excise men or "gaugers" (tax collectors). Some would set up a complete network of pipes from a woodland still to a nearby cottage so the smoke would come out of the cottage and the gaugers wouldn't know what was going on.'

They created their own portable stills, which were easy to dismantle in minutes, and had canny ways of hiding Scotch from the taxman, keeping it in caves, coffins or stashed in the church by members of the clergy. The clans and Jacobites united the people behind the smugglers and bootleggers, turning them into heroes of 'free trade'.

GRAHAM

It's funny because Scotland's much-loved poet Robert 'Rabbie' Burns (1759–96) worked as a gauger (tax collector) in his later years to pay the bills. Burns said, 'Taxes were seen by Scots as oppressive and resistance to them positively patriotic.' And I'm guessing they were especially loathsome given they were indirectly imposed by the English. The Act of Union in 1707 created levies on some goods seven times higher than in England and this 'VAT' remained high throughout the eighteenth century to line the crown's coffers to fund dust-ups with the French.

In 1786 Burns wrote 'The Author's Earnest Cry and Prayer' in which he coined the immortal line: 'Freedom an' whisky gang thegither', which was used as an episode title in Outlander (Season Three, Episode Five). Addressed to The Right Honourable and Honourable Scotch Representatives in the House of Commons, it is essentially a plea for tax reduction.

Although he didn't like his occupation he must have been good at it because he was promoted to the Dumfries Port Division in 1792. And as Richard explains, Burns would have been busy. 'Before the Excise Act of 1823, which halved the amount of duty on whisky, there were records of over 14,000 illicit stills confiscated in Scotland.'

That's a still for every other Highlander!

And, everyone was drinking it. Apparently, even King George IV requested an illegal dram of Glenlivet on a state visit to Scotland in 1822.

SAM

I was brought up near Rabbie Burns' hometown in Dumfries and it was at the 'Burns Centre' (an art house cinema and not a hospital!) that I first went to the cinema. *Turner and Hooch* with Tom Hanks was the first proper movie I remember. The local cinema in Castle Douglas had a cracked screen and would pause the movie halfway through for an intermission to sell melted ice cream and penny sweets. I don't remember them playing a single McTavish film! *[Sam: Right, that's enough talk of swally, we've got some fighting to do . . .] [Graham: I need a lie down.] [Sam: That can be arranged.]*

★★★

Sam's Top Tipples

SAM

We were by the beach at Fairmount Miramar, Santa Monica, for the BAFTA Los Angeles Burns Night 2020. And we asked a good friend of mine, Tim Robinson of Twist London, a genius medal-winning mixologist, to create some Sassenach cocktails. He came up with these two beauties:

SASSENACH HIGHBALL

60ml Sassenach whisky
60ml lemon verbena tea (brew to taste)
7.5ml honey
Top up with approximately 80ml Fever Tree elderflower tonic (or similar)
Dash of lemon bitters
Garnish with a lemon 'horse's neck'
Serve over a single ice block 'spear' in a highball glass

THE RABBIE

50ml Sassenach whisky
10ml Tio Pepe sherry
15ml sweet vermouth (Cocchi Torino or similar)
10ml Sangue Morlacco cherry liqueur (or Cherry Heering if not available)
Mezcal mist (use atomiser lightly over top of drink)
Garnish: Luxardo maraschino cherry
Stir and serve in a Nick and Nora glass or a coupette

And here's a timeless one with minimal fuss:

SASSENACH OLD FASHIONED

50ml Sassenach whisky
1 sugar cube/teaspoon of sugar/sweetener if preferred
4 dashes Angostura bitters
1 orange slice

Garnish: orange peel
Serve over a single ice block in a highball glass

Duncan Lacroix's Top 10 (make that 11)
Tips for a Legendary Night Out

1. Before you leave the flat line your stomach with a loaf of bread and a pint of full-fat milk (none of this 'trim' shit).
2. Take a vitamin B12. God knows why.
3. Fill your pockets with stuff that would make 'Black Jack' wince, in case you get 'lucky'.
4. Drink two of anything alcoholic just before you close the door of your flat.
5. Find a mate who's even more mental than you, e.g. 'The Irishman'.
6. Get to the bar early. Double up with pints and chasers.
7. Sink 'depth charges' in your mate's pint, and then drink it yourself anyway.
8. Be sure to urinate outside the window of the restaurant in which your director is enjoying dinner with his wife.
9. Break into your own flat because you've forgotten your keys.
10. Start a fight with the person you've invited back to your flat for 'more wine'.
11. Threaten to execute your boss.

CHAPTER THREE

The Land That Begat Me

From 'Scotland the Brave' by Robert Wilson
High in the misty Highlands,
Out by the purple islands,
Brave are the hearts that beat
Beneath Scottish skies.

SAM

Returning to Scotland to shoot *Outlander* after living in London for twelve years, I realised I had the opportunity to really learn more about my heritage and the country in which I was born. I'd toured the Highlands and Islands years before, working in Scottish theatre, and loved the language and stories of the past. Yet, I knew very little about my own heritage. Whilst shooting episodes, each week I'd find myself in another terrific location: a castle ruin, an ancient house, a sweeping glen or a pine forest. At the weekends I'd go into the hills, exploring the peaks and walking or cycling the length of the country. I really began to fall in love again with the land and history. I had been working on producing and creating my own TV show and movies, at which point Graham and I discussed our *Men In Kilts* idea (over a cafe latte in LA). It got me thinking and, after a great deal of work, a few months later I had assembled a crew, cameras, drones, hotels, guests, costumes, locations, the odd stuffed toy and even managed to get the bearded one to jump on a plane from his home in New Zealand. Don't ask me how I managed to convince him to ride in a camper van, with me driving.

So while Graham is drinking an emergency lady latte in a Glencoe layby in order to restore his sugar and caffeine levels to 'safe', I want to go right back to the beginning of Scotland, which started with the glaciers tearing their way across Britain. Scotland was inhospitable until the ice melted around 9600 BC . . . Okay, we don't need to go quite that far back! But we do need a bit of history as context for our journey and to get our 'heids' around the people known as Highlanders, so let's start with the Roman Invasion in the first century AD. When the Romans reached the modern-day Borders they met the locals – the fearsome Picts and Gaels (known as 'Scoti' by the invaders). The Romans didn't think much of these savages so they built a vast stone wall – Hadrian's – in 122 AD to keep these brutes away from their designer togas and Gucci sunglasses. The Scoti and Picts behind the wall didn't think much of these slick-haired Romans with their pasta and newfangled ways, and these ancient tribes weren't about to give up their lands without a fight, nor would they become slaves or tax monkeys to the Romans, so they kicked their Italian arses. There were many raids and battles until the Romans, fed up with these cranky 'Caledonians', pushed the troublesome ones right up above the Central Belt of Scotland between the Firth of Forth and Firth of Clyde and built another wall – the Antonine – in 142 AD.

Graham: That was very good. Did you go to the library?
Sam: No, I mainly got it from Asterix books, Mr Vitalstatistix.
Graham: Right.

GRAHAM

I mean it's extraordinary to think that the Roman Empire had successfully conquered the length and breadth of Europe but never taken Caledonia (the Romans' name for Scotland). The Scots laughed at Hadrian's hurdle and dabbled in border cattle raids and some general violence until the end of Roman Rule (383–410 AD) when the Romans finally buggered off home, battered and bankrupt. And that's when the Gaels took over Western Scotland and Wales, establishing Dál Riata, whilst various Pictish kings controlled the rest of Scotland.

In the sixth century, missionaries were sent to Scotland from Ireland and Rome (with Augustine in 596 AD) and the Picts converted to Christianity (and shinty). Frictions between the Picts and pagan Gaels increased, with many skirmishes, but the two sides eventually united in the ninth century against one common enemy: the Vikings, who invaded Scotland on and off between the eighth and fifteenth centuries. The Vikings were people who liked a dust-up too and they left much of their culture behind in Scotland.

SAM

Including me. [*Graham: I think violating a local peasant girl after burning down her village doesn't really count as 'leaving behind your culture'.*] Obviously way back there was a fair Heughan wench who had the hots for a Viking raider because I'm proud to reveal I'm 3.7% Norwegian, not enough to claim it as my home but there are certainly many similarities in the landscapes of my two claimed nations. You just need to look at the Great Glen (Loch Ness) and the Fjords of Scandinavia to see that. In fact, the word Firth comes from the Norwegian 'fjord', which is an estuary. And, many clans carry the names of their forefathers: MacIvor (son of Ivor), Macaulay (son of Olaf) and MacAskill (son of Asgeir). It's always fascinated me to hear Scottish words being used that are Norse in origin, such as 'greet' (cry), 'een' (eye), 'keek' (look) and perhaps the most Scottish term of all, which derives from Old Norse: 'kilt', meaning 'to tuck'.

I was obsessed by the Vikings as a child. In the nearby borough of

Kirkcudbrightshire, a Viking archaeological dig had been established and I vividly remember being allowed to help slowly brush away at the bones of a Viking settlement. Although I found no buried treasure or ancient magical weapons, I did find pieces of bone that the patient archaeologist assured me had been the supper of a bearded Viking warrior.

GRAHAM

Around the time of the marauding Vikings, Kenneth MacAlpin, the first king of Scotland, united the Kingdom of Scotland in 843 AD. Also at this time, the Highland clans were emerging (although the majority of clans cannot be authenticated until the twelfth or thirteenth centuries). Early Highland clan life drew its roots from the Druids and Celts with the Gaelic word 'clann' meaning children. Built around kinship (blood ties), identity and a sense of belonging, you were essentially part of a huge extended, if sometimes highly dysfunctional, family. Clans had more to do with survival in a harsh land full of tumult rather than race or nationality. Members organised themselves around a 'chieftain', a territorial leader ruling over classless free men of equal rights. (There were slaves but these were never from the tribe, just some poor unfortunates they rounded up.)

Most chieftains were elected, and if they didn't come up to scratch they could be deposed. One such clan chief in the seventeenth century was deposed because while on a cattle raid to the neighbouring clan in freezing winter he had the temerity to make a pillow out of ice to sleep the night on. The rest of the lads were so appalled and disgusted by this weakness, they simply got rid of him. 'Did you see Willie – an ice pillow?! Probably wants a wee teddy bear too, and for us to tuck him in! SLIT HIS THROAT!!!'

The clans lived in 'black houses', many built of turf, not stone. Later medieval castles, like the MacKenzie clan's Castle Leoch in *Outlander*, were built on the profits of international trade which, from the thirteenth century onwards, was massive. Cod and salmon were shipped in large barrels from Aberdeen to Hamburg; hides and wool were traded for wine and other luxuries in Flanders and Bruges and cattle were raised to be sold (and exported) and were to become a great source of wealth for many chieftains. But cattle were also the prime cause of inter-clan violence.

Inheritance was through something called 'Tanistry', where a cousin or a brother would inherit before a son and, as for marriage, the early Celts believed in free love. There was no marriage and children were raised by the whole clan. No one really knew who anyone's father was, and they didn't care. Boys were given independence at fourteen, but were not regarded as men until they'd grown a full beard.

Sam . . . ?!

However, it's worth mentioning that meanwhile, the Picts on the eastern side of Scotland, also of Celtic origin, were actually big on marriage and were 'matrilineal' so lands, goods and titles all passed through the mother's line.

But the Gaels lived in a big old hippy commune, just with eye-watering violence and slavery thrown in. Land belonged to everyone, not to any individual. However, scraping a living off marginal and harsh terrain, with a constant battle for resources and territory, made for ferocious violence and the opportunity for clan chieftains to assert dominance over local families, who accepted their protection in return for food and money.

Later Scots' emphasis on physical strength, courage and stamina owes much to these early Celtic tribes. Druids were given terrifying ordeals in order to become ordained. One example was that they had to compose a song, and play it with musical accompaniment, to one of the many complex bardic metres. Sounds simple enough. But oh no, not the Druids. Some wag, somewhere in the mists of time, decided to tell the prospective ordinant the chosen meter, moments before he was immersed up to his nostrils in a tank of cold water *for the entire night*. The next morning, he was taken from the ball-freezing tank and told to play his chosen song, with his chosen instrument *immediately!*

Not, 'Here's a towel, and a cup of tea. Get your breath back. Take your time.'

No, it was, 'Play the bloody song or we may sacrifice your gonads to that oak tree over there.' They revered oak trees and gonads. (I honestly think Sam should attempt this for Season Two of *Men In Kilts*. In fact, if he'd known about it I'm pretty sure he would've volunteered straight away, while trying to get muggins here to do the same.)

However, by the sixteenth century clan life had begun to change. Marriage alliances became a means of strengthening political pacts and consolidating wealth and power. There were no elections to chiefdom, common ownership continued to survive, but now they levied increasing rent and class structures began to appear. 'Tacksmen' were those who had smallholdings, working farms held by rent from the chief. They could sublet them to others. Below this class were 'cottars' arranged in townships (tiny clusters of homes), each with enough land to sow some oats and have a couple of cows. The chief wasn't just a landlord, he was way more powerful; with 'heritable jurisdiction' he could enforce the law. Along with the charms of 'pit and gallows' (to drown women and hang men) he could hang and imprison *anyone*.

Out of this clan system came warriors quick to attack and savage in close combat. This led men to push themselves as individual champions. Men were encouraged and expected to fight like ferocious animals in battle. They instinctively surged forward, running quickly to fight, trusting to being chancy rather than canny. If there was no combat to hand the Highlanders had no hesitation in triggering one; a cattle raid, or the least excuse seized upon to start a 350-year feud, for instance . . .

SAM

1300–1600 were some of the most violent years in the Highlands during what became known as the Clan Wars – tribal gangs feuding and generally knocking seven bells out of one another in a mafia style, governed by codes of absolute loyalty, respect and honour. And, 'Thou shalt not steal thy neighbour's coo, or I'll cut yer heid off!'

One notable clan feud was between the MacLeods and the MacDonalds. In 1577 there was a terrible massacre on the Isle of Eigg and here's what happened. Three young MacLeod men were banished from the island after trying out a number of dodgy

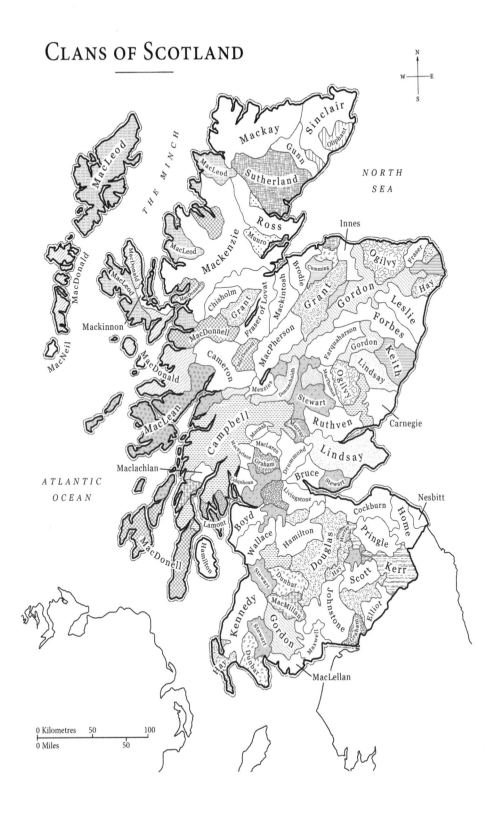

CLANS OF SCOTLAND

N
W • E
S

THE MINCH

NORTH SEA

MacLeod

Mackay

Sinclair

Gunn

Oliphant

MacLeod

Sutherland

Ross

Munro

Innes

MacDonald

MacLeod

MacLeod

Mackenzie

Brodie

Cumming

Ogilvy

Fraser

Hay

MacDonald

MacLeod

MacDonnell

Chisholm

Grant

Fraser of Lovat

Mackintosh

Grant

Gordon

Leslie

Mackinnon

MacDonnell

MacPherson

Farquaharson

Forbes

Gordon

Keith

MacNeil

Cameron

Donnachaidh

Ogilvy

Lindsay

MacDonald

Menzies

Stewart

MacDougall

MacLean

Campbell

Macnab

Murray

Ruthven

Carnegie

Maclachlan

MacFarlane

MacLaren

Graham

Drummond

Lindsay

ATLANTIC OCEAN

Colquhoun

Livingstone

Bruce

Stewart

Nesbitt

Lamont

Boyd

Wallace

Hamilton

Cockburn

Home

Pringle

Douglas

Murray

Hay

Scott

Kerr

MacDonell

Hamilton

Stewart

Dunbar

Johnstone

Graham

Elliot

Kennedy

MacMillan

Gordon

Maxwell

Hay

Stewart

Dunbar

MacLellan

0 Kilometres   50   100
0 Miles   50

chat-up lines on a few local ladies. The MacDonalds didn't mess around and the MacLeod youths had their hands and feet bound and were bunged in a boat and cast adrift until they finally washed up at Dunvegan. The MacLeod chieftain was livid at the MacLeod boys' treatment and immediately set sail for Eigg with a number of his men to 'have a word' with the MacDonalds. Knowing the MacLeods were on their way, like a Mexican cartel out of *Narcos*, the entire MacDonald clan hid in the Cave of Frances to the south of the island. However, the MacLeods tracked their footprints to the cave. The MacDonalds refused point blank to come out and 'have a chat' so the MacLeods lit a bonfire 'of turf and ferns' at the entrance and suffocated all 350 MacDonalds inside.

Incidentally, I spent many a summer during childhood on the Isle of Eigg and visited the cave many times. Walking across the Singing Sands (the sand squeaks with every footstep) and past a large rotting whale carcass, the entrance to the cave is hard to spot. Squeeze through the small gap and you find yourself in a large cave. It opens up and goes quite far back. In the darkness it's hard to see how big the cave is, but some old sheep bones on the floor reveal it's claimed more than the lives of the MacDonalds.

A year later, in 1578, the MacDonalds' and MacLeods' beef continued, this time on the Isle of Skye. Hell-bent on revenge for the Eigg cave massacre, the MacDonalds who had survived landed eight ships at Ardmore Bay, surrounded the local church and torched it. All the worshippers were burned alive, except one young lady who escaped out of a window. Seeing the smoke, the MacLeods rushed to the church and the MacDonalds legged it back to their boats *but* the tide had gone out! So the boats were on the rocks and the MacLeods had them surrounded and, yet again, all the MacDonalds were slain. (Hey, but they bounced back centuries later with the Golden Arches, right?)

'Their bodies were range in line alongside a turf dyke . . . and the dyke was tumbled over on the top of them – a quick but unfeeling form of burial.'

Alexander Cameron, *The History and Traditions of Skye* (1892)

It was properly brutal stuff.

GRAHAM

With such a fearsome reputation for violence it's no wonder James VI of Scotland (1566–1625) believed the Highlanders were barbarous and there was wicked blood in the isles. He recommended that Highlanders should be 'treated like wolves or wild boar'. This was a Scottish king and a Stuart, by the way!

Of course, the Highlanders were not complete barbarians, and by the fifteenth and sixteenth centuries many had travelled abroad, could speak French, and often Italian, too. Their children were educated, their homes lavishly furnished and their drink of choice was likely to be claret over whisky. They were apt to boast. MacLeod of Harris bet James V he had finer candlesticks and a bigger table. After the King had shown him his banqueting table, MacLeod invited the King to Harris and had a hundred men stand in a circle around the cloth-covered table carrying flaming pinecones for illumination. MacLeod won the bet.

The perceived 'romance' of Scotland simply refuses to fit the reality of a deeply practical race of people who made decisions out of hard-nosed self-interest and loyalty to their kith and kin.

SAM

When William Wallace started a revolt against Edward I in 1297, brilliantly brought to life by Mel Gibson's epic movie *Braveheart*, Scotland was ruled by (King) Robert the Bruce, a supporter of the Wallace Uprising. Robert 'the badass' Bruce went on to famously defeat the English army at the Battle of Bannockburn (1314), securing Scotland as an independent and sovereign kingdom. Get in! But of course we know it wasn't to last. There's a memorial erected to Bruce near the dramatic and seriously fortified Stirling Castle.

SCOTTISH KINGS AND QUEENS TIMELINE

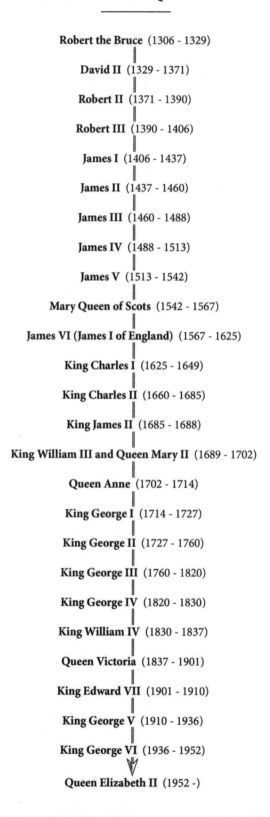

Robert the Bruce (1306 - 1329)

David II (1329 - 1371)

Robert II (1371 - 1390)

Robert III (1390 - 1406)

James I (1406 - 1437)

James II (1437 - 1460)

James III (1460 - 1488)

James IV (1488 - 1513)

James V (1513 - 1542)

Mary Queen of Scots (1542 - 1567)

James VI (James I of England) (1567 - 1625)

King Charles I (1625 - 1649)

King Charles II (1660 - 1685)

King James II (1685 - 1688)

King William III and Queen Mary II (1689 - 1702)

Queen Anne (1702 - 1714)

King George I (1714 - 1727)

King George II (1727 - 1760)

King George III (1760 - 1820)

King George IV (1820 - 1830)

King William IV (1830 - 1837)

Queen Victoria (1837 - 1901)

King Edward VII (1901 - 1910)

King George V (1910 - 1936)

King George VI (1936 - 1952)

Queen Elizabeth II (1952 -)

Whilst running the Stirling marathon in 2018, and in the eighteenth mile as my legs were really starting to burn, I caught sight of the Wallace monument. It marks the site of the Battle of Stirling Bridge where Wallace defeated the English and became a national hero and was given the sobriquet 'The Guardian of Scotland'. He was purported to hold a Claymore double-handed sword measuring five feet four inches – taller than Dwalin the angry dwarf – and he was a fearsome warrior. His memorial can be visited today and, via a narrow spiral staircase of 246 steps, you can reach the top to receive a dramatic and windy view. It's a rewarding climb; just don't do it after running a marathon.

And so we come to the House of Stuart (the same family as Bonnie Prince Charlie) which came to the throne in 1371, ruling Scotland for three centuries with James VI inheriting the English throne as well, becoming James I of England, in 1603. Then there's the bit in the middle where Charles I (also a Stuart) is beheaded in the midst of the chaos of the English Civil War in 1649. Oliver Cromwell presides as Lord Protector until the Scots proclaim Charles II (a sequel Stuart) King of Scotland, which makes Cromwell raging mad and leads to several bloody battles in the 'Scottish Campaign', including the Battle of Worcester, after which Charles II is deposed. *However*, Charles II leads another Stuart comeback in 1660 and is restored to the thrones of England, Scotland and Ireland and all is well again. *Until* it's James VII's (James II of England) turn to mess everything up again by converting to Catholicism, which gets the English Protestants' knickers in a twist, so they depose him in 1688 and install first cousins from the House of Hanover, William and Mary, meaning inbreeding was totally fine just so long as they weren't Catholics! James VII (II of England) flees to France and tries to return by invading Ireland but loses the Battle of the Boyne in 1690 and spends the rest of his life in France, living off Louis XIV. The Stuart Family would be trying to do a David Hasselhoff comeback for the next fifty-six years . . .

In a nutshell this 'Glorious Revolution' of sectarianism, king nobbling and incest goes down like a shite sandwich in Scotland, and it leads directly to the first Jacobite Rising of 1689 and subsequent unrest, as those 'loyal to Jacob' (Hebrew for James) are determined to put a Stuart king back on the throne and keep Scotland independent. The 1707 Act of Union, which created the Kingdom of Great Britain, further inflames the Jacobites, so much so that when Graham playing Dougal MacKenzie (a diehard Jacobite) discovers Jamie's and Claire's plot to kill Bonnie Prince Charlie in 1746 (in order to change history and prevent the slaughter at Culloden occurring), there is a fight to the death.

Needless to say I won and Graham became unemployed again. *[Graham: You had HELP!]* A sore point to this day. In the book, Jamie kills Dougal himself. By involving Claire, it makes the two complicit and binds them in his death. I fear Diana was not best pleased . . .

But that's quite enough history. Let's go and get a drink!

Key Dates in Scottish History

1314 – Battle of Bannockburn

1300–1600 – Highland Clan Wars

1494 – Earliest Written Record of Whisky

1688 – Glorious Revolution – William of Orange

1689 – Early Jacobite Uprising

1690s – Little Ice Age, slump in trade, famine:
    collectively known as the 'Seven Ill Years'

1692 – Glencoe Massacre

1694 – Dougal MacKenzie born 29th May

1715 – Jacobite Rising of 1715

1701 – Act of Settlement – secured succession of
    only Protestant monarchs to the thrones of
    England and Ireland

1707 – Act of Union – creating the Kingdom of
    Great Britain

1721 – Jamie Fraser born 1st May

1745 – Jacobite Uprising, Charles Edward Stuart
    (Bonnie Prince Charlie) returns to Scotland

1746 – Battle of Culloden

1750–1860 – Highland Clearances

1755–83 – American War of Independence

1789–99 – French Revolution

1799 – Graham McTavish born

1846–56 – Potato Famine

CHAPTER FOUR

Scotland Was Born Fighting

'Lament for the Old Highland Warriors'
by Robert Chambers (January 1835)
Oh, where are the pretty men of yore,
Oh, where are the brave men gone,
Oh, where are the heroes of the north?
Each under his own grey stone.
Oh, where now the broad bright claymore,
Oh, where are the truis and plaid?
Oh, where now the merry Highland heart?
In silence for ever laid.
Och on a rie, och on a rie,
Och on a rie, all are gone,
Och on a rie, the heroes of yore,
Each under his own grey stone.

SAM

It's the winter of 180 AD and General Maximus Decimus Meridius wants to go home. Ancient Rome is thriving. Somewhere in Western Europe, he sits upon his trusty steed ('Rusty', whom Russell Crowe tried to steal and take back to the US; we rode Rusty in Season One of *Outlander*) and contemplates what may be the final battle against the Germanic tribes. Crowe, dressed as Roman General Maximus, has a clipped military accent and haircut to match. He's trained, hardened and resolute, as he surveys the land across to the forest beyond. Suddenly, a huge figure appears on horseback, a mighty Germanic warrior, with a long beard and enormous axe; he is holding a Roman soldier's severed head. He stands in defiance opposite the mighty Roman army and issues a guttural scream. The sound echoes off the trees and makes the hairs on the viewers' necks stand up on end. A mass of mighty warriors thirsting for blood answer his unintelligible cry and a horde of German barbarians appear along the treeline, ready for war and bloodshed. Things don't look good for Russell . . .

The mighty German warrior in Ridley Scott's *Gladiator* is played by Charlie 'Chick' Allen – a battle re-enactor and the leader of the Clan Ranald Trust for Scotland. The trust stages re-enactments and has its own fully functioning Highland village, which appears in countless TV shows, films and commercials. As terrifying in real life as he is on screen, Charlie is tall, broad and bred from the very rock itself. He naturally commands respect from the other re-enactors, who are as hard as nails but are too terrified to fight Charlie themselves, because of his fearsome reputation. On *Outlander*, he taught me how to wear a Great Kilt and fight with a sword, dirk (long knife) and targe (spiked Highland shield). He gave me my first dirk, used in Season One, and I learnt to spin it on the palm of my hand. It now sits in pride of place in my living room in Glasgow.

GRAHAM

Charlie arrives at Loch Achtriochtan in the heart of Glencoe on a 'Sons of Anarchy' style hog that you could probably hear in Inverness. He's wearing a bandana with a skull on it, and a black helmet fashioned to resemble that of a storm trooper. Now, while on others this might appear hopelessly desperate and perhaps sad, on Charlie one can't help feeling he wrenched it from the head of an actual Nazi after headbutting him to death.

One thing about Charlie Allen is, he doesn't look like a 'Charlie Allen' – he really looks like more of a Ruaridh McMurderer or Angus Og McBludgeon. As he walks up the bank of heather surrounded by the menacing Bidean nam Bim massif on the southern side of Glencoe – the ridges of Stob Coire Sgreamhach, Stob Coire nan Lochan and Aonach Dubh glowering down – Sam and I instantly feel emasculated. 'He looks like a f*cking beast!' says Sam, who visibly shrinks in his presence. I suspect Dwayne 'The Rock' Johnson would start to cry.

Charlie's beard is of legendary proportions, right down to his nipples. Thick, luxuriant and menacing, it is tempting to think that without his beard Charlie would look benign, but I'm pretty sure under the beard is . . . another beard.

I have a beard, Sam has something resembling facial hair, but this is a *real* beard, not crinigerous folly. And then he speaks. While Richard, our whisky man, had a softly modulated Scottish accent, soothing and mellifluous like a whisky liqueur, Charlie's is the sound of heavy boots on gravel, a different timbre entirely. There is no attempt at putting you at your ease, it is simply a blunt instrument, like an axe. I have known Charlie for twenty-five years and he still greets me with the same wary suspicion, as if he may need to set about me with anything that comes to hand. Of course, this initial impression belies a soft interior, a Wildean wit, a habit of breaking into song and a love for Rodgers and Hammerstein musicals. Just kidding. I can't remember his handshake. I've probably blanked it from my mind because it was so painful.

SAM

He emerges at the top of a wee hill, dirk and targe in hand. 'Ahrrrrr! The modern Highlander,' I say in my deepest, manliest voice.

Graham is at it too. 'Arrrr!' he says like Long John Silver. 'The man himself.' I bet Charlie can smell lady latte on his breath. (He had one on the way over – well, of course, he did.) I, however, have gargled whisky from my hip flask and have the breath of a warrior.

'Good to see yer. Good to see yer,' I start to jabber, trying to stop looking like a pathetic actor. 'So here we are.' My inner voice is as Scottish and as fierce as Charlie. 'Get a grip, yer jessie,' it barks.

Oowwww!

Yup, his handshake is pretty terrifying, my manly resolve now crushed in his enormous hands. I subtly shake the pain out of my knuckles as we dive in to talk of Highland weaponry. Charlie tells us in his deep Scotch burr, 'There was a lot of warring going on between the clans so they weren't short of fighting practice! Over the centuries we were our own worst enemy. There were a lot of feuds between families and between clans, and when one clan's in, we're all in.'

We learn that a father wouldn't have taught a son how to sword-fight; that would have been left to the uncle. In *Outlander*, Jamie Fraser was trained by Uncle Dougal MacKenzie, played by Graham. At the age of fourteen he had gone to foster at his uncle's house. Dougal taught him to fight with both hands; they were both left-handed but capable of using both. We decided on the show to let Jamie use both hands when writing and fighting as solely using my left hand would prove difficult and unconvincing. However, I try to use both when I can.

[Graham: No comment.]

Charlie lifts up his targe and tells us the circular shield (or Highland target) is one of the primary weapons of a Highland warrior. Made of wood and covered in cowhide, with an iron or leather handle and arm strap, they were sometimes highly decorative with intricate Celtic patterns in brass or silver. At the centre was a spike, which mercifully Charlie hasn't screwed on today.

Charlie says, 'A lot of people mistake the shield as just being for defence but it is a weapon. The spike on the targe was really long and you could use it to slash and impale the enemy.' It was common to hold a dirk (or 'biotag', a long knife) in the targe hand, the blade sticking out below for more slashing and stabbing. Charlie demonstrates, 'So you'd come in over the top with the dirk, smashing through with the targe and impaling with the spike. It was just like a big thrashing and meshing machine. It was block, slash, cut; block, slash, cut with the targe alone.'

When defending, the Highlander would stop the point of a sword or bayonet with their targe and then lunge low for an upward thrust into the enemy's torso with their sword, held in their other hand. The Highlander's sword of choice was a basket-hilt Highland broadsword (or another dirk for some of the poorer Highlanders). These broadswords were really brutal weapons. Charlie holds out his for us to inspect.

'They were three-foot razor blades. *Very* sharp with two blade edges – they could cut right through anything. The one I'm holding is a bit heavier, for re-enactment purposes, and it's got a blunted edge to keep people safe, but the real ones were much lighter and easier to handle for slashing and cutting.'

GRAHAM

Charlie really is a man born in the wrong time. As he describes how the Highland warriors would fight with dirk, targe and broadsword, you see a wistfulness pass over his face, as if wondering why he's not allowed to do this in his local Marks and Spencer's.

I tell him I'd read that reports of the wounds at the Jacobite battles of Killiecrankie (1689) and Prestonpans (1745) were horrific because of these weapons, with skulls cloven in two, tops cut clean off, people split in two with a single blow right down to the guts. It was unbelievably brutal stuff.

'Yeah,' he nods, unfazed. 'And they also had the basket at the end of the sword, which not only protects the hand but is a good weapon – like a steel boxing glove, so if you got in really close you could use it for upper cuts or pummelling down.'

He explained that, in battle, the Highlanders didn't just go running in with swords. 'They would stand and "loose off" arrows at the opposition. Some would go in with claymores [two-handed swords] or battleaxes before the line. The whole point of the line and the way the Highlanders fought was about protecting the man next to you, which is what the British [Redcoats] sussed out at Culloden, so when the Highlander's arm was up, that's when they came in underneath to stab them.'

The Highlanders ran forward in groups of twelve forming part of a greater wedge, with Gaelic battle cries of 'Faster, faster', booms and blood-curdling screams to invoke fear and shock in the enemy. The famous Highland Charge was all about speed. Once in musket range of the British, the Highlanders, armed with muskets, would fire at the enemy, gun smoke obscuring the enemy's line of sight. The Highlanders would dive down to the ground at the return of fire and, whilst the Redcoats were reloading, or plugging their bayonets, the Highland Charge would continue thundering forward until they battered through the British lines.

'They were incredibly fit men,' says Charlie. At the Battle of Killiecrankie (1689) when the British let off the first volley into the Highlanders, they didn't even have time to plug in their bayonets before the Highlanders were on them. They ran that fast. Imagine the panic in the British ranks when they saw wild plaid-wearing warriors roaring towards them, screaming, with all that weaponry . . .

The Charge, however, was to prove fatal on the boggy moor of Culloden (1746). The old warrior style of fighting could not contend with modern weapons, nor British tactics, and approximately 1,500–2,000 Highlanders and 300–400 British soldiers were slain in a battle that lasted no more than an hour.

Over a hundred years after Culloden echoes of the Highlands were heard on the Battlefield of Gettysburg (Pennsylvania) in 1863 as the Confederates thundered towards the Unionists in Pickett's Charge shouting their 'Rebel Yell'. Given the predominance of Scots and Irish settlers in the Southern states (particularly after the Clearances of 1750–1860, when the landlords and clan chiefs 'cleared' their tenants by force to make way for sheep), the tactics would seem more than just a coincidence. And just like at Culloden, war cries and speed were no match for modern weaponry. The Confederates were defeated in the bloodiest battle in US history, with 10,000 men killed and 30,000 wounded on both sides.

SAM

During a shirtless Highland Charge in Season Two of *Outlander* (a few episodes before our re-enactment of Prestonpans), Graham and fellow actors playing Rupert and Angus, along with a melee of extras, were required to run at us in full cry. I distinctly remember Graham with his long johns slipping down from under his kilt during each take (not a true Scotsman this time, mate!). Moments before, he had been seen doing press-ups to get himself and his impressive chest pumped. Duncan Lacroix stood smoking a cigarette watching the War Chief knock out some reps. As the pack of clansmen charged towards us, all in varying states of exhaustion, baying for blood, some not in great shape, wheezing, panting and being pummelled in the face by their own bouncing moobs – I couldn't help notice they were covered in mud: a tactic to make them look even more wild and terrifying. However, Graham's mud seemed to have been perfectly placed to enhance his muscles and six-pack. A mud pack. Don't get me wrong, the man is in great shape . . . for his age . . . but I'd never seen a Highland Warrior use mud in this manner.

[Graham: Says the Kim Kardashian of contouring.]

After maybe two takes, Graham starts to complain he's cramping and his quads are seizing up. It happened *every* time he was required to ride poor old Lambert, his faithful horse in the show. Graham gives 100% . . . for a couple of takes. And then, as soon as he feels he's done enough or he thinks the director has enough footage, he suddenly gets cramp or an injury and has to have a wee sit down. And a latte. And definitely a snack. 'And could I possibly trouble you for a copy of *The Times* – thank you so much.' And perhaps a shoulder massage from a fair wench . . . There is a lot I can learn from Maestro McTavish.

GRAHAM

The wonderful Lambert was my horse on *Outlander* and possibly the most patient horse in the equine world. His twin was called 'Butler'. Named after a brand of cigarettes, Lambert & Butler – only in Scotland! Lambert covered up *all* my shortcomings. I'm sure he'd look up at me and wink with his big winky horse eye before a take as if to say, 'I've got this, buddy.'

There was a shot at the end of Season One, Episode Four – with me in the front, leading a long line of Highlanders away from Doune Castle (aka Castle Leoch). As I rode, hand on hip, I could hear the screaming of Stephen Walters (Angus) behind me, arguably even less happy with a horse than I am. His horse was careering back and forth, with him holding on for dear life, shouting, 'Woah, woah, *woah!*'

I resolutely stared ahead, I didn't want to give Lambert ideas, my only concern being whether I was in focus on camera. As Lambert and I passed the lens, Stephen's voice fading in the background, I gave Lambert a thankful pat on his neck. He'd managed to make me look vaguely competent, yet again.

Another time we were riding in a long line and this time I'm singing a song (Season One, Episode Five). Now, I've never said I'm a singer. Nor has anyone else. I once auditioned for, ironically, *The Hobbit* (the musical) back in 1990 and after I had sung my song the director said, 'You have a great voice – struggling to get out.' I was later asked by Brian Cox to be in *Richard III* at Regent's Park Open Air Theatre. The theatre has a musical as part of its repertoire every year. They like you to be in two shows in the season. After my singing audition, Ian Talbot, the artistic director, said, 'I think we could put you in the children's summer show instead.' So I ended up doing *Richard III* and playing the Sheriff of Nottingham in *Kids from Sherwood*.

So when I was asked to sing 'The Maid Gey to the Mill ba Nicht' in *Outlander* I thought, *This is my chance!* However, Grant O'Rourke, who played the wonderfully named Rupert, had other ideas. (I don't think I've ever met a Rupert in Scotland, unless he was having his head flushed down a toilet.) Grant fancies himself as a bit of a singer, among other things, but he did not approve of my singing ability. He constantly corrected me and offered advice (all, of course, ignored by me). Instead, sitting astride my trusty Lambert, I belted out the song, in the wrong key, but with all the pent-up frustration of a man repeatedly denied his chance to sing. If I wasn't going to get naked in *Outlander* (more on that later . . .) I was bloody well going to sing my lungs out. So when you watch that moment, remember the singing voice that had so long been denied its chance was finally being set free, while four horses back Grant O'Rourke was shaking his head in disbelief. The only silver lining was – Grant got thrown from his horse.

Thanks Lambert.

SAM

Do you remember Duncan's horse? At the first arrival at Leoch it had *severe* flatulence. *Every* time they called 'Action' it would let rip! You can almost see Caitriona covering her face in the scene as she couldn't control her giggles. It would *have* to be Duncan with the farting stallion!

And the lovely 'Sleepy' – my black Friesian on *Outlander*. Ah Sleepy, I miss you. Slender and elegant, he looked after me in Season One. Luckily, the stunt team saw through my 'bull' regarding my ability to ride – I'd lied about being raised on a farm and riding horses since I was a bairn to land the parts in *Alexander the Great* and *Billy the Kid*, having previously only stroked a donkey! But this time I was going to learn how to ride properly, or at least trust Sleepy and let him do the work. I now feel confident on a horse (Sleepy in particular). The horses are so well trained and generally make us look better than we are. Sleepy likes to look around a lot; he's a curious horse but guns don't bother him, nor do loud noises, blustering actors, lighting rigs, mud, cobbles or rain. He loves a mint and a scratch under his mane, particularly on his withers (the ridge between the shoulder blades of an animal). He *loves* that. The only thing he really doesn't like is goats. (Graham's a Capricorn 'goat' – I don't think he liked him.) Sleepy and I parted ways when Jamie set sail for the New World (Season Three) and I had a new companion, Pinocchio. Occasionally dyed a different colour to make him double for various equine friends, he's beautiful and he knows it. We are similar in personality: slow in the morning, overly enthusiastic at times. His only failing is he will *always* trip up on his own feet or a tree root. Even though we may pass the same tree each take, he really doesn't get it. Either that or he's testing me, which may be closer to the truth.

But back to fighting, before Charlie knocks my block off . . . As he's been in *Rambo* with Sly Stallone, I have to admit Graham is a good fighter. I like to think I'm pretty good at stage-fighting too, having performed many action scenes on *Outlander*, as well as other stage, film and TV shows. God knows what Charlie Allen *really* thinks of our poncy fighting, but I'm not asking his opinion anytime soon. Anyway, Graham and I share a unique skill – we're not masters of the choreography, we are masters of the sound effects. Jedi warriors in vocal fighting. During a fight scene, vocalising can help the other actor by indicating you're hitting them, so that they can react in time. The vocalisation also helps to add power and strength; it looks and feels stronger. However, we always take it too far . . . groaning, blustering, seething, panting and shouting, Dougal MacKenzie is particularly ferocious and you can definitely hear it! But it's short-lived, the magic lasting for only a take or two before Old Graham needs another sit-down. And another latte and a protein bar.

I wonder if he's the same in the bedroom department. 'Er, Beryl, angel, we've done it twice now – and it was spectacular, darling, earth-moving – but let me have a little sit in the armchair. I don't want to get injured – it's not really worth the risk, is it?' *However*, two hours later, after food and caffeine, I guarantee Beryl will be cooing like a pigeon in the strong arms of the Silver McFox.

GRAHAM

I was making action movies and television whilst Sam was still potty training so it's not surprising that I've developed a degree of caution as a result. Sam is quite correct. Two takes and I'm thinking, *We're all pushing our luck now.* Generally if you haven't got it in two takes, someone isn't doing their job properly. I've learned that directors will ask you to do things that they would never dream of doing themselves. (Sam's romantic sodomy scene with Tobias Menzies in Season One proves that.) And sadly I know too many actors (and stuntmen) who have been seriously injured or killed because they were too afraid to say no. If I have *any* doubt about the safety of something, I stop.

[Sam: Er, safety is of paramount importance, Beryl, we could slip in the shower . . .]

Strangely enough, Sam is a safe fighter. I always feel he knows what he's doing (unlike on this trip where he's embracing a cavalier approach to driving and drinking, but thankfully never the twain together). The red mist doesn't envelop him on the word:

'Action!' But there was one fight on *Outlander* where the rule-book went flying out of the window. Sam wasn't in this particular scene. It was in a bar scene with Stephen Walters (Angus), Duncan Lacroix (Murtagh), Grant O'Rourke (Rupert) and several stuntmen. Some of the locals were watching us and basically, it kicked off. We'd rehearsed the action and everyone seemed to know what they were doing, but just before the take, Dominic (our stunt coordinator) utters the immortal line, 'Just go for it! The stuntmen will be fine.' Big mistake when you're addressing Walters and Lacroix. On 'Action' it was mayhem. Duncan grabbed a guy and threw him against a wooden post. I started throwing him back and forth screaming, 'Bastard! Bastard! Bastard!' (not in the script) and Stephen Walters actually bites the stuntman's nose. When we cut, Stephen apologised to the stuntman who said, 'No mate, it's great, do it again!' And that's all you need to know about stuntmen. *[Sam: It must be mentioned that my character Jamie wasn't allowed to be in this scene as he'd easily have beaten everyone. Fact.]*

And Charlie Allen is from the exact same mould of nutters. He's a lovely guy but having seen him fighting . . . I stay well clear. We first worked together on Jeremy Freeston's film of *Macbeth* in 1997. At the beginning we recreated the battle against the Norwegian king and were given weapons such as axes and maces, which had solid cores with a thin rubber outer layer. Charlie insisted we use them at full force during this sequence.

My most action-packed experience was *Rambo 4* with Sylvester Stallone, the godfather of action heroes. Working with him I realised how hard it is to make everything seem as effortless as he does. He is a true master. I suppose I've always enjoyed pretending to fight; I find it strangely therapeutic. However, I have rarely been in punch-ups in real life. Possibly only three. Which, given my role as a World Peace Tartan Ambassador, might be three more fisticuffs than Desmond Tutu or Susan Boyle have been in. They, along with Malala and the Dalai Lama, are recipients of the blue peace tartan (I even have my own peace kilt). And yes, considering the roles I play, the irony is indeed heavy.

Sam: World Peace Ambassador? Can I have some of what you're smoking?

Graham: You're plainly jealous and I forgive you.

SAM

Seeing as we are name-dropping here, let me tell you about working with Vin Diesel, spending a week or so in a swimming pool in South Africa, trying not to punch him in the face. In Sony's *Bloodshot* from the Valiant Comic series, Vin plays the title character, an ex-soldier killed in action but given new nano-technology that regenerates him. I play an ex-Navy Seal called Jimmy Dalton who has suffered extreme trauma in an IED explosion. He lost his legs (and much of his humanity) and is pissed off that Vin gets all the new technology. Jimmy is angry at the military, his boss and most of all, 'Bloodshot' (Vin), who gets new toys to play with. I actually did most of the fight scenes, with great help from my amazing stunt double. The stunt crew were from the *Fast and Furious* films, and we really wanted to impress Vin's fans. We trained for weeks and I was happy to do some aerial stuff, too (similar to the 'Batman Live' Cirque-style show I performed in, all around the world, a couple of years earlier). Vin does occasionally message me or send a video, usually when he has downtime and is with his gorgeous family. His kids performed a traditional tribal dance they had learned especially for the whole crew on *Bloodshot*, whilst shooting in South Africa. His last name is actually Sinclair and he has some Scottish heritage. I last saw him online, in Edinburgh on the Royal Mile, whilst filming *Fast and Furious 15.5* or whichever one it is, singing 'Oh Flower of Scotland' at full volume – he knew all of the words too!

I had barely dried off from the South African swimming pool before I started on *SAS: Red Notice in Budapest*, based on Andy McNab's series of books. Andy is one of the most decorated UK special forces operators, having famously been captured in Iraq during the Gulf War. He was our military advisor and I spent many days with him training. Two things to understand about Andy: 1) he is genuinely one of the most charming people you'll meet; 2) he is a certified psychopath. Really. He has written a book about it and conducted multiple studies with Oxford University on the subject. Luckily for me he's a 'good one'. I had to spend a lot of time with him alone, with various military weaponry, and at first I found this rather unsettling. I have countless stories about him but one sticks in my mind: whilst showing me how to dominate and control a civilian, he made me hold a porcelain mannequin and pretend to be a neutral. Then, at the top of his voice, with controlled aggression, he smashed the mannequin into my nose, almost knocking me over. My eyes started to water and I thought, 'Shit, I better not cry, he's a bloody psychopath, might think me weak, maybe kill me, or eat me . . . fuck, that *hurt*.' I mean, I was alone with him, what if he just decided to break my neck? He had just shown me how to kill some-one with a mobile phone . . . (old flip phones are the best). Fortunately, I survived the experience *somewhat* intact and at the time of writing, the movie is due to be released soon, in all its psychopathic glory.

Ahem.

Charlie Allen is looking right at me as his men unfurl an enor-mous amount of plaid (checked or tartan twilled woollen cloth). As I said, Charlie taught me how to wear a kilt and now two of his Clan Ranald assistants – already in plaid – have brought me a four-metre 'Feileadh Mor' (meaning 'great plaid') to climb into.

Charlie tells us there is no set length or width for plaid. 'I guess if you were portly you would have fewer pleats, thinner, more pleats and richer, more material.' The Highland warriors wore their plaid as a kilt with the extra material tucked in at the sides and back or pinned above the left shoulder to a jacket. It's a really adapt-able piece of clothing – by folding it in various ways it can also be used to carry food, children, hidden weapons and it can be pulled up over the head for shelter or warmth. Being traditionally dyed using local berries and plants, it would act as a natural camouflage from enemy soldiers. And these kilts kept us surprisingly warm during winter shoots, my body and legs never getting cold whilst wearing them.

It's been a while since I have worn a belted kilt; after Culloden in 1746 (and Season Three, Episode One in *Outlander*), the wearing of plaid and tartan, along with all weapons and other symbols of

Highland culture, were banned by the British until 1782. Folding the pleats is hard to do in the heather. Charlie tells me, 'You can actually gather it on your arm.' He can probably do this in his sleep . . . if he does sleep.

I sit down on the plaid, which has been pleated by Charlie's helpers. 'Put your bum in the middle with your ankles facing me,' he says as I begin to fumble with the folds of my kilt, trying to show him I know how to dress myself. I fear his silence is a mixture of annoyance and disappointment and am ready for him to just punch me in the face for being rubbish, or not being naked while I dress.

My plaid became my daily ritual every day on set in *Outlander*. I'd lay out the cloth in my tiny trailer, then meticulously fold the material into pleats. Despite it being extremely early in the morning, it was a form of meditation and preparation. Once maybe a third of the material was pleated, I'd lie down in the middle so the material was just above the knee, and fold the right-hand section across my naked body, then the left, and then I'd line them up at the front. A belt placed underneath the plaid is done up to secure it around the waist. Standing up it looks like a large dress but then I would fold both sides up into the back of my belt to give the traditional Jamie Fraser look.

Generally speaking belted kilts were worn well above the knee, much shorter than how we wear them today. And, according to the Highland dress historian, Graham McTavish, everyone in *Outlander* wore their kilts 'way too long, with the honourable exception of Stephen Walters [Angus] who wore his kilt like a Mary Quant miniskirt.' But then he has got the legs for it. His new book *Men in Skirts* is out in 2021.

[Graham: Another little gem is that tartan actually developed during the Roman occupation, with various patterns denoting certain districts and ranks.]

In battle, many Highlanders tied their plaid between their legs to allow them to move more freely as they stormed the enemy lines in a Highland Charge, which must have felt like a big nappy. In the Battle of the Field of Shirts (Blàr na Léine, Kinloch-Lochy) in 1544 they removed their plaid altogether and tied their shirts between their legs before running into battle because it was an unusually hot day! Fought by Clan MacDonald of Clanranald, assisted by their cousins the Camerons, against the Frasers and Clan Grant, there were 800 men at the start of the battle. By the end, only thirteen men were left standing.

'They'd almost committed genocide on each other's clans,' says Charlie. 'There were lots of bloody feuds and oath feuds that went back generations, which made that battle exceptionally nasty,' he explains.

'A lot of people wonder how they identified each other at the Battle of the Field of Shirts without their plaid but they never looked at the cloth but the badge they wore on their hat, such as an oak leaf for Clan Cameron. You're not gonna look at another man's kilt as you're trying to take his heid off!'

Sam: Especially if he's not wearing one.

Charlie: Exactly.

GRAHAM
WHAT'S UNDER YOUR KILT . . . ?!

If I had a pound for every time someone has asked me that I'd . . . well, I'd have a few quid more than I do. I love wearing a kilt. I've worn them since I was a teenager. I now own five: the McTavish, the Campbell of Argyll (from when I thought we were connected), the MacDonald (from my mother's side, a modern-style grey tweed) and, of course, the kilt for my role as a World Peace Ambassador, with my mate the Dalai Lama.

Sam: We had a friend of the family that helped Tibetan monks escape Tibet and come to Scotland. Now, get on with it!

Plaid is a contentious issue amongst Scots. Some embrace tartan and are proud to wear a kilt; others regard it as a lot of nonsense made up by nineteenth-century gentry. What is undeniably true is that the tartan, or 'breacan' as it was known in Gaelic, was indeed a true Highland look. In Skye there is a rock named 'Creag an Fheile', the 'Rock of the Kilt', dating from the seventh century, showing a kilted Highlander with a sporran. I can't help wondering if this was sculpted from life – some budding artist getting his mate to stand still while he carved it into the rock. 'Stop moving, Angus, you're going to love it when I'm finished.'

And plaid is referred to throughout history. In 1512, John Major, (not the ex-British prime minister who famously wore his shirt tucked into his underpants) described the Highland Scots as, 'having their body clothed with a linen garment manifoldly sew'd and painted or daubed with pitch.' There were three classes of tartan: clan, dress, and hunting. The hunting tartan was, as George Buchanan says in 1612, 'For the most part . . . brown, near to the colour of the hadder [heather], to the effect that when they lie down amongst the hadder, the bright colours of their plaids shall not betray them.'

In 1703 in the book *Description of the Western Isles of Scotland*, the author Donald Munro told how, 'Every Isle differs from each other in their fancy of making plaids as to the stripes, breadth and colours. This humour is as different thro the mainlands of the Highlands, in so far as that they who have seen the plaids are able, at the first view of a man's plaid, to guess the place of his residence.'

In other words, depending where you lived the tartan looked the same or very similar. It was a form of identity and I love the idea of moving from the Isle of Lewis to Harris to the mainland and roughly knowing where you were based on what people were wearing. However, it's safe to say it wasn't rigidly uniform. I think there would have been room for individualism within a generalised look for each clan. Perhaps some wore it long, others short like Stephen Walters, and maybe his mates would wear it short to show they were part of his gang. I have images in my head of me, Stephen, Duncan Lacroix and Sam all in tartan minis prancing around like Scottish Harajuku boys.

It was only after the repeal of the Act of Proscription in 1782, and particularly after George IV's visit to Scotland where his corpulent frame was bedecked in tartan, that the rigid clan tartans of today came into being. And now I have five kilts in different tartans and I wear them all in the traditional way. That's right. No pants. And landing the part of War Chief of the MacKenzie clan I looked forward more than anything to sporting a kilt, charging through heather, the wind blowing free and generally having a rare old time in the Highlands. However, our costume designer, Terry Dresbach, had other ideas. Apparently, as a man of status, Dougal would not have worn a kilt. Trews (trousers) was the verdict and so it was that I spent two and a half years (with the exception of the Prestonpans bare-chested episode) wearing trousers with a kilt wrapped around me like a cloak, denied the opportunity of wearing the outfit that I loved.

[Sam: And he always wore his little woollen hand warmers and thermal long johns. FACT.]

Still, at least I had no trouble in the bathroom. You'd think it would be more straightforward. It's not.

Kilts exert a strange power over people. Despite the resemblance to a skirt, they are to my mind the most masculine thing a man can wear and the reactions of some women seem to confirm this.

Sam: Oh dear Lord. Make it stop.

SAM

I have been photographed 'up my kilt' a few times (not by myself!). Generally it's when I'm on a panel at a fan convention or Comic Con and I forget the audience below can afford a pretty decent but rather terrifying view. The first kilt I bought was from Howie Nicholsby, the amazing modern kiltmaker from 21st Century Kilts, in Edinburgh. He's done away with the rather nasty Victorian creation of traditional high-waisted kilts and has made them a great deal more comfortable to wear. Along with his modern design, complete with denim or leather kilts, he has added pockets for iPhones or hip flasks (essential). Although the sporran has become less fashionable I still enjoy wearing one. Whilst doing some research on *Outlander* we found that a sporran was worn (pre-Victorian times) to one side, more of a manbag than a 'bawbag' to hide yer privates.

Outlander created our own coloured tartan, to reflect the wildlife of the area the clan was from. There would have been an unofficial uniformity due to the very nature of the natural dyeing materials that grew nearby. For instance, clans in the north might not have had access to certain plants or berries that they had in the south. I have five kilts at the moment, one a 'beer kilt' that could be akin to a hunting one; fine to get it dirty and covered in beer when attending a rugby game or rowdy party. I actually lost my most recent kilt,

in Sassenach tartan, somewhere between Las Vegas and Mexico. I
do hope someone in the highlands of Mexico is distilling tequila
whilst wearing a fine grey and black plaid. Most dear to me is my
father's kilt, which I received after he passed away whilst I was
shooting Season One of *Outlander* in 2014. I haven't worn it yet. It's
MacDonald, as our family descends from the MacDonalds and
comes with a plain but well-used brown leather sporran. I'll honour
him one day by wearing it – just need to lose some weight first, he
was rather slender!

GRAHAM
CUT TO: Rome

I'm filming *Empire* (a TV show for ABC) when Stephen
Graham, a wonderful actor, persuades me out to a Roman night-
club. And, as usual, my kilt came too. It was time to go to the
toilet. Now, I know what you're thinking. Graham, there seems
to be a pattern developing. Well . . . yes. I was followed in there
by a man who seemed quite insistent on seeing what was under
the plaid. After much grappling and several stern words from
yours truly, I escaped. Stephen Graham still laughs about this.
Bastard.

At *Outlander* events, wearing a kilt is almost a requirement. Sam
was the first to break ranks (something he still no doubt gets shit
for) but I persevered, giving up only recently, but not before I found
myself doing a fan convention with Diana Gabaldon (the novelist
who created the *Outlander* series) in Iowa. I was asked to deliver a
thirty-minute speech about my own life (terrifying), and while I
stood at the lectern, wearing, of course, a kilt, a particularly drunken
fan ambled up and lay down *underneath* my kilt.

SAM
Both Graham and I share a very grand title, one we have fought
over for years. He received it first but mine was obviously way
better. We have both been Grand Marshall of the New York Tartan
Day Parade. It comes with little responsibility and the benefit of
walking down the centre of 6th Avenue and not getting a ticket for
jaywalking. I bet the local NYPD officers would be too nervous to

give you a citation as you're followed by several thousand proud, flag-waving, kilted Scots. Each year, the procession is led through New York and celebrates all things Scottish and our influence in the USA. Previous alumni have included Sean Connery, Billy Connolly, KT Tunstall, Brian Cox and Kevin McKidd. Actors, musicians, politicians and athletes have led marching bands et al., in every weather.

The day I was Grand Marshall it was dreich and typically Scottish. I'd been sent a vast selection of whisky by Laphroaig, which filled the hotel room, and I proceeded to share it with my friends, including Howie from 21st Century Kilts, an ex-Grand Marshall himself. A *Variety* magazine photographer joined in, documenting the event and throwing himself into the celebrations, donning a warm cashmere tartan scarf and toasting our small 'clan'. We all 'filled our boots' with whisky, smelling of peat fire and damp wool, and fell out onto the street, gathered up by the crowd. The turnout was incredible; despite the pouring rain, spectators lined the streets and cheered as we marched past; Highland dancers performed a Highland Fling and I toasted the crowd from the top of a NYC tour bus. *Slainte Mhath!*

GRAHAM

And the crucial difference between both of us receiving the honour of being Grand Marshall of the Tartan Day Parade (apart from them choosing to give me the honour first) is that my New York parade was bathed in sunshine, with the Avenue of the Americas glorying in the blooms of spring, the fans dressed scantily for early summer, enjoying the warmth of the sun, while Sam's parade was marked by relentless, pissing rain. Mine was apparently the largest turnout they'd had. [*Sam: They told me the same. Apparently, I had the largest turnout!*]

One could almost call it Dougal MacKenzie's revenge . . . He kills me in *Outlander*, you know. Horribly. But we'll come to that a bit later.

Our plaid and fighting lesson over, we leave the *Clanlands* crew to film some savage fight re-enactment with the kilted ones while Sam and I slope off with Charlie to do some still photographs. Charlie duly poses with us but I can't help feeling that this sort of namby-pamby shite is beneath him. Eventually, after another bone-crushing handshake, he stalks off back to his waiting motorbike. He pulls up the bandana, rams his Nazi bucket on his head, guns the beast into life and thunders off down the Glencoe pass, leaving our wilting masculinity in his wake.

CHAPTER FIVE

The Massacre of Glencoe

Forgive your enemy but remember the bastard's name.
Old Scottish Proverb

SAM

When I was twelve, we moved to Edinburgh. It was an exciting place for a teenager with little experience of cities, with its dark alleys, ancient spires, hidden closes, and dimly lit pubs with dark corners and even darker histories. There was one watering hole called the 'Cask and Barrel' on Broughton Street, where every Thursday night my friends and I would gather in our late teens. A blind man with a white beard, resembling a seer or Druid (Graham's wise doppelganger), would sit quietly near the window, with only a half pint of ale as company, seemingly waiting for someone. The bar would be full of regulars who wouldn't give him a second glance. My friends and I would pull up a small barstool as close as we could and wait for him to sing. For a few hours each night, he'd sing old Scottish folk songs, his voice powerful, filled with sadness, his only payment the occasional half pint from a thankful audience. After I worked up the courage, I'd lean close and ask him to sing 'The Massacre of Glencoe', a mournful lament. He could always transport me to the bleak, cold glen and the demise of the unsuspecting MacDonalds on 13th February 1692.

The Massacre of Glencoe

Chorus:
Oh cruel is the snow that sweeps Glencoe
And covers the grave o' Donald
And cruel was the foe that raped Glencoe
And murdered the house o' MacDonald

They came in a blizzard, we offered them heat
A roof for their heads, dry shoes for their feet
We wined them and dined them, they ate of our meat
And they slept in the house of MacDonald.

Chorus

They came from Fort William with murder in mind
The Campbell had orders King William had signed
'Put all to the sword' these words underlined
'And leave none alive called MacDonald'

Chorus

They came in the night when the men were asleep
This band of Argyles, through snow soft and deep
Like murdering foxes amongst helpless sheep
They slaughtered the house of MacDonald

Chorus

Some died in their beds at the hand of the foe
Some fled in the night and were lost in the snow
Some lived to accuse him who struck the first blow
But gone was the house of MacDonald

Chorus

It is a very ancient and important Scottish song. Well, I *thought* it was ancient but it was actually written in the 1960s by Jim McLean and performed by the Corries! It's still beautiful though.

Walking along the Old Military Road in the sunshine, it feels a very different Glencoe to the one in the Corries' song. The story we were about to learn was far more complicated and nuanced than the tale I'd learnt in various bars off the Royal Mile. And by my side is a trusty grey companion – neither wise, nor blind but definitely still moaning about me starting off with the handbrake on again.

We walk up a hill to a pile of stones, which our guide – Derek Alexander, Head of Archaeology at National Trust Scotland (NTS) – tells us was the settlement at Achtriochtan, one of the MacDonalds' turf houses furthest up the glen. Turf blocks were used to construct walls, insulate the roof and act as mortar. It was a perfect solution if you lived in a landscape without trees (and therefore had no timber). Dry-stone was used internally to stop animal damage – because during the winter you were *living* with all your animals – cattle, goats, hens, you name it, all in the byre, which was a cowshed in your living room. Given there was no TV I suppose it was a primitive version of *Countryfile*.

Derek and his team excavated the whole thing and plan to build a replica turf house at the Glencoe Visitors Centre in 2020. He leads us to where the entrance would once have stood and shows us remains of a turf wall that runs around the settlement. 'We uncovered flagstones and drains this end so we think this was the byre. The animals would have kept the people living here warm. As the wind howled up the glen, the cattle at this end would absorb the cold air and pass warm air into the house. And there would be a fire in the middle so it would be warm, sometimes too warm . . .'

Graham: . . . And fragrant. Like our camper van toilet.

Indeed.

Achtriochtan is one of five poorly preserved remains of houses, barns and byers at Glencoe, with people living in some form of structure here until the mid-nineteenth century. 'When you go back to the seventeenth century we know there were 400–500 MacDonalds in the glen, with possibly forty or so people living at each of these houses,' says Derek.

The massacre that happened here at Glencoe is a subject close to Graham's heart and was the seed which started our *Clanlands* journey, so I'm going to let him tell you the story, as he will tell it well.

GRAHAM
Thank you, Samwise.

As we enter the Glen my thoughts turn to the books I have studied and treasured. One called Ward Lock & Co's *The Highlands of Scotland*, a red illustrated guidebook that doesn't have a date but must be from the 1940s, says, 'Glencoe maintains its air of wild grandeur, despite the new highway [built in the 1930s], and its increasing stream of motors. On a little elevation stands a modern monument [erected in 1883] to the victims of the Massacre of Glencoe, while for a mile or two up the Glen on the same side clusters of green mounds and grey stones mark the sites of the ruined townships of the clan. At the head of the wider part of the Glen rises the Signal Rock, which owes its name to the tradition that it was the spot from which the signal for the massacre was given.'

Close above this spot stands the Clachaig Inn where only days before we got hammered on whisky at 9am.

Sam: Er, that was this morning, Graham.

Graham: It's been a long day.

One of the things I've learned about history is that it's rarely simple. This is definitely true of Glencoe. The received wisdom is that the peace-loving MacDonalds were murdered in their beds by a bunch of treacherous evil Campbells: 'The Bloody Campbells' as they became known. As if a group of choristers had been set upon by a collection of Satan worshippers. It was even the case that, until recently, the Kingshouse Hotel (where we are staying), like the Clachaig Inn, bore a sign above its door with the words 'No Hawkers or Campbells!' These people have long memories. But received wisdom hides a bigger picture; many paths led to Glencoe and it's worth looking at them all.

The MacDonalds of Glencoe (a branch of the larger Clan Donald tribe) came to Glencoe in the 1300s after supporting Robert the Bruce. Due to the hostile terrain, terrible weather and even crappier soil, they were known to be light-fingered, rustling their neighbours' cattle and generally getting a bad name for themselves (along with the MacGregors and the Keppoch MacDonalds). This is also partly why they were set upon at the Glencoe Massacre: they had few friends and had amassed a great deal of enemies over the years.

And the same people who were murdered that night in February 1692 were guilty of many acts of violence for and against the Campbells, and others. The Glencoe men murdered MacGregors for Campbell paymasters in the sixteenth century, and then later, *joined* with the MacGregors, who were then serving the Campbells. In short, they burnt, killed, and stole across the region for whoever it suited them to at the time. Sometimes the alliances of these men beggared understanding. MacIain (chieftain of the MacDonalds of Glencoe) fought alongside Camerons against Mackintoshes and he also helped the MacLeans against the Campbells of Argyll. In other words, there were no Gandhis in them there hills.

In late January 1692, 128 soldiers from the Earl of Argyll's Regiment of Foot were billeted (assigned temporary accommodation, often in a civilian's house) with the MacDonalds of Glencoe. Robert Campbell of Glenlyon commanded one troop of men; Thomas Drummond, from south of Athol, commanded the other.

The Earl of Argyll (later made a Duke in 1701 by William II) was a leader of the Campbell clan. Now, the Argylls were one of the most powerful noble families in Scotland for hundreds of years – let's just say the Campbells knew how to play politics and how to amass land. Rather like Lord Sandringham in *Outlander*, played by the fabulous Simon Callow, they knew when to keep quiet, when to drip poison into a carefully chosen ear, when to make alliances and when to remain neutral.

And it is worth noting that of the 128 soldiers billeted with the MacDonalds, a third were from the Lowlands, who definitely had no love for any Highlander, the other two-thirds were from the

Argyll region and were by no means all Campbells; only thirteen of the 128 were actually Campbells. The rest were a plethora of clans – no McTavishes, I might add – but Camerons, Alexanders (my mother's maiden name), MacCallumms, MacIvor, MacLean, MacKinlay, MacNeill, MacEwan, and even, if you look closely at the list, a certain James Fraser . . .

The soldiers spent twelve long days with their hosts the MacDonalds, breaking bread together, gambling, drinking and trading stories by the fire. They had wrestled each other, tossed the caber, practised archery, played shinty . . . they would have become friends, some may have been related. I mean if you spend two weeks with people you'd get to know them well. Sam and I have only spent a couple of days together in the camper van and already he wants to massacre me. And the feeling is certainly mutual.

So what marks out the Glencoe Massacre as so heinous was that the 'Redcoats' had arrived under the protection of Highland hospitality and the MacDonalds had no idea that the soldiers in their midst were vipers about to strike. *But* the soldiers had no knowledge of the impending slaughter *either*.

It was only the night before that their leader, Robert Campbell of Glenlyon, received the order. It is worth quoting here in full:

'You are hereby ordered to fall upon the rebels, the MacDonalds of Glencoe, and to put all to the sword under seventy. You are to have a special care that the old fox and his sons do upon no account escape. You are to secure all the avenues that no man escape. This you are to put in execution at five of the clock precisely; and by that time, or very shortly after it, I'll strive to be at you with a stronger party. If I do not come to you at five, you are not to tarry for me, but to fall on. This is by the King's special command, for the good of the country that these miscreants be cut off root and branch. See that this be put in execution without feud or favour, else you may expect to be dealt with as one not true to King nor government, nor a man fit to carry Commission in the King's service. Expecting you will not fail in the fulfilling hereof, as you love yourself, I subscribe these with my hand at Ballachulish.'

Robert Duncanson, 12th February 1692

It's chilling stuff, isn't it?

In short: do as you're told, kill them all, don't wait for me, and if you don't do as you're told, you're a traitor and will be hanged.

They had Robert Campbell by the proverbial balls. He was sixty, a drunkard with a very expensive gambling habit *and* he was also married to Maclain's niece. Imagine the scene: Duncanson writes the order by candlelight, quill scratching on paper, signs and seals it in wax, dispatching the epistle up the glen to Campbell. Duncanson also places the burden of action on Campbell. 'If I'm late, don't wait for me. Just carry on slaughtering.' As it was, Duncanson *was* six hours late. Long enough for many of the clan to escape into the hills in the blizzard.

Now imagine Campbell reading those orders. Did he know what was coming? Did his men? I doubt even they could have imagined such an order. If he followed the order he would be breaking that most inviolable code of honour: that of Highland hospitality. You see, it was fine to lay in ambush and kill a Highlander from a tree, or thieve from him, or burn hundreds of them in a cave (see the MacLeod and MacDonald feud), but definitely *do not* have dinner with him and *then* kill him.

Strange, but true.

Campbell would have passed on the order to his junior officers and, in turn, to the men along the five-mile length of the settlement, that the killing should begin promptly at 5am on 13th February in what is supposed to have been a simultaneous strike. These orders could not have been passed on within the walls of a cottage, for fear of being overheard. They would have been whispered outside, in the dark, in the icy wind. The darkness would have at least hidden the horrified faces of the men receiving the news.

Just imagine what that night was like for those who knew – wrestling with what they had to do in the morning, because if they didn't comply they would be hanged. It would have been torture, so it is small wonder that Glencoe is known as the 'glen of weeping', given what was about to happen.

Derek tells us, 'There are various tales of soldiers giving hints to the people they were staying with. Achtriochtan is one of the sites mentioned where a soldier, sitting by the fire petting the dog was heard saying, 'If I were you, grey dog, I wouldn't sleep here tonight. I would go and sleep in the heather.'

[Sam: Did he really just say 'grey dog'! I try not to smirk and look at my grey-bearded companion.]

The rank and file knew nothing till just before 5am. Were there warnings? Perhaps, but maybe only one warning that has since been multiplied into many. It was even said that Glenlyon's piper, Hugh MacKenzie (yes, he was a MacKenzie), played the lament called 'Women of the Glen' knowing any MacDonald hearing it would understand it as a warning.

There was also a rather unsubtle warning – a great fire was lit on Signal Rock signalling the slaughter to begin.

'Eh, what's that bloody great fire for?'

'Oh, that's to let us know when to start butchering our hosts.'

BANG!

Derek says, 'Where the superior officers were staying the orders are carried out on time at the far end of the glen but some are slow to carry out orders and, as smoke and the noise of gunfire travels up the valley, it perhaps warns clan members further away. Many people at the Achtriochtan end would have escaped into snow up and across to Appin where they had relatives.' Several soldiers, Campbells included, refused to carry out the order to execute on that fateful February night, quite literally looking the other way as MacDonalds escaped into the hills.

MacDonald of Kerrigan (the house in which Robert Campbell was staying) and his household had already been bound and gagged to prevent any warning. Duncan Rankin died first running towards the river. Next came MacIain, woken by a banging on his door. He rose, ordering his wife to bring a dram for the officer outside. He was standing with his back to the door in his shirt, his trews untied, when the officer entered. MacIain was found with a bullet hole through his body and one to the back of his head. His wife was stripped naked, the rings gnawed from her fingers, but she was spared.

Elsewhere the slaughter began in earnest. Some were herded onto dunghills and shot. A certain Captain Drummond executed more, even when Glenlyon tried to call a halt. Some homes fared worse than others. John MacDonald of Achtriochtan was thrown on a midden with the bodies of others. Here, the soldiers stabbed, hacked and shot as frightened MacDonalds fled from their homes. It was said that when they were too tired to raise their muskets they burnt fourteen alive in one cottage. They even killed an eighty-year-old, and nothing was found of the man except a bloody hand in the snow.

Three of the Argyll men found themselves on the receiving end, however. In their haste to follow the fleeing MacDonalds, three turned on them with their dirks and put an end to them. Sometimes there is nothing more satisfying than hearing about the moment that the predator becomes prey.

In all, thirty-eight members of the MacDonald clan were murdered.

'The reason government forces chose Glencoe to set an example was because it was so confined. It's difficult to escape,' explains Derek. 'The plan was to send another 400 soldiers over from Fort William (led by Duncanson) who would come down the Devil's Staircase and block the top end of the glen.'

SAM

If you haven't climbed the Devil's Staircase, I'd recommend it. There is an ultra marathon (forty miles) held each year, that runs along the Great Western Way, and this particular part is extremely tough. However, once you get to the top, it's a great place (for Graham to catch his breath) and to admire the spectacular views.

GRAHAM

It was also the plan for another 200 troops from Ballachulish to catch the escaping MacDonalds at the other end. But none arrived before 11am because of a snowstorm. Can you imagine a line of 400 men coming down the glen? There would be no escape in winter, the desolate ridges impassable on either side. If they'd got here at five in the morning everyone would have been wiped out. And, as we have seen, those were the orders.

'People tend to think it was a Campbell–MacDonald thing but it was more about the government trying to make an example of a small clan so they could stop posting troops to a costly garrison in the Highlands and relocate their soldiers to conflicts in Europe,' says Derek.

The idea was to get the clans to sign an oath of allegiance and those who didn't (who refused or were too slow) were to be made an example of with the 'utmost extremity of the law'. Another arch-villain of the massacre was John Dalrymple (made 1st Earl of Stair in 1703 by Queen Anne), Scottish Secretary of State and a Protestant Lowlander with a particular dislike of Highlanders. He used the situation to fit his agenda.

After the battle of Killiecrankie in 1689, Lord Stair met with Jacobite clans offering them a pardon for their part in the first Jacobite uprisings in return for swearing an oath of allegiance to King William of Orange. The deadline was 1st January 1692, however, paperwork was delayed and distrust grew, with Stair believing the Jacobite signatories would not keep their word. The brutal weather of Glencoe also delayed the Head of Clan MacDonald of Glencoe, MacIain. Sir Colin Campbell confirmed his arrival (at the wrong place) before the deadline and his attempt at signing was known by the government, but with the deadline missed Stair seized the opportunity to send a murderous message to the other Highlanders he so despised.

John Prebble writes in his seminal work, *Glencoe*, 'The MacDonalds of Glencoe were victims of what Highlanders called Mi-run mor nan Gall, the Lowlanders' great hatred . . . Highlanders were regarded by Lowlanders as an obstacle in the way of the complete political union between England and Scotland. Many believed that their independence of spirit had to be broken.'

And in the end it was.

As I stand at Achtriochtan looking down at the remains of that house, knowing that it was here, in this glen, where so many stained the snow scarlet, just for a moment I can feel the chill of that February night and the haunting notes of MacKenzie's pipes floating across that scarred valley.

SAM

Chastened, we drive in silence for the first mile to the Glencoe Folk Museum in Glencoe village, situated on the southern shores of Loch Leven. I park up and enter a long white thatched building, a genuine eighteenth-century croft cottage built five years after the massacre. Graham and I duck on our way in (for actors we are very tall – Graham's six foot two inches and I'm six foot three inches, an inch shorter than Jamie Fraser, which, as I've said, is still a bone of contention for some diehard *Outlander* fans!).

The croft cottage would have had roughly the same layout as the Achtriochtan turf house but one level up with thick stone walls and a roof thatched with moorland heather. We meet Catriona Davidson, the museum's curator, and Jimmy 'The Bush' Cormack, a volunteer who shows us several Jacobite artefacts, including a Jacobite flintlock pistol found on Culloden Moor battlefield and two Highland broadswords found hidden in the thatch of local cottages, possibly concealed after weapons and plaid were banned by the British government following the Battle of Culloden (1746).

To close your hand around the butt of a pistol used at Culloden is a very moving moment. The chances are it belonged to a Highlander. During the ill-fated charge against the government troops, they would have had one shot (those who were fortunate enough to own such a weapon). In their fury and urgency many fired their weapons well out of range of the British lines, and then threw the weapon away, at the same time drawing their basket-hilted broadswords for the close combat ahead. In my hand, there-fore, sat a man's only chance to fire at the enemy. He had probably fired it, chucked it away, and run on, in all likelihood to meet his death.

The carnage at Culloden was truly awful.

In twenty minutes the Highland troops were destroyed.

Graham: Connecting to an object like this really brings it home. I can almost feel the sweat around the pistol butt.

Sam: That may have been mine. Or Jimmy's. Sorry. The weapons are very similar to the ones we used in *Outlander*, the basket-hilted sword and the pistols. My personal favourite was a set of solid steel pistols I used in Season One. One would always be attached to the front of my belt and the other hidden at the back beneath my jacket. Jamie was always armed and prepared, including a bone-handled Sgian Dubh (small dagger) in my right boot. Later, when Claire and Jennie (Jamie's sister) go to find Jamie, you see Claire carrying the pistols. It's special to hold the real thing and I wonder whose hand was clasped around this grip and what they did with it. I look at the notches on the blade of the broadsword acquired from fighting.

I pass it to Graham who holds it aloft. 'It's still reasonably sharp, not at all blunt.'

I don't like the way he's wielding it with a glint in his eye. 'I have memories of our previous encounter,' he says with a pinch of menace, still banging on about the time I killed him in Season Two. As if I somehow planned it with the writers. I didn't, *but* I did enjoy killing him. And that's the rub because he's a competitive old bastard who wanted (and wants) to vanquish me, just like his maniacal character, Dougal MacKenzie.

GRAHAM

'It's surprisingly light to hold. Even now you can feel the superb balance.'

Its weight meant that it could deliver horrific blows to the head and body. At the battle of Prestonpans (which we went on to recreate in *Outlander*), the majority of the dead British soldiers were found with the tops of their heads taken off, like an egg, or simply cleaved in two. [*Sam: There's a real macabre side to McTavish, isn't there?*] I saw a broadsword demonstrated on a side of meat once. It carved a diagonal line straight through it. [*Sam: Just a usual Sunday for Big G.*]

SAM

He's holding a Jacobite glass now and looks as if he's about to have a Meg Ryan moment. 'Wooaaahhh!' Cue more heavy breathing noises and gasps. I love his enthusiasm – it's infectious. Enough for me to politely socially distance myself.

'Ohhhh, the spirals down the stem. It's beautiful and the weight of it . . . it looks like it could have been made last week.'

Jimmy 'The Bush' points out the white rose, which he says was a secret symbol of Bonnie Prince Charlie. 'He raised his standard in Glenfinnan, his army marching to Fort William, when on the way they came across a field of white roses at Fassfern. The Prince made his soldiers wear a white rose in their hat so when they went into battle you could see who was your friend and not attack them.'

Just like the emblem (or clan badge) – usually a plant – that Charlie 'Chick' Allen was telling us about at the Battle of Shirts. No one looked at another man's kilt, they all knew who to protect from the flower or spray in their hat.

The significance of the white rose is conjured by Neo-Jacobite poet, Andrew Lang (1844–1912) who wrote 'The Bonnie Banks o' Loch Lomond'.

White Rose Day – 10 June 1688
'Twas a day of faith and flowers,
Of honour that could not die,
Of Hope that counted the hours,
Of sorrowing Loyalty:
And the Blackbird sang in the closes,
The Blackbird piped in the spring,
For the day of the dawn of the Roses,
The dawn of the day of the King!

White roses over the heather,
And down by the Lowland lea,
And far in the faint blue weather,
A white sail guessed on the sea!
But the deep night gathers and closes,
Shall ever a morning bring
The lord of the leal white roses,
The face of the rightful King?

There were many other secret symbols the Jacobites used to communicate, from painting their houses pink, to the famous secret toast to the 'King Over the Water', in which those loyal to Charles

Edward Stuart subtly passed their wine glass over a vessel of water, like a finger bowl – the reason why water was often removed prior to the Loyal Toast at military dinners. You see Jamie Fraser witness this in Season Two of *Outlander*, the fine Jacobite glasses holding the secret rose emblem. Wearing the now infamous French knee-high buckle boots that took a good ten minutes to put on each morning – each boot had around fourteen buckles, which made 'intimate scenes' rather difficult to direct. (How does Jamie get his boots off so quickly?) They lasted two whole seasons, including boat journeys to the Caribbean and America.

Myself and Duncan Lacroix enter the French brothel dressed in our newly acquired French fashion finery, on a secret meeting with his Royal Highness, one Charles Stuart. I remember shooting for days on the boiling hot set, in Cumbernauld, outside of Glasgow, that doubled for Madam Elise's high-class brothel, where we would be entertained by a variety of buxom girls and a large assortment of variously sized dildos. According to Duncan, or was it Murtagh, he believed the French were 'a sorry bunch who can't please their women'. Can't take him anywhere. Despite his strong words, Jamie gains the confidence of Charles Stuart, played wonderfully by Andrew Gower, imp-like with a slight speech impediment and catchphrase 'Mark me!' Fans now play a drinking game whilst watching Season Two: every time he uses those words, they take a shot. It gets messy, surprisingly quickly. Words used that carry more weight though are: 'The King over the water': the secret Jacobite oath, pledging allegiance to Charles Stuart. Jamie is in France to try to stop the rebellion, as he knows that history reveals the defeat of the Jacobites and the loss of many lives. During one of the scenes – I believe it was in the brothel, though I can't find the scene, maybe it was never used in the final edit? – the characters swear the oath, whilst passing their hand over a Jacobite glass, complete with the Jacobite rose inscription on the glass.

And now we too are off 'over the water' to the Glencoe island of Eilean Munde, where 300 MacDonald graves lie and where clan chieftain MacIain is thought to be buried. 'They were buried on an island to stop the wolves digging them up,' explains Jimmy as we are leaving. 'There were wolves in Scotland in those days. And bears, lynxes and wildcats too.'

With all the conflict, feuds, marginal farming, famine, disease and general hardships in those days, there were wolves as well! Life truly was a perilous path. The last wolf of Scotland was supposedly shot by Sir Ewan Cameron in Killiecrankie, Perthshire in 1680 but many thought small numbers survived into the eighteenth century, with tales of sightings into the late nineteenth century. I imagine the howl of a solitary wolf echoing around the glen.

We drive the camper van the short distance to the shores of Loch Leven to catch a boat to the Isles of Glencoe. I clap my hands. It's time for some action and a little levity of mood! I had managed to wangle a brand-new two-man kayak that we'd been towing around, along with bikes and other random paraphernalia in the camper. I've done a lot of kayaking in the past and am very confident in the water, but I didn't want to let Graham know that. *The more he panics, the better for TV,* I thought. But maybe I was going too far.

I pull on my wetsuit and life jacket and get ready to jump in the sea loch. It's our last location of the day and by now my companion has sobered up and is hungry, bordering on hangry (hungry and angry). In fact, he is metamorphosing into Grumpy Graham before my very eyes. The light is dropping as is his blood sugar, so we have to move fast. Despite all my pleas and mild manipulation, Grumpy Graham will not be kayaking with me today. He boards a small boat and refuses to budge, wedging himself firmly in the middle of the boat, so I am forced to bend to his wishes. This time.

Perhaps Graham and I need to head to the Island of Discussion (Eilean a' Chomhraidh). It was used a lot in those times when clan feuds were a regular occurrence. I love the rather simplistic, very Scottish way of resolving things. Two men or clans have an issue or argument so they're taken out to a small island in Loch Leven and left to 'work out their differences'. When their disputes had been settled satisfactorily the disputants sailed up the loch to Eilean na Bainne (about one and a quarter miles west of Kinlochleven). This is the Isle of Covenant or Ratification; here the agreements were drawn up and sealed. However, they wouldn't return until the matter was settled. Or one of them was dead.

I wonder if we would ever return?

GRAHAM

It seemed appropriate that our first day should be ending with a trip to the place where they buried the dead. After surviving Sam's driving, and the risk of alcohol poisoning at 9am, it seemed the logical conclusion. I couldn't help wondering if this was all part of Sam's larger diabolical plan – lure me to an island and leave me there? Probably with a coconut and a GoPro. [*Sam: And it's only day one!*]

Sam does a complete costume change (and make-up touch up) and somehow transforms into something resembling James Bond in the underwater sequence of *Thunderball*. His initial idea is that we kayak to the island. And sure enough there is a two-man kayak.

How can one man hate me so much?

It's been a very long day, the air is cool, the sun is setting and I'm not getting in a kayak with a ginger hulk who can barely handle a manual motor vehicle on dry land, let alone a canoe on a sea loch. Did I mention he's set off with the handbrake on *five times* today? That's how long it's taken for him to work out what is causing the beeping noise! Every time he gets behind the wheel he doesn't recall the other four times he's set off with the handbrake on because his default mode is more speed, less haste. I decline his kind invitation to go sea kayaking citing the rapidly fading light as an excuse. But I know this will not be the last I see of the coffin made for two.

Our guide, a classically dour Scot called Robert, issues us with our life jackets and we clamber aboard the boat and head for Eilean Munde, the largest of the Glencoe Isles, known as the burial isle. I am dressed in what I woke up in, Sam is auditioning for *Thunderball*.

(Attention Barbara Broccoli, there are some serious hints being dropped here.)

It's a truly breathtaking journey across the loch. The sun is dipping in the west, casting shadows that film-makers the world over describe as 'the golden hour'. We're followed by our camera crew who bellow at a distance to try and keep us in shot. We arrive at an outcrop of rocks covered in lichen. *[Sam: I think it's more likely seaweed, Grey Dog.] [Graham: Thank you, Monty Don.]* Robert explains getting off might be treacherous as the rocks are very slippery. This is where Sam's outfit comes into its own. He is wearing some specialised gripping rubber booties, turning him into some sort of ginger salamander. I think I might be wearing tap shoes. Sam duly hauls us in and I gingerly (no pun intended) step off the boat, managing to reach dry land without making a complete arse of myself. The boat securely tied, we set off.

SAM

I am the first to jump onto the slippery rocks. Thick seaweed obscures them from view. I scramble across and find dry land, pull-ing the rope and boat with me. Graham tentatively looks over the edge of the boat and, yet again, refuses to budge. 'No, it's too dangerous,' he squawks at the crew on a separate yacht, filming the action. Odds on Graham taking an early bath look slim. With some cajoling and a little encouragement, he takes his first step. I have to turn my back so he can't see me laughing. I pray the crew are record-ing this as he yells at them again, while Alex Norouzi tries to apply some Germanic common sense to the situation. 'Ja, ja, take your time, und be wery careful, Gray-ham.'

'I *am* being careful, it's just bloody treacherous, Alex!' Gray-ham howls. 'Jesus Christ!' He's puffing and sweating even more than usual as he, inch by inch, makes his way over to me, like an ancient bald crab, until he is finally on the burial island.

Small and hidden from the mainland by thick trees and rocks, it's claimed Alasdair MacDonald (MacIain of Glencoe) was buried here after the massacre in 1692, along with many others. It was also the burial site of local families such as the MacInneses, MacDonalds, Campbells and Stuarts. As we near the peak of a hill and come out of the trees, a dramatic sunset is framed before us and we are greeted by a truly breathtaking sight: rows of headstones, all facing east (towards Jerusalem in the Christian tradition), the setting sun illuminating them from behind.

Uninhabited, the island has an ancient chapel, first built by Saint Fintan Munnu in the seventh century. The last service to be held in the church was in 1653, with the last burial almost fifty years ago. We have literally stepped back in time. There's an eerie feeling; the only inhabitants are seagulls overhead, screaming at the living. To walk in the same footsteps of those clansmen carrying the remains of their loved ones who had fallen in battle or died in the massacre hundreds of years before is discombobulating.

Our guide explains that, depending on your status you could have been just left on the ground; those more important would have been buried, but with no depth of soil the remains were barely covered. Mercifully, no bodies are visible in the long grass and we stick to the trail in case we stumble upon some . . . body.

The gravestones, hundreds of years old, look as unruly as their inhabitants, sitting at various angles, now crumbling away. We are led to one in particular, which reads:

> *My glass has run.*
> *Yours is running*
> *Be wise in time*
> *Your hour is coming.*

Graham: Can't beat a bit of black humour from beyond the grave. My tomb will bear the inscription: BLAME SAM HEUGHAN.

I wonder if I shouldn't be so cavalier with my friend's sensibilities. I will go easier on the Grey Dog, I think. As we enjoy the peaceful and beautiful sunset together, we feel lucky to share this moment with the inhabitants of those graves. I look at my good friend and smile. Instead of smiling back he looks at me with distrust. All he had to do was smile. But he didn't so I immediately decide I will continue to f*ck with him for the rest of the trip.

As we scramble back to the boats I leap aboard the crew's yacht and break open a bottle of whisky for everyone to share. 'Where's Graham?' I ask, sitting on deck. I can now see him clambering back into the small boat, holding on with both hands, his life jacket bulging over the side. Nah, no need to take it easy. You can be sure, Mr Sensible will look after himself. 'Cheers Graham!' We raise our cups as the yacht accelerates away, leaving Graham looking mortified he's missed out on the whisky and is stuck in a slower boat with a dour Scotsman. Ya snooze, ya lose!

And just wait until he sees what I've got planned for him tomorrow. I smirk into my dram.

CHAPTER SIX

Mounting Mountains

From 'Night on the Mountain' by George Sterling

The mountain seems no more a soulless thing,
But rather as a shape of ancient fear,
In darkness and the winds of Chaos born
Amid the lordless heavens' thundering –
A Presence crouched, enormous and austere,
Before whose feet the mighty waters mourn

SAM

It has been an epic day and Graham is hungry and thirsty. No surprise there. After a quick shower and change, I find him already seated at our table in the hotel restaurant, fingering the wine list. He knows what he's going to order and is pairing the wine. Of course, he is. The waitress brings him a large glass of Sauvignon Blanc and I see him visibly relax from uptight grandpa to his more debonair self.

I order an Oban whisky (a clean Highland spirit from the sea port) as the others start to come down for dinner. Wendy plonks her handbag on the chair next to me and I have Alex the German on the other side. Graham is flanked by Michelle and . . . Duncan Lacroix, who announces his entrance loudly with 'Good evening, bastards!' No one knew he was still here. And, at our expense.

Duncan tucks a napkin into his T-shirt and starts to scrutinise the menu. I can see he and McTavish are ready to do some culinary and alcoholic damage tonight. They go on little romantic holidays and gourmet breaks together, not that I'm jealous, but I've never been invited. Actually, I believe Duncan ends up being turned into a glorified babysitter for Graham's children and resident chef, cooking most nights whilst Graham reclines with a fine wine. What a romantic couple!

What *has* Lacroix been doing all day, I wonder?

Wendy reads my mind. 'What have you been doing with yourself, Murtagh the Squirter?' she shouts at full Glaswegian volume.

Lacroix: Climbed a Munro, chased some sheep, had sex . . .

Wendy: Poor wee lamby.

Wendy laughs her arse off and high-fives Lacroix. The banter is classically blue as the crew starts to get the drinks in. Wendy orders a Jack Daniels and Coke (full fat), whilst Lacroix's nose is buried in the wine list. He consults Graham. 'Yes, I thought that one too. Excellent choice, Duncan,' says Graham nodding in approval.

'A bottle of Domaine Jean Monnier & Fils Puligny-Montrachet,' says Lacroix in perfect French looking me straight in the eye and raising one of his thick black eyebrows. I raise my whisky glass at him as we order our food. I am eating vegan for thirty days so I go for the roasted root Wellington, with wild mushrooms. The abuse comes thick and fast.

McTavish and Lacroix have ordered a feast. I make a mental note to double the budget on *Clanlands 2* to accommodate Lavish McTavish's tastes.

Graham gobbles:

Hebridean scallops, seaweed tartar, parsnip puree, shallot crisp

Roast Atlantic cod, cockle & fennel broth, vitelotte mousseline & a side of spice roasted Brussels sprouts & crispy bacon

The Cheese Board with Isle of Mull Cheddar, Hebridean Blue, The Highland Minger and Blue Murder cheese with oatcakes and plum chutney.

All washed down with two bottles of white for the first courses (shared with Lacroix) and a couple of bottles of red with the cheese. I have a couple of whiskies and join everyone at the bar for a nightcap afterwards. High-maintenance Graham is now regaling us with tales of 'a certain Elf' on *The Hobbit* who used to go crazy during stage fights suffering from 'the red mist'. 'He used to go mental at the stunt guys; he's a really unpredictable guy.' I always thought the actor in question looked like he needed feeding up but Graham makes him sound like Schwarzenegger.

It looks as though Lacroix and McLavish are settled in at the bar for the night but suddenly Graham looks at his watch, announces it's been a long day – 'a magnificent, life-changing day but it's time for bed.' Lacroix is as stunned as me. And off the grey goat saunters, trotting up the stairs like an eager billy.

What *is* he up to?

[Graham: Escaping alcoholic carnage, mainly.]

In the TV show we pretend Graham sleeps in the camper van but I'm not even going to try and spin that line because as you well know by now, the likelihood of him doing anything below five stars is truly remote.

Ten minutes later Wendy returns from a call to her husband. 'Yous'll never guess what?! Aye saw bug Graham smuggling a wee hairie in his room.'

★★★

The next morning I watch Graham like a hawk, hoping he will give away 'a tell' or a clue. I want to know what he's been up to. He's particularly energetic, humming his way around the breakfast buffet with his extra large Alan Partridge plate. I have finished my porridge and black coffee but Graham has a lot of work to do. He's going for a 'full Scottish' cooked breakfast, followed by toast and preserves, granola, natural yoghurt and berries and . . . Is he doing what I think he's doing? Yep. He's wrapping a hard boiled egg and bread roll in a napkin along with most of the fruit bowl, and packing it in his knapsack for later. Clearly the man needs to replenish his energy after the night before. I'm sure I heard his guttural groaning and wheezing, much like an *Outlander* fight scene; I had buried my head in the pillow and longed for it to stop. The whisky (or lack of oxygen) must have knocked me out and I awoke the next morning.

I wonder if it's time for him to have a blood sugar test. I mean he *is* fifty-nine, going on a hundred. He should definitely get a Well Man check-up. He's in the prostate danger zone, too . . . I'm going to suggest it. Maybe even arrange for him to have one in the camper van, without his knowledge. Little surprise . . .

But not now.

Twenty minutes later we're in the van. I look over at my camper companion who is now peeling a tangerine. It suddenly dawns on me I am doing all of the driving. I ask him if he would like to drive. 'Absolutely not,' he says picking the tiny white strands off an orange segment, which for some reason really annoys me.

I set off with the handbrake on again. Graham doesn't say anything but I feel him silently judging me.

Sam: Soooo, early night . . .

Graham: Yes.

Sam: Up to something?

Graham: No.

Sam: Hmmmmm . . . are you sure?

Graham: I don't know what you mean.

I narrow my eyes at him. I know what he's been up to . . . Graham McTavish has been enjoying some how's yer faither!

GRAHAM

Sam is scratching around trying to work out what I was up to last night but I will keep him guessing. It will drive him to despair, which is what his driving is doing to me. Yet again, he has set off with the handbrake on which is making me come to the conclusion that he might be *terminally* stupid. I mean many good-looking people are often not very bright, because, well, they don't have to be. My theory is backed up by Sam's tenuous understanding of a gearbox – like the numbering of 1–5 is somehow a riddle. And, if his driving isn't bad enough, Fiat has failed to factor into their design of the Auto-Roller that anyone over six foot might consider sitting in the front. Perhaps it was designed for the vertically challenged Italian customer, but for Sam and me it is akin to being crammed into a shoebox. My knees are grazing the dashboard, my feet are starved of blood and my poor back feels as if it is propped against a particularly rough plank of wood. *[Sam: Yet I have photographic evidence that he fell peacefully asleep, having a mid-morning, post-elevenses nap.]*

Not that I can really complain amidst the majestic scenery. *[Sam: Bloody good attempt, though.]*

We are on our way to Glencoe Mountain Resort because, although Sam thinks it's a surprise, Michelle, our eminently sensible executive producer, told me at dinner. Upon arrival, I unfold myself from the van and stretch myself back into my original shape. Allegedly there is snow here in winter good enough to ski on. I don't ski. I have attempted it twice: once aged fourteen, and once a few years ago with my kids. The last attempt did not end well. Now I prefer to enjoy watching my children ski while I sip a latte and read a book. However, today the land is bereft of soft powder and instead, a rocky slope tufted with grass rises before us. I am staring up at the misty Munro, Meall a' Bhuiridh when fans Glenn and Delilah the daughter heave into view wearing matching T-shirts with Sam's face on it.

Graham: Hello ladies!

Glenn barely gives me a second glance but her daughter waves so I smile back. She's a good-looking lass and they've only come to wish us well . . . Sam walks to the back of the camper – Delilah's whole face lights up and Glenn swoons. They only have eyes for the Young Highlander – which is quite frankly ridiculous.

Sam is ruffled. 'Morning ladies. Er, what brings you here?'

It *is* a pretty random place to be at 8am. For a moment I think the ladies might be joining us at the top of the mountain. Sam is posing for photos and is certainly more relaxed than he was at the Clachaig Pub. Or in the stairwell in Prague.

Photos over, Michelle starts to escort us to the chairlift. However,

Glenn is insistent she comes along too 'with the king of men' and, her not being one to take no for an answer, we are soon breaking into a jog towards the chairlift, which is not something I have ever contemplated doing because I *loathe* chairlifts. There are two men helping at the lift. One is a corpulent Scotsman, purple of face and broad of waist. He is the operator. If we get to the top without him suffering a massive heart attack we'll be lucky. His assistant is, well . . . a child. Literally a child. Maybe eleven years old. What happened to school? He is there to assist us in getting into the chair-lift. Hmm. I fear he will be too busy 'assisting' his father/uncle/ brother (or all three?) into an ambulance.

We are told to stand on a line and prepare to board the chairlift. I watch as the metal instrument of torture spins towards us. Sam insists on exchanging banter with the Artful Dodger, possibly slip-ping him money to make my journey as miserable as possible. The large man operating the lift controls the speed. This is the first time I realised that you could speed these things up. I'm pretty certain I detected a conspiratorial wink from Heughan. It's time to get on board.

Strangely, moments later, I decide to tell Sam that I'm afraid of heights. *What am I thinking?* 'It's something I've dealt with quietly for a long time . . . I don't like to make a fuss.'

The chair approaches. I look behind me. It swings around a tight 180 degrees and thunders towards us (well, 'thunders' may be an exaggeration). I lower myself backwards and hope for the best. The chair slams into my backside and I am swinging in mid air before I've even had a chance to hurl abuse at the Fat Controller! Sam glances across and smiles. Yes, one of those smiles. I look ahead, focusing on the chair in front (containing our camera department), and refuse to look down. 'So you're afraid of heights?'

'Yes. I'm not as bad as I used to be but I'm still nervous in certain situations. Like now. So whatever you do please don't start rocking the chair!'

Sam bides his time.

We chat. It's actually quite fun. I look out across the hills. It's beautiful. We are passing through the clouds to emerge into the light above. This is not too bad at all, methinks. Then he starts to shake the chair. I yelp, perhaps whimper. Then I adopt my stern father voice: '*Stop* shaking the chair, Sam!'

'Sorry, buddy. Of course.'

We go on. Sam shakes the chair. This pattern more or less continues to the top only interrupted by me singing 'Misty Mountains' from *The Hobbit* just to stop the chair shaking.

SAM

As we get on the chairlift Graham tells me he's scared of heights. I'd already suspected vertigo, which was why I suggested the chairlift in the first place. I sit down saying it's like a comfy chair. Graham murmers, 'Oh God,' as he falls back heavily.

We glide up the mountain. 'Don't look down,' I say leaning over and looking down.

Graham: 'Don't do that.'

Sam: 'These chairs actually look quite old.' I shift my weight.

Graham: 'Don't.' I lean out to the left and back towards Graham.

Graham growls, 'I mean it, Sam.'

He really does. So I behave myself. Well a bit. I want to get to the bottom of who was in his room last night.

Sam: Come on, who was the lucky lass?

Graham: There is no lucky lass.

Sam: Sure, okay you said it. Look at the waterfall below! We're still yet to go in the water, big man.

Graham: Are you determined to make me suffer?

Sam: Only for my own amusement.

Graham starts singing 'Misty Mountain' from *The Hobbit* in revenge and it's working. He is as far away from a 'Triple Threat' (when actors can act, sing and dance) as is humanly possible. He sounds like an injured tomcat. Make it stop. 'I was on the album you know,' he says. *Dubbed out*, I think. He regales me with stories from his time playing Dwalin the dwarf as we disappear into the heavy cloud.

GRAHAM

We were filming in Te Anau on *The Hobbit*, nearly at the bottom of the South Island of New Zealand, with the 'scale doubles' (the long-suffering shorter people who doubled for the dwarves on a few occasions, and 'Tall Paul' the seven-foot-two-inch policeman from Auckland who doubled as Ian McKellen for some key over-shoulder shots). It was 'talent night' at the pub. A local started playing his guitar. Another local then punched him in the face. One of our short friends remonstrated with this individual which set off a full-scale pub brawl. Thirteen people under five feet tall fighting with local farmers, with a seven-foot-two-inch giant literally throwing people into the street.

You couldn't make it up.

SAM

I'm not really listening. I have reminiscing of my own to do because Glencoe was the first place I learned to ski on snow. I had some lessons on the dry ski slope at Edinburgh, which was a mixture of mud, glass and razor wire because when you fell over it always seemed to cut you into pieces. I was skiing with some friends in foggy conditions, like the cloud we are in now; you could barely see your hand in front of you. I crashed into a sign that said: 'Danger Cliffs!' but I carried on and then fell off said cliffs about 10–15 feet into deep snow.

Graham is appalled. 'You just kept going? Of course, you did. Such a safe sport, isn't it? Like tiddlywinks.' He looks at my hands. 'And no gloves or hat – you're very hardy, Heughan.'

I look at him and think the exact opposite. He's wearing a cashmere grey hat, which must be beautifully soft against his sensitive bald head, combined with a midnight-blue felted jacket with a fine orange check and a scarf.

GRAHAM

I may dress like someone who drinks lattes [*Sam: Understatement!*] but let me describe the Mountain Goat's attire. A high cream turtleneck and khaki-green sailing smock with wooden toggles – like he's Kirk Douglas in *Heroes of Telemark* about to save Norway in WWII. I imagine him jumping off the chairlift in wooden skis (no, I imagine pushing him off) and attacking the slopes like a born skier (or him falling like a sack of spuds). You could rely on him in an avalanche . . . Only to find out later he's caused it in the first place.

He asks where my scarf came from and is utterly astonished that I *bought* it from Dovecot Studios, Edinburgh. I ask him the last time he *bought* his clothes. He dodges the question; even his underpants are freebies.

Sam: I don't wear any.

Graham: Any chance to be shirtless or butt naked. Those poor cameramen [on *Outlander*] having to look at your chocolate starfish for hours on end.

Sam laughs: The cameraman's seen my arse more than me.

Graham: Everyone's seen your arse more than you!

Mercifully we are not ascending the Matterhorn and arrive intact. *[Sam: I've skied there too! Yet to climb it, though Cameron McNeish has!]* Sam gracefully alights from the chair like a gazelle in Gore-Tex, while I throw myself off and scramble for safety like that gazelle at the back of the herd in a David Attenborough documentary. You know . . . the one about to be eaten. We walk to a rocky outcrop and look out across the truly stunning landscape below us. The clouds have parted. I'm not sure how far I can see but it's a bloody long way.

It's at this point that the trip pauses for me to remember my dear friend, Martin Graham Scott.

Marti died tragically at the age of forty in an awful car crash in 2004. His wife, young daughter, and infant son were in the car with him but mercifully survived. It's an awful thing to lose a friend prematurely. I remember the moment I heard. A mutual friend called me when I was in Spain on a shoot. It was truly terrible.

I've brought the engraved whisky flask he gave me, which I take with me whenever I wear a kilt or return to Scotland. The top of Meall a Bhuiridh is a fitting place to bring it because he loved the mountains and he loved skiing, so I wanted to raise a toast to him here on our *Clanlands* journey.

Martin had always been a staunch and wonderful supporter of

my early career. We had met when I was twenty and he was eighteen at a private airport where we both worked doing odd jobs in the summer – firemen duties, haymaking, carpentry, aircraft refuelling, and an array of dogsbody employment. He looked like a young Robert Redford. I've since lost a few more friends (my father had died the previous year – in fact Martin read at his funeral), but the loss of Martin has always been particularly hard. To this day I keep a photo of him on my fridge so that I see him every day.

I am glad to share a quiet moment with Sam on the ridgeline, looking out across the valley. Martin would have liked him. In fact, they are alike in many ways. Not that I'm going to tell Sam any of that. I remain buttoned up like a true Scotsman and take a nip of whisky. I want to offer Sam one but instead I'm churlish saying, 'You're not having any.'

'Martin wouldn't have approved,' Sam says gently.

'He hated your work,' I say in spiky banter.

Truth is, I miss Martin terribly; he was a 'brother from another mother' and that bond is hard, if not impossible, to replace.

'This is for you, Martin.' I take another sip and hand the flask to Sam. He takes it from me and smiles, understanding my pain.

SAM

It's a fitting tribute and a heartfelt moment, because despite his gruff exterior and dwarfish ways, Graham is an old softy at heart. 'To you, Martin,' (beat) 'and this is to a friend of mine,' I say, taking a swig.

'What friend?' he says with a pang of curiosity. Or is it jealousy?

'To Graham McTavish.'

GRAHAM

It is a lovely gesture. We toast each other and I glance at Sam, feeling grateful that I'm standing with a new friend celebrating the memory of an old one. Life is indeed a strange journey, for who would have thought that I would be at the top of a mountain toasting Martin with a man I met in a Soho casting office six years ago. But then you can pick up all sorts of things in Soho. [*Sam: I'm sure that's not the first time Graham has picked something up in Soho – same joke twice, I know, but I can't help it!]*

I decide to tell him who was in my room last night. 'A physiotherapist came to sort my back out.'

Sam: What?

Graham: Ask Michelle [beat]. Heughan's magic 'blunderbus' has buggered my back. Mainly because my knees are forced up around my ears. She says I need to take little breaks to stretch it out. Or take a different mode of transport entirely.

SAM

His cantankerousness tickles me and I stifle the sniggers. He's now chuckling too and, very soon, we are belly-laughing on top of Meall a Bhuiridh, Glenn and the crew (save Merlin and John) under the mist somewhere below. He takes another swig from his hip flask and passes it to me. Whisky is for savouring and sharing with others. As a tradition, whenever I climb a Munro – one of 282 Scottish mountains that are at least 3,000ft, named after the famous Scottish mountaineer Sir Hugh Thomas Munro, 4th Baronet (1856–1919) – I take a small whisky flask and toast the adventure at the top. It's who you are with and where you are that makes a dram really special and memorable.

And this dram with Graham is unforgettable. Despite his broken back.

CHAPTER SEVEN

The Sweetest Morsel I Ever Tasted

'Porridge' by Spike Milligan
Why is there no monument
To Porridge in our land?
If it's good enough to eat,
It's good enough to stand!

On a plinth in London
A statue we should see
Of Porridge made in Scotland
Signed, 'Oatmeal, O.B.E.'
(By a young dog of three)

SAM
We've been rattling along a single-track road towards Glen Etive
this morning for over an hour and seen no sign of life, until now.

There is only one road to Glen Etive and the area is sparsely popu-lated, apart from the clans of belligerent sheep. As Graham says, it's so rural you canna just pop out for a carton of milk. Or a ramen. One such woolly Highland gang is standing defiantly in the road, staring us down with unblinking eyes, like the MacLeods did to the MacDonalds before they lit the fires at the entrance of the cave and suffocated all inside.

I consider sending Graham out to move them on but see he has a date with the boiled egg butty he packed at breakfast. The man's insatiable. He offers me a bite. I shake my head. He opens the hotel fruit bowl in his knapsack, gesturing at it. I tell him I'll take an apple later.

There's no way *I'm* getting out because Scottish sheep are not like sheep anywhere else, they are as hard as nails, have real attitude and will come at you . . .

Graham gives sheep commentary:

Graham: (thick Glaswegian) I am in the road. I am not gettin' out of the road. So yous can move yer motorhome and *do one!*

We don't move.

Graham: Come on then bring it on, man! What yer doin'? Oh, you think yer sooo hard, don't yer? In yer four by four . . . Run me over, go on run me over!

Sam: I dare yer, I dare yer. I dare ewe!

Graham: My wee lamb can take yoo. *Ewes* are nothing! (See what I did there?)

Sam: I already did 'I dare *ewe*'.

Graham: Oh.

The sheep clear off and we carry on in silence down the road made famous in *Skyfall*. I feel far away from the glamour of James Bond and hit a pothole to confirm it. Graham perks up to point out 'Loch Choke-on-my-coch' to his left. (Really Loch Etive.)

We finally arrive at our RV (rendezvous point) in the stunning Glen Etive valley, protected by some impressive peaks including Ben Starav and the popular Stob Dubh. As we park up, Wendy wanders over to the driver's side and I wind down the camper van window.

Wendy: All right? How's it handlin', beg man?

Graham: (Glaswegian) *Superb, absolutely superb!*

Wendy: Can I have a coffee and bag a chips, pal? One fish supper and a single sausage supper . . .

Sam: We're out of sausages, I can do the chips.

Wendy: And a pie.

Graham: One pie and chips coming up.

We jump out of our 'mobile fast food van' (perhaps a means of balancing Graham's fine dining budget) and wander over to the camp our crew has set up for our next filming segment. There is a large canopy and Graham's army-issue 1940s canvas tent from his schooldays. Little does he of the shiny bonce know he's contractually obliged to sleep in it for one night because neither he, nor his agent, read the agreement properly! I cannot wait to see his face when I tell him the good news. I will wine and dine him first, otherwise he might 'do a Jeremy Clarkson' and punch me on the nose – because when Graham and Jeremy aren't fed on time, people get decked.

To be honest I'm a bit nervous about how he'll react. It's like standing in the queue for a roller coaster. I'm nervous, excited. But before we deliver more sh*ts and giggles, we have work to do. This fine morning we are interviewing Gaelic singer and storyteller Gillebride MacMillan, about language and Highland culture. Gillebride played Gwyllyn the Bard (Season One, Episode Three) singing traditional Gaelic songs at Castle Leoch. Gaelic is his first language and, after learning to recite a little of the language on the show, I was keen to find out more.

I give Graham his stage directions: when Gillebride arrives he is to emerge from the tent after spending a sleepless and uncomfortable night. I will busy myself making Graham a Highland breakfast. Graham disappears into his tent whilst I start cooking porridge over the campfire. Traditionally made with oats, water and salt, porridge is the best way to sustain one's energy, as it is a slow-release carbohydrate. I swear by porridge. Growing up, we had a friend of the family who would make it religiously for breakfast. With so much salt added, he'd let it cool and solidify. 'One slice or two,' he'd ask, serving it up like a soggy cake. It never put me off though. I find if I eat it daily, it sustains me for hours of filming. It actually has a reasonable protein content and is very filling; even Arnold Schwarzenegger would demolish the stuff.

And, you can add anything to it to spice it up: protein powder (chocolate flavour), banana, nuts, berries, jam, peanut butter, even whisky. Although perhaps not all together. I've been known to scramble an egg and eat that on it too. *[Graham: And that's why you've never been invited on any gourmet getaways with Duncan and me.]*

If you're as serious about porridge as I am, I suggest you buy yourself a spurtle. Shaped like a thistle, it's used to stir the porridge (in a clockwise direction, to ward off the devil). Sometimes, the Highlanders of old would bleed their cattle and mix blood into it for variety. Or they might add boiled cabbage water. *However,* unfortunately for Graham these extra ingredients aren't available to spice up his porridge today so he will have to make do with plain lumpy gruel. I actually dropped the spoon so there is a little Highland soil and grass in there, too.

Upon Gillebride's arrival, Graham crawls out of his tent, stands up holding his back dramatically and yawns. I hand him his third breakfast. I'm not sure he wants to eat it but the camera is rolling and Graham will do whatever the camera wants. He shoves mounds in and pretends to like it. I shake hands with Gillebride. Graham can't speak. 'Sorry, my mouth is full of Sam's porridge,' he splutters.

There is nowhere to sit so Graham can't help showing off his superhuman strength and acting skills to impress our new guest. Finding a large rock, he proceeds to puff and gasp a great deal, trying to lift it. I'd seen this kind of performance before on set, the sound effects alone worthy of an Oscar.

'Ta-*da!*' A mock rock, used for set dressing, was placed beside the fire for Gillebride to sit on. I'm not sure why Graham carries fake stones around with him but maybe it was exactly for this moment. I ignore him and continue to stir his congealed breakfast.

Gillebride sits down and Graham perches on his pet rock. Gillebride is originally from the Western Isles where Gaelic is still spoken as a community language. 'Gaelic was my first language and I only learnt English when I went to school,' he says.

Scotland has always been a mix of cultures. The place names especially interest me. Many villages, mountains and lochs are a mix of Gaelic, Norse, English or Old Scots. The old languages are very descriptive and can help you understand more about a place and its history. In Gaelic, *Beinn Ruadh* are the red/russet-coloured mountains, *Creachann Mor*, the great bare rocky hilltop, and *Greusaiche Crom*, the crouching cobbler (shoemaker), which you can see from the shape of the hill. *[Graham: And Huighe Bhum Crachen – the giant parted arse cheeks!]* Fort William was initially created as a garrison for the British army to help tackle unruly clans such as the Camerons. In Gaelic, *An Gearasdan Dubh* is the black garrison. Instantly you see the dark and negative connotations.

Gillebride explains, 'The Highlanders and Islanders would have spoken Gaelic all the way up until the mid-eighteenth century and the language differences, as well as the geographical dislocation, would have fuelled differences.' (That and nicking each other's and the Lowlanders' cattle!) 'Chieftains of the clans often had French and English but the people under them were monolingual Gaelic speakers,' he says.

After Culloden, the British tried to eradicate the Gaelic language and the Highland culture, such as the wearing of Highland dress and all weapons. 'They tried to assimilate the people (the High-landers) into another form of culture, which has historically happened in many parts of the world.'

The Clearances, road building and other factors all took their toll, diluting language and culture; however, miraculously (and with lots of effort, education and funding), Highland culture lives on and is in fact thriving with 70,000 Gaelic speakers registered in Scotland. 'With the fluent speakers tending to live in the Highlands and islands,' says Gillebride.

'In part the culture has survived thanks to storytelling,' explains Gillebride. 'One thing that we did when I was growing up was go to a ceilidh house. We now think of a ceilidh as a dance but the Gaelic word means "to go visiting" and when you're visiting you tell a story, sing a song and if the gathering is going well, at three in the morning you might have a dance in the kitchen.'

So essentially a ceilidh was a social visit, encompassing storytelling, music, dance and of course, whisky. 'And one of the things they did was tell ghost stories or "An Dà Shealladh" (literally "The Two Visions" or "Second Sight") – premonitions of the future taken seriously by all who heard them,' he says.

There are plenty of examples of foretelling the future which were (and still are) taken very seriously in Scotland. I have first-hand experience of people telling me about a death or an incident that they were warned of through 'An Dà Shealladh'. This could be a foretelling of death by seeing a shooting star, or being gathered up into the vision of the future – you'd then have three days to make your peace with the person who is going to die or with everyone else if you are the one who is destined to die. There is definitely a great film script in the stories I heard growing up about that whole thing – it is still very much a living part of the culture in some of the island communities. The film *Sixth Sense* would have nothing on these supernatural tales!

Gillebride says, 'Imagine a glen not too dissimilar to this, on a road not too dissimilar to the one you came along. You see a group of people you recognise, you see your neighbour Donald, your neighbour Callum and neighbour John, but they don't recognise you and they are carrying something. Your good friend Michael isn't in the group and what they are carrying is a box. That tells you have three days to make your peace with Michael.'

All the families would sleep in one room so the children would hear the stories and premonitions and the oral traditions would continue. Our forebears' ability to recall songs and poems was incredible. Many would only need to hear scores of verses just the once before recounting them to new ears. Graham can't even remember where his bus pass is.

> *Early on Sunday morning I climbed the brae*
> *above the castle of Inverlochy.*
> *I saw the army arranged for battle,*
> *and victory in the field was with Clan Donald.*
> *The most pleasing news every time it was announced*
> *about the wry-mouthed Campbells, was that every company*

of them as they came along had their heads battered with
sword blows.
Were you familiar with Goirtean Odhar? Well was
it manured, not with the dung of sheep or goats, but by the
blood of Campbells after it congealed.
To Hell with you if I feel pity for your plight, as I
listen to the distress of your children, lamenting the company
which was in the battlefield, the wailing of the women
of Argyll.

This poem is by a seventeenth-century Scottish poet called Iain
Lom, from the MacDonald of Keppoch clan. Because a lot of people
had the same names, many were given nicknames based on looks or
features. Lom is Gaelic for 'bare', 'bald' or 'as bald as a coot'. But it
also can mean someone who is plainly spoken . . . so it fits Graham
'Lom' McTavish on both fronts!

Gillebride asks us to sing the chorus with him. We do. And
'Graylom' kills it. Stone dead.

GRAHAM

Sam's warbling is reminding me of Pierce Brosnan in *Mamma Mia*.

[*Sam: Funnily enough, I did an audition for that movie, to play the
young lad 'Sky'. At the time I had a natty 1940s 'tash' from starring in
Noel Coward's* Vortex *at the Manchester Royal Exchange with singer Will
Young in the lead role. Will, who had won* Pop Idol – *a British talent show
in 2002 – then went on to have many platinum albums and Brit Award
nominations. He kindly offered to help me learn the song. Yet when he tried,
he couldn't make the top notes and suggested I didn't try; transposing the
song an octave down was a better idea. I walked into the audition with my
newly grown tash perfectly manicured. The casting director looked at me in
shock. I hesitated and took a deep breath, 'I'm going to sing this an octave
lower, Will Young said that's a better idea.' The casting director pulled her
eyes away from my top lip and, unblinking, replied, 'No you're not. Sing it
as it's written.' The sweat started to run down my back. 'Okay, if you're
sure,' I gulped. 'I am,' she replied, folding her arms and giving the pianist
a nod. I think you can guess the outcome and clearly I didn't find myself
travelling to Greece to appear in a Pierce Brosnan / Meryl Streep sandwich.*

The result in the audition room was very similar to a cat being strangled,
with a furry top lip. I wonder if Will Young could grow a tash as well?]

GRAHAM

I weirdly enough dated one of the leads of *Mamma Mia* in the West
End, Helen Hobson. We met doing a stage version of *Persuasion*
directed by the wonderfully named Michael Hunt. (Never call him
Mike . . .)

Although I admit to having Van Gogh's ear for music (the one he
cut off), to hear that music in the landscape of Glen Etive is
profound . . .

But this is a TV road trip and we don't have endless time for
reflections and pondering on the profound because we are on a
schedule and need to beat it to Achnacarry Castle to learn all about
Clan Cameron who, let's just say, were a notorious bunch.

I've already spoken of the enmity between the Camerons and
the Mackintoshes, which lasted a mere 300 years! (It's ironic that
one of the West End's greatest musical producers is called
Cameron Mackintosh. I wonder if his parents knew about the
feud?) Anyway, by the mid fourteenth century this feud had gone
on so long that it had come to the attention of the King, Robert
III, who decided to end it once and for all via a sort of gladiatorial-
style pitched battle in 1396. The ground was selected in Perth by
the River Tay, on the island of North Inch. (The battle was later
known as the 'Battle of North Inch'.) A huge trench was dug and
an amphitheatre was erected with the King placed in the centre to
judge the combat. Thirty Camerons and thirty Mackintoshes
came to the battleground. They were to fight to the death to settle
the feud.

The Mackintoshes were one man short but this small detail
wasn't going to stop a good old battle. So they went to the pub and
offered money to anyone who would volunteer to make up the
numbers. Henry Wynd, probably having downed prodigious quan-
tities of cask-strength whisky, rose to the challenge. In some reports
he was a harness-maker, in others a blacksmith. Either way, Henry
was someone used to working with his hands and he soon got busy
on the battlefield.

At this point I'll let that little-known Scottish writer Sir Walter Scott take over:

'The trumpets of the King sounded a charge, the bagpipes blew up their screaming and maddening notes, and the combatants, starting forward in regular order, and increasing their pace, till they came to a smart run, met together in the centre of the ground, as a furious land torrent encounters an advancing tide.

'Blood flowed fast, and the groans of those who fell began to mingle with the cries of those who fought. The wild notes of the pipes were still heard above the tumult and stimulated to further exertion the fury of the combatants.

'At once, however, as if by mutual agreement, the instruments sounded a retreat. The two parties disengaged themselves from each other to take breath for a few minutes. About twenty of both sides lay on the field, dead or dying; arms and legs lopped off, heads cleft to the chin, slashes deep through the shoulder to the breast, showed at once the fury of the combat, the ghastly character of the weapons used, and the fatal strength of the arms which wielded them. When the battle was over, eleven men of Clan Chattan stood, though wounded, and one man of Clan Cameron was left. He promptly fled for his life and Clan Chattan was declared winner.'

From Sir Walter Scott's novel, *The Fair Maid of Perth*

Did you catch what Walter was saying there? Basically these two groups of lunatics actually had a half-time! Like a football match. You can just imagine it . . . 'How's it going out there, Donald?'

'Well, I've split two heads in two, and left my axe in a third, how's about you? Pass the whisky, bastard!'

Needless to say one of the survivors was good old Henry Wynd, who no doubt returned to the pub bathed in gore to finish his pint. Of whisky.

Now the Mackintoshes were part of a 'Federation', Clan Chattan. *[Sam: Why are those raincoats named after them?] [Graham: Allow me . . . the waterproof raincoat, made of rubberised fabric, was first sold in 1824 and named after its Scottish inventor, Charles Macintosh, without a 'k'.]*

Clan Chattan was a group of like-minded head-cases who all got together and formed a kind of 'Super-Clan'. It certainly helped with the numbers. So it was that in 1370 the two teams came to the pitch – the Camerons and Clan Chattan. Now, to pursue the footballing analogy a little further, this would be like an FA Cup Final where one team fielded eleven men while the other had forty lads kicking the ball on the other side. Slam dunk for Clan Chattan, you would think? (Excuse the mixed metaphors.) But no! Where you stood on the line of battle was an excessively big deal for the average Highlander. You wanted to be on the right-hand side. If you were on the left-hand side, this was akin to putting you on the subs bench, or even locking you in the dressing room! The Mackintoshes were the clan leaders of Clan Chattan and on this occasion chose to place Clan Davidson on the right. This so infuriated and outraged the MacPhersons (remember these guys are *all on the same side*), that their leader took his men and walked off the pitch. So what had been a battle where Clan Chattan outnumbered the Camerons, suddenly became the opposite.

Clan Chattan were heavily defeated, which went down like a mocktail in Motherwell, and that night a drunken Mackintosh went to the MacPherson camp and taunted them for their cowardice. Probably something along the lines of 'Ma granny's harder than youse!' This set the MacPhersons into a collective homicidal rage, whereupon they marched off that very night and slaughtered the Camerons. It was just another day amongst the heather.

Then we come to the Battle of Bun Garbhain in 1570. This is where we get to meet a real-life Dougal MacKenzie. The wonderfully named Donald Taillear Dubh na Tuaighe Cameron (Black Taylor of the Axe), uncle to the infant chief of Clan Cameron – not that I'm saying Gary Lewis (Colum) is like an infant, but you get what I mean. What a name, though. I mean, come on, try saying that after a morning of drinking with Sam Heughan. Black Taylor of the Axe, so called because of his terrifying ability with a Lochaber axe. In this battle, Black Taylor, henceforth to be known as just 'The Axe', killed the chief of the Mackintoshes with the aforementioned giant head chopper. But he didn't stop there, oh no!

'The Axe' went on to kill a couple of dozen more Mackintoshes with his hefty tool like some whisky-fuelled grim reaper. Those that survived fled to a small hollow called Cuil nan Cuileag, thinking themselves safe. But our dear friend 'The Axe' was only warming up.

He led his Camerons to the hideout and slaughtered every last one of the Mackintoshes. Yes, you read that correctly. Not 'he killed a lot of Mackintoshes.' Or, even 'most of them'. No, Donald Taillear Dubh na Tuaighe Cameron (Black Taylor of the Axe), killed *all of them*.

After the battle (or massacre, depending on your point of view), 'The Axe' went back to tell the mother of the infant chief of Clan Cameron the good news.

'They're aw deid! I killed every last bastard Mackintosh there, what do you think of *that?*'

Perhaps in his enthusiasm for slaughter, 'The Axe' had forgotten that the said mother of the infant chief was in fact a Mackintosh herself. Needless to say she didn't take the news of the slaughter of everyone with her surname well at all and tried to throw the infant son onto the fire.

'The Axe' saved wee Allan Cameron (bit of a small name that one), and banished the mother from Lochaber territory forever by tying her naked to a horse, her face to the tail. The horse was whipped and off she went, leaving 'The Axe' no doubt to quietly clean the mountains of gore from his well-used weapon.

By the way, he was nicknamed 'Black' because of his bad temper.

SAM
And why this senseless violence and carnage? Well, mainly because they were nicking each other's cattle . . . or it was unbridled revenge for something someone said about someone's mum? Just like the gangsters throughout time, you can't say a bad word about their mums. But the Battle of Palm Sunday (1429) between the Camerons and the Clan Chattan was started 'cos word on the moor' was that the Camerons had taken a 'spreagh' of cattle from Strathdearn.

spreagh n. plunder, especially cattle taken as booty.
Origin: Scottish Gaelic **spreidh**, cattle.
Derived terms: **spreagh´ery**, cattle-lifting.

(Possibly the origins of the word 'spree', which Graham now uses for shopping.)

The Camerons were attacked while worshipping in church, the whole tribe nearly cut to pieces. John Major (1467–1550) in the *History of Greater Britain* writes: 'Clan Chattan put to death every mother's son of the Clan Cameron.'

It's hard to picture now that when you hike or drive through the Highlands you are crossing a land quite literally soaked in blood. At some of the more famous locations, such as Culloden, the Isle of Eigg, the North Inch, if you close your eyes you can almost hear the battle cries of the warriors and the screams of the dying and wounded. It is a race forged in the crucible of death. For a Highlander, fighting was as natural as breathing, and all of this is in our minds as we arrive at Achnacarry Castle, at the western end of the Great Glen. Seat of the Camerons and home of the current Lochiel (every Cameron chief is known as 'Lochiel'), we approach the castle along a beautiful wooded avenue. The Cameron lands stretch as far as Ben Nevis and the estate is still one of the largest at 70,000 acres.

The original castle was burned down by the Hanoverians (British) after Culloden in 1746 and, after lands had been restored in 1784, a new one was built designed by the architect James Gillespie Graham in 1802. We park up in our Terry-and-June wagon to greet Ewan Cameron, the 27th Lochiel. I can't help thinking of his fearsome predecessor, Sir Ewan, the 17th Lochiel, known as the 'Ulysses of the Highlands', such was his enormous strength and size. He lived until he was ninety (1629–1719), was a vigorous Jacobite, married three times and is credited as shooting the last wolf in Scotland in 1680. In a fight with the English he was about to be stabbed on the ground when he leant up and bit his aggressor's throat out and said of the incident afterwards: 'It was the sweetest morsel I ever tasted.' Maybe he was bored of porridge?

Ewan is a wonderful host – just to be clear, I'm talking about the current 27th Lochiel and not the throat-biter! He explains, 'All

My wonderful mum
and dad, Alec and
Ellen McTavish,
around 1947

Dad, Susan, Alec,
and Mum holding
a bewildered infant
Graham, 1961

Aged 1, trying to make
sense of life, 1962

On holiday in
the Grand Canyon,
USA, 1981

Doing the 'half
nash' playing
Jem Merlyn in
the 1986 touring
production of
Jamaica Inn

Persuasion with Helen
Hobson. I played Captain
Wentworth in Mark
Healy's adaptation
in 1999 at Exeter
Northcott Theatre

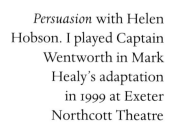

Filming *Rambo* with Sylvester Stallone in 2008

Kitted out as Dwalin with my brilliant Stunt Double 'Moo' on location in *The Hobbit*

Astride my ever-patient horse Lambert in *Outlander* (Season 1), 2014

The premiere of *Plastic*, April 2014, at London's Odeon West End

Outlander mid-season premiere at the Ziegfeld Theatre, New York, April 2015

New York City Tartan Day Parade in 2016, judging the dog competition

In my role as The Saint of Killers in AMC's *Preacher*

Sandwiched between my *Outlander* co-stars, some chap called Sam Heughan and the lovely Caitriona Balfe moments after they'd murdered me

With my dear friend Duncan LaCroix, a wonderful guy. Being upstaged, as usual, by Sam and Caitriona

The cast at the premiere of *Preacher* Season 3 in Los Angeles

Quietly sobbing with joy whilst holding the prized second edition of Shakespeare's Folio at Cawdor Castle during *Men in Kilts* filming, 2020

Sam and I resting with our bikes and my aching backside outside Cawdor Castle

The valley of Glencoe – rich with history! Stood with Sam and Richard Alexander

The Fiat Fiasco on the road and our 'home' during the *Men in Kilts* shoot

Cosy amongst the Badenoch Waulking Group. I have no words

Whisky tasting at 9am, it's a tough job…

Fighting talk at Glencoe between me, Charlie Allen and Sam

This picture taken moments after Sam and I had learned about his 'toys'

About to climb into the death trap, otherwise known as a sidecar

Cameron clan chiefs are known as "Lochiel" – it's not a title, just a patronym. There were Jacobite peerages but they got wiped out (after Culloden)!'

As we enter the castle, Graham and I stop in our tracks, immediately struck by Highland and Jacobite weapons on display such as the famous Lochaber axe, claymores, basket-hilted broadswords, pistols from Prestonpans and the actual broadsword that the 19th 'Gentle Lochiel' used at Culloden. Like eight-year-old boys, we gaze up, mesmerised. Having recreated the struggles, politics and battle scenes of the era in *Outlander*, seeing the Gentle Lochiel's sword really brings the history home. And, it's moving because the Battle of Culloden signalled the end of a whole way of life and culture in the Highlands.

GRAHAM

I've already experienced some powerful, moving moments during this trip (not counting the bowel-loosening moments at the hands of Heughan), but none has affected me quite as much as seeing the actual broadsword wielded by Donald Cameron, the 19th chief of the clan, on the battlefield of Culloden. He led about 700 men that day. It was a matter of pride to him that their pipes were the first heard when the Prince's standard was raised at Glenfinnan. It was their piper who sounded in the sleet on that fateful day, 'You sons of dogs, of dogs of the breed, O come, come here on flesh to feed!'

Chlanna nan con thigibh a so's gheibh sibh feoil!

As I say, these guys didn't muck about.

Over the staircase the Cameron flag flown at Culloden is framed. '*Pro Rege et Patria* – For King and Country,' says Lochiel. 'A chap called McLaughlin wrapped it around his body and escaped from the battlefield and gave it back some years later.'

I imagined the Gentle Lochiel on that day. (Known as the Gentle Lochiel because of his humane treatment of prisoners taken at the Battle of Prestonpans.) The sword hanging at his side, soon to be unsheathed, the standard fluttering in the icy sleet, and the voices of 700 men raised singing that blood-curdling chant to the tune of the pipes as they began their charge towards the British lines. I can see Sam is moved too. It's moments like this, when something so unexpected happens, that you must simply stand, absorb it and recognise its profound effect.

A Highlander needs thirty inches or more around him to swing his broadsword. Lochiel and his men were among the first to charge. They stood on the right of a line that stretched a thousand yards. The line took an oblique angle with the left standing 800 yards from the British troops while Cameron and those on the right stood 500 yards away. It was only the right that made it to engage with the British. It was being in this situation, impatient and angry after being shelled for half an hour, that prompted the men on the right to charge first, and Lochiel was among that group. They had waited like children on their father, for the order 'Claymore', and finally it came.

The Camerons started second, after their bitter rivals the Mackintoshes had charged first. The piper would have played the rant, and then passed his pipes to his attendant boy, at the same time unsheathing his broadsword. Again I imagine Lochiel beginning that 500-yard dash. Imagine the sound, the screaming, and the panting as hundreds of men ran forward like hungry wolves. If you've ever sprinted 500 yards you know how hard that is. Now imagine doing it with cannons packed with grape shot (a mixture of lead balls, iron nails, anything that could be packed into the mouth of a cannon and fired like a shotgun), with the withering platoon volley fire of disciplined, battle-hardened British troops. Some Highlanders held their plaids in front of them in the vain hope of shielding themselves from the rain of lead tearing through them. And now imagine doing it over rough ground, carrying a sword and shield. All of this ran through my mind looking at the weapons assembled in Achnacarry Castle.

By the time the Camerons got to the British line, their hacking at the barrels of muskets could be heard all down the line as metal clanged on metal. Lord Robert Kerr, Captain of Grenadiers, received the first charging Cameron on the point of his pontoon, before a second cleaved his head down to his chin. (Lochiel tells us that Captain Kerr is an ancestor of his wife. He once made a joke about his gory end and ended up wearing her homemade chocolate mousse!) Some Camerons even made it to the rear, where a

Lieutenant Colonel Rich held out his slender sword to parry a blow from a Cameron, only to have his hand and sword severed at the wrist. James Wolfe went on to describe the Camerons as the bravest clan among them. The Gentle Lochiel, still carrying the sword now present at Achnacarry, was carried from the field, both ankles broken, by four Camerons, hidden in a cottage and then laid across a stray horse and led away to the mountains to hide. He joined the Bonnie Prince in his escape through the heather taking a route through the north-west Highlands, Western Isles and Skye, eventually fleeing to France from Loch nan Uamh, near Lochailort.

Through the window of his drawing room, Lochiel points to some beech trees. 'When Bonnie Prince Charlie landed, the Gentle Lochiel went to tell him that he hadn't got a hope and should give it all up.' He argued that the Jacobites now controlled Scotland, and with French support they had a much better chance of beating the British. 'Before he left he chucked the young beech trees into a trench down the river and, of course, he never came back because Prince Charlie persuaded him to join him on the march south. So the trees have grown up higgledy-piggledy down the river; planted in 1745.'

SAM

One of the Gentle Lochiel's brothers, Archibald Cameron, also escaped to France with the prince but he was sent back to Scotland to search for the lost Jacobite gold by the money-mad Prince. Spain had pledged 400,000 livres (the currency of the time) to Charles and the Jacobite cause. The Mackays, loyal to King George II, captured the first instalment. In 1746, two ships (*Mars* and *Bellona* – both gods of war) arrived with 1,200,000 livres from the Spanish and the French, leaving the money and gold at Loch nan Uamh Arisaig on hearing of the defeat at Culloden. It was the same place from where the prince would escape to France and it was on Cameron land.

Whilst in Scotland, Archibald Cameron was betrayed by the infamous 'Pickle' Alasdair Ruadh Mac Dhomhnuil, 13th chief of Clan MacDonell of Glengarry, who became a Jacobite double agent for the British. Thanks to 'Pickle' (what a bastard) Archibald was arrested for being a Jacobite traitor and sentenced in 1753 to be hanged, drawn and quartered (hanged until almost dead, emasculated, disembowelled, his entrails and heart thrown into an open fire, beheaded and cut up into four pieces. Who thought this shit up?). It was the same way they killed William Wallace and others guilty of 'high treason'. I mean even a cat doesn't mess about with a wee mouse like that. It is said Archie approached his demise with bravery and resolution. 'The gold is supposed to be buried along Loch Arkaig,' says Lochiel. 'There are lots of people with metal detectors but no one's ever found it.' Yet. I can see wily old Graham already mentally ordering his metal detector. He'll be back, I guarantee it.

Achnacarry also played a significant role in WWII when the government commandeered the castle and estate, establishing a training headquarters and putting 25,000 Army and Royal Marine Commandos through their paces here between 1942 and 1945. On the banks of the Loch and River Arkaig, with Ben Nevis just eighteen miles away, Achnacarry was the perfect terrain to train an elite fighting force to defeat the German foe. Here they learnt physical fitness, survival, orienteering, close-quarter combat, silent killing, signalling, amphibious and cliff assault, vehicle operation and various weapon and demolition skills. And in those days they didn't mess around in training. Oh no, they recreated night operations on the loch with boats and men under machine-gun fire from real live rounds. Several were injured or killed in training here and Lochiel says they are still finding unexploded ordnance.

Around a mile from Spean bridge is the Commando Memorial, overlooking the training areas of the Commando Training depot. There's a terrifying photo of men practising stabbing each other in the neck with a large knife, much like the dirks our Highlanders would carry. The Commando Memorial at Spean Bridge is a constant reminder of their endeavours and with a few veterans still with us now in their nineties they, like the Highlanders, were a breed apart.

He wears the kilt of the Cameron Clan,
Fierce and proud in Lochaber lands,
Ancestral home of the great Lochiel,
And above on a hill a memorial stands –

It honours the memory of those who have gone.
For freedom and justice so many have died
For king and country they gave their lives,
And the piper plays with sorrow and pride.
From 'Spean Bridge' by Barbara McPhail

I've often wondered what kind of soldier I'd make. But then I realised you can't take your make-up artist with you in a real battle. Joke! But it isn't that much of a stretch because I've always loved the outdoors, working out and getting stuck in – mountain biking, hiking, climbing – everything you can do as a Marine or soldier. During the shooting of Season Two of *Outlander*, four members of the crew and I entered the 'Tough Mudder' race. Ten miles of running, slipping and falling into thick mud, plus twenty-five obscenely muddy obstacles. It was a fun weekend challenge and we felt pretty confident, attacking it with great enthusiasm, a welcome change to shooting in the glorious but extremely warm 'French Apartment in Versailles' (reimagined by our genius set designer Jon Gary Steele).

The promise of free beer at the end spurred us on. Fifteen-foot jumps, running through fire, scaling large walls, swimming in freezing water and all whilst covered in thick, clay-like mud – it's quite a test. The first obstacle was an ice-filled pool that you had to submerge in, chilling your bones and soaking your clothes, and it was the sign of the things to come. Each hurdle covered us in yet more mud or submerged us in freezing water – and the driving rain didn't help either. Yet surfacing from the murky freight container filled with an assortment of fluids, someone called out: 'Go on Sam!' A small, hardy group of *Outlander* fans had arrived to cheer us on and it gave us the boost we needed. Our *Outlander* crew are tough, the best, possibly the hardest in the business, having to face the outdoor elements most days, for almost ten months straight, for fourteen-plus-hour days. However, we lost two of them around a mile in, claiming they 'needed a breather' – or a cigarette break. Those of us remaining cracked on like a military unit – running and slipping in unison was the only way to keep warm. The only time we wavered was at the electric shock trap. With a rumoured 10,000 volts of electricity, it reportedly packed quite a punch. Like being tasered, still damp and wet from the course, it at least keeps your insides warm whilst frying them. There was no way around it but to run through. I closed my eyes and ran. Bang. Like being kicked in the head. I made it to the finish and, amazingly, back to work the next day, relatively unscathed. Jamie Fraser's hair may have stood a little more on end. Having completed this, I've always wanted to try an army assault course or compete in one of those Special Forces shows on TV.

As we walk up the line of interwoven trees, known as The Dark Mile, or 'Mile Dorcha', passing the remains of the original burnt-out castle, it's time to say farewell to our host Lochiel and take a look around the Cameron Museum.

Inside is the last kilt worn in battle, at Dunkirk in 1940. Given the significance of WWII in *Outlander* (the story starts in 1945), Achnacarry actually connects those two significant periods of history in an extraordinary location. Graham beckons me over to look at Prince Charlie's waistcoat, which is very small. 'Not a big man,' says Graham disappointedly. 'A bit on the diminutive side for my liking, if I'm honest. Like following Tom Cruise into battle, without the CGI.' It would never fit Graham's 'muscular' figure. It would hardly fit a young boy, slender and slight; he must have been a small yet striking figure. A cherub standing in the Highlands surrounded by these hardened, brutal men. My character had many meetings with the Young Pretender, beautifully played by the actor Andrew Gower. Jamie Fraser feared this young man didn't have the experience or bravery needed to lead an army and would be overpowered by his confidants and advisors. And Jamie wasn't wrong about that, was he? I say he should have listened to the wise and Gentle Lochiel and waited for the French (which is what I was trying to sort out with Claire in most of Season Two!).

Hanging in the museum is a print of a famous painting of Bonnie Prince Charlie by the artist John Pettie, painted in the 1800s (it now hangs in Holyrood Palace). In the picture, to his right is Cameron of Lochiel and Alexander Forbes, 4th Lord of Pitsligo. It was actually this painting that we used as a reference on *Outlander*, looking at how kilts were worn and depicted. Many an argument was had in the early days, our creative team insisting that Highlanders would always wear the jackets indoors. To me this made no sense. Obviously for warmth and comfort, but most paintings were staged and there was little formality in the Highlands, if living from hand to mouth. Even this painting was embellished by the artist many years later than the event. However, one character I'd studied, standing loyal in the shadows behind the Bonnie Prince, was an ancestor of the man I'd just been talking to, his sword still hanging in the hallway: Cameron of Lochiel.

GRAHAM

There was one scene where I was making a speech inside a cottage with a roasting fire. Trying to gather money for the Jacobite cause. I suggested to the director I do it in my shirtsleeves, very 'Obama Town Hall meeting' style, a man of the people!

We started shooting the scene this way. After we'd shot half the scene we were told that I 'had to have the jacket on'. Word had come through. So as a result if you look at Episode Five of Season One, I keep jumping between jacket on and jacket off, in the same scene!

SAM

We have run out of time and like the set of Jacobite glasses with the Latin inscription 'Redeat' (to comeback or reappear) we will, like their king, return. Outside, we are ambushed. Not by government forces but by a cloud of hungry midges. I *wondered* where they'd been. This trip has been too sunny, too painless but here they are, the sun setting and gone 6pm, prime midge-munching time. They gobble at our faces and necks and Graham's main course of a bald heid. Small and annoying, their bite is no more than an itch, but they like to hunt in clouds of thousands. On set, they find their way under your wig, anywhere warm and slightly moist, they feast on your scalp and it's so hard not to itch or scream during your close-up . . . darling. Sometimes as soon as a take is called 'Cut', you'll find me or a co-star jumping up and down, wailing and tearing at our heads. Then the poor make-up team has to come and fix the damage. For some, like Graham, the damage is irreparable. They took all of his hair!

We scramble into the camper, bang the doors shut and that's when it dawns on me: I have to tell Graham he's sleeping in the tent tonight, under the stars and swarms of midges. He's looking 'wabbit' (tired) so I'll take him out for dinner first; I'm not a cold-hearted bastard . . .

CHAPTER EIGHT

Sleep No More!

GRAHAM as Macbeth:
Methought I heard a voice cry, 'Sleep no more!
McHeughan does murder sleep' – the innocent sleep,
Sleep that knits up the ravelled sleave of care,
The death of each day's life, sore labour's bath,
Balm of hurt minds, great nature's second course,
Chief nourisher in life's feast.
Macbeth: Act Two, Scene Two

SAM

Less Bear Grylls, more Teddy McTavish, Graham crawls slowly out of his tent into the morning light of Glen Etive. Damp with dew, he is broken and alone.

Until I turn up. Honking the un-macho horn on the wagon of despair.

'Morning Graham!' I yell, parking the beast next to the rest of the gathering crew. It's time to pack up and get going because we have a long, action-packed day ahead.

Graham: You *absolute* bastard.

Sam: I've brought you breakfast . . .

Graham: I hate you.

Sam: Here's a sack of goodies from the breakfast bar. And, your latte.

He sips it, eyeballing me, not even a flicker of an involuntary smile. The crew takes down the tent and packs up Graham's pet rock. Everyone thinks I'm a bastard because I didn't sleep out here too; however, I *did* suggest we both sleep in the camper van, but Graham insisted he wouldn't fit. I mean he's tall, but he's not Gandalf. I had every intention of sleeping under the stars but stayed up talking nonsense to Lacroix (yes, he stayed yet another night) and, well, it's a bit hazy after that.

McTavish opens the breakfast bag hungrily like he's been in the wilderness for forty days, not seven hours. 'It was bloody awful in that tent. Never again.' He tucks into croissants and preserves. 'What else have you got up your sleeve? I'm serious; tell me.' He wipes away some flakes from his well-kept whiskers.

Sam: Nothing.

Graham: Tell me.

Sam: A spot of kayaking.

Graham: No.

Sam: It's totally safe.

Graham: I've already told you – a two-man canoe with you in it, forget it. Next . . .

Sam: Motorbike and sidecar.

Graham: Who's driving?

Sam: Me.

Graham: Over my dead body. (Beat.) Anything else?

Sam: No.

Graham: Sam? What about today?

Sam: There's a bike ride.

Graham: Okay, a bike ride but on what *kind* of bike?

Sam: A normal one? (Beat.) It's on the back of the camper – go see.

Graham: And, no surprises?

Sam: Absolutely none.

He is hilarious when he's grumpy. He stares at me with all the menace he can muster, like a bearded Lady Macbeth . . . which is appropriate because that's who we are off to meet this morning. Well, almost . . . we have an appointment with Angelika, the Dowager Countess Cawdor, who is Thaness of Cawdor, too. I kid you not.

FIRST WITCH
All hail, Macbeth! Hail to thee, thane of Glamis!
SECOND WITCH
All hail, Macbeth! Hail to thee, thane of Cawdor!
THIRD WITCH
All hail, Macbeth, that shalt be king hereafter!

'I think it wise not to stay for dinner,' I say, climbing into the driver's seat of the camper.

Graham nods. 'Especially if she tells us we can stay in the Duncan Suite.'

GRAHAM

We are back in our usual seats in the Fiat Turd, or whatever it's called, and are on our way to Cawdor Castle, which I would be excited about if I could actually see through my eyes and didn't feel like a giant bat had shat in my head.

Given Sam's mistreatment of me last night, I shall start the day with a little revenge of my own revealing Sam's middle name. Drum roll . . . wait for it . . . wait for it . . . his middle name *is* . . . **Roland**. Yes, like the rat. Mine is James, like the 'true king'. You see, I was destined to play a Jacobite. Not sure what Roland is going to lead to . . . although, I have an image of Sam behind an 80s 'Roland' keyboard. The Biopic of Duran Duran maybe? Or George Michael. I see great things in his future. Roland is not the worst name – Agrippa, Gawain and Barry are far uglier, but it does sound so much better in Italian – Orlando. I mean everything sounds better in Italian, doesn't it? *[Sam here! Roland is French, Graham. I'm apparently*

27% French. Roland was a legendary military hero who served under Charlemagne c.778 AD. Put that in yer pipe and smoke it, History Man.] [Graham: I fart in your general direction.]

In spite of my sleep deprivation there is much jolly banter and laughter with my captor. I think I am beginning to develop Stockholm Syndrome. You know the one, where hostages start to actually enjoy being in the company of terrorists. And, as we drive along yet another narrow road I even begin to forget that Sam's clear intention is to make me as nervous as possible. Amid the grinding of gears, boat-like steering, and the GPS conspiracy to lose us as often as possible, I am actually smiling. Beaming like a lobotomised psychiatric patient.

We talk about the significance of the 'Scottish Play' in our acting lives. When I was sixteen I wrote two comic adaptations, one of *Macbeth* and the other of *Antony and Cleopatra*, which I directed, and acted out at school. I was obsessed with Monty Python at the time and somehow I got a copy of the script for *Monty Python and the Holy Grail*. Incidentally, Doune Castle, where the *Holy Grail* was filmed, became Castle Leoch, seat of the MacKenzie clan in *Outlander*. Little did I realise back then that I would be war chief of the very castle in which the Python team enacted legendary sketches such as the Black Knight ('Tis but a scratch') and the Insulting Frenchman:

I fart in your general direction.
Your mother was a hamster and your father smelt of elderberries.

It was Python's writing that inspired me and I started writing sketches with my best friend, Neil Graham, a kid from my school who had no television (*unheard of!*), and a passion for photography. We would sit and write stuff and then perform it for the school, but only because we didn't trust anyone else to perform it. These performances led the school drama teacher, Des Margetson, to continually ask me to be in the school play – something I consistently refused to do.

Then, when I was seventeen, he came to me explaining that one of the actors in his production of Sheridan's *The Rivals* had suddenly become ill and would I take over? Bear in mind there were three days before the performance. To this day I have no idea why I said yes. I suspect there was a girl I felt I could impress, or one in the cast that I fancied. But I learnt the lines and went on stage at France Hill Comprehensive School in Surrey as Bob Acres, the simple country bumpkin. People laughed. And then, at the end . . . they applauded. I remember thinking, 'Mmm, this is good,' and the funny part was, I found it easy. I had no nerves (well, hardly any), and I could retain all the lines. It was like I'd stepped into something that fitted me. I was quite shy at school, very studious. What would be called a 'nerd' nowadays, and suddenly I was 'cool', and funny, and the centre of attention. [*Sam: What happened, mate?*]

SAM

Macbeth was the first play I was ever in. I was a soldier in the Tom McGovern production at the Lyceum in Edinburgh 1999. One night I remember being a bit hung-over, running across the stage in the pitch dark with a group of chain mail-clad warriors, over stepping stones, between two vast rotating walls (operated by a stage manager secreted inside the fake stone). I bumped into one of the walls and ricocheted off Eric Barlow (the actor playing MacDuff, but in this scene doubling as a Scottish warrior escaping the battle-field.) The lights came up and I was on stage – a lost soldier in the wrong scene.

Eventually I got promoted to 'Spear Carrier Number 2' in the main stage version, which at the time was like winning the theatrical lottery because I was in awe of Tom McGovern and had followed his career. He was athletic and his command of the language muscular, his delivery distinct.

Months earlier, during the Edinburgh Festival, I had wangled myself a job as a stage-hand at the Traverse where Tom was in *Shining Souls*. [*Graham: Stalker?*] I was helping to lay deck to the temporary stage (they had three spaces that were all used and rotated almost hourly for numerous productions during the festival). Distracted by the cast and trying to eavesdrop on their conversation, I let go of some decking, which dropped heavily on the stage manager's hand, causing a large flesh wound needing several stitches. He and I both realised in that painful moment that stage management wasn't for me and, as I quickly exited stage left, I found myself outside Tom's dressing room (a dressing room that would soon become familiar about three years later as it would become mine for *Outlying Islands* by David Greig, which won an Edinburgh Fringe First award and earned me a Laurence Olivier Award nomination). Tom was lounging in a chair, his feet up on the dressing table, reading a script (or maybe picking his nose). Addressing him in the mirror (like a ghostly reflection foreshadowing what was to come) I told him I was a big fan and hoped to be an actor one day. He was gracious and kind, encouraging me to get as much experience as possible, which drove me to join the Lyceum Youth theatre months later and to find myself on stage with him as Spear Carrier Number 2.

And finally, I was sitting at the same table as him, promoted to 'Scottish Lord Number 4' at the Lyceum Theatre, as Banquo's ghost appeared and Tom hurled his fake clay drinking vessel at the apparition. At the table, the lords would shake their heads and mutter in bemusement at Macbeth's erratic behaviour, whilst secretly giving Tom the footie score.

I would love to do a production of *Macbeth* with Graham. He would make an outstanding Lady M.

GRAHAM

Well, if Fiona Shaw can portray Richard II or Helen Mirren Prospero, why not? I'm game for everything. I said that when I signed with *Outlander* and ticked the nudity clause with great enthusiasm. Never got to take my kit off, though, a source of consternation and regret.

Sam: I can arrange for you to strip off . . .

Graham: No, because what you will arrange will hurt or involve freezing cold water that will cause my testicles to retract.

Sam: And, helps with your performance of Lady Macbeth.
Ahem.

Graham as Macbeth:
There's comfort yet; they are assailable;
Then be thou jocund: ere the bat hath flown
His cloister'd flight, ere to black Hecate's summons,

The shard-borne beetle, with his drowsy hums,
Hath rung night's yawning peal, there shall be done
A deed of dreadful note . . .

I really would love to play Macbeth but it's been a case of 'always the bridesmaid, never the bride'. I have been Macduff once, Malcolm once and Banquo twice, including in Jeremy Freeston's 1997 film, cunningly entitled *Macbeth*.

Banquo
O treachery! Fly, good Fleance, fly, fly, fly!
Thou may'st revenge – O slave!

Arguably my favourite Shakespeare play, it's like an action movie. Written specifically for King James I (James VI of Scotland) who had just come to the throne, it is in many ways the ultimate high-class job application. And it worked because shortly afterwards Shakespeare's Company, the Lord Chamberlain's men, became the King's Men. It deals with witchcraft, one of Jimmy boy's favourite subjects (he'd even written a book on it – *Daemonologie*, in 1597, a copy of which resides – of course – with Lady Cawdor. Coincidence? I think *not*.) [*Sam: Just to be clear, it's* not *a biography of Matt Damon.*]

The play does a terrible disservice to the real Macbeth, who was actually a bit of a star in Scottish history and not an ambitious psycho with a power-hungry wife who loved to wash her hands. [*Sam: Er, Macbeth did still kill King Duncan in real life. AND Duncan's dad!*]

My first experience was the best. It was in 1989 at Dundee Repertory Theatre. I had just come off doing the movie *Erik the Viking* and had moved back to Scotland to be with the woman I loved – only to be dumped shortly after I arrived! I ended up sharing the huge three-bedroom tenement flat with . . . myself. And, instead of starting a new, exciting chapter with my girlfriend, I spent three months feeling pretty shit about life in general.

Then I got the audition for Dundee Rep. It was to do the whole season (sadly this is now a thing of the past – actors in repertory, learning lines and rehearsing one play, while performing a different play at night. Hard work but bloody good fun, and a great training ground). When I auditioned I was seen by all three directors, all of whom couldn't understand why I wanted to do rep in Dundee after being in a big movie. I think it was difficult for them to understand, but I just really loved to work, to act! I didn't want to sit around waiting for the phone to ring like so many actors. It's why I've done about sixty stage plays while many people have only done four or five. I had written and performed my own show, I'd done fringe, but this was my first 'proper' theatre gig, and I couldn't wait.

SAM

Sorry to interrupt but, yes, Dundee Rep was every young actor's dream. They were still one of the few theatres to run an ensemble company and you could see your favourite actor play in multiple productions, throughout a season. From comedy, to new writing, farce and pantomime. I was lucky to play Dundee Rep in *Romeo and Juliet*. Unfortunately not as Romeo (I did that at drama school and think he's a precursor to Macbeth; you can see some of Shakespeare's early writing in the character, comedy and great philosophical tragedy). Macbeth feels like a more refined and experienced man, as if Shakespeare, too, has grown with the experience of writing. Carry on, Graham!

GRAHAM

Macbeth was played by a wonderful Scottish actor called Hilton McRae (married to Lindsay Duncan). His is still the best Macbeth I've ever seen, and I've seen a lot. Hilton is a wee guy, wiry, and febrile. The director had the inspired idea to surround him with big guys in all the other main roles. Me as Banquo, Kenneth Bryans as Macduff and Liam Brennan as Malcolm. Both of those guys went on to have distinguished careers in Scottish theatre. I remember the ghost scene in particular where Macbeth is visited by Banquo's ghost. A piece of 'scrim' or cloth was stretched across the back of the set. Whenever I appeared as the ghost, I pressed my face against the cloth, stretching and distorting it. With a lighting change it was very creepy indeed. As if the room itself was rising up against him. The witches were played by local children. Terrifying. It's been much imitated since, but this was the first time I remember it. The curse of Macbeth struck when one of the kids was tragically killed in a car crash on the way to do the show.

The second show, where I played Macduff, was by the same director. His view of the tragedy seemed to have changed along with his lifestyle. He had taken to driving around in an old VW camper van with a giant face of Buddha painted on the front. The show was set in a psychiatric hospital where the therapy was to 'act out' the play. A clever idea and with a better overall cast it could have worked. But with the exception of a handful of us, including Liam Brennan again as Macbeth, it was a depressing experience. Liam was so riled by the actress playing Lady Macbeth, it was all he could do to stop the banquet scene turning into a full-on brawl. Liam sat in the van that night driving home drinking a bottle of gin. [*Sam: I played Malcolm in a production at the Lyceum Edinburgh with Liam in the title role. He's a terrific and intense actor who doesn't go anywhere without a copy of David Mamet's book* True and False: Heresy and Common Sense for the Actor *in his pocket, and a wry smile.*]

I worked with that director one more time, in *Twelfth Night*, a production so riven with acrimony and hatred that Orsino actually knocked Feste out in the climactic reconciliation scene in front of an audience of 400. The actor used to stand next to me at the curtain call bowing, while muttering the words, 'Only fifteen more performances to go!' – happy days!

My third *Macbeth* incarnation was again as Banquo. This was a film version with Jason Connery as Macbeth. Jason is a wonderful guy, and a very fine actor and director. In *Macbeth* he had the second worst case of forgetting his lines I've ever seen (Billy Connolly in *The Hobbit* beat him for that!). It was tough to witness but he triumphed in the end.

It was a pretty good film though. I learned a lot about film acting on it. It was directed by a lovely fella called Jeremy Freeston for a film producer called Bob Carruthers. Bob had made his name making films in Scotland using 'investors' to help finance the making of them. This was in 1994 and he got these 'investors' to put in £1,000 to be an extra in the film. In return they got a credit, and minimal screen time. They even had to bring their own lunch and costume. These guys couldn't give him their money quick enough! They were queuing up!!

This was where I first met Charlie Allen and his gang. He didn't have the storm trooper head gear and hog back then, but in every other way he was just as formidable. Everything was directed by Jeremy apart from the witches scenes. Hildegarde Neil was one of the witches so these scenes were directed by that colossal legend, Brian Blessed.

I've worked with him three times. He doesn't drink, but is incapable of constructing a sentence without swearing. He'd just returned from an ascent of Everest (at sixty!), without oxygen wearing the same clothes as George Mallory in the 1920s (basically hobnailed boots and tweeds – he clearly used the same costume designer we had on *Clanlands*). He was directing us in a scene when he suddenly started to stare into the distance, muttering, 'Hmmm, ahhh, ohhh.' After several moments of this alarming behaviour his attention snapped back to the gathering of appalled actors in front of him: 'Ah, so sorry. I was back on the mountain for a minute. It's the altitude you know, thickens the blood. I have visions.'

All of my experiences with Brian have been similar. I've seldom laughed so much as I have with the stories he has regaled me with. Laughing so much I nearly wet myself (similar to experiences with the Ginger Nut, but for different reasons). Brian once turned on a particularly annoying 'amateur dramatics' performer who was his stand-in. He had been pestering Brian for about fifteen minutes at 5am during make-up. His patience finally exhausted, Brian was then calmly heard to utter the words, 'You're a lovely bloke, John, but you were born a c*nt and you'll die a c*nt. Now fuck off.' As I say, a legend. Read his autobiography immediately, going by the wonderful title of *Absolute Pandemonium*.

Sam: Is that Cawdor Castle I see before me?

Graham: Indeed it is. And quite beautiful, but does it have a drawbridge?

Drawbridges always make me think of films like *Robin Hood* (multiple versions), *Warlord* (a great Charlton Heston flick if you've not seen it) and *Ironclad* (very good too). Bad shit always happens on the wrong side of a drawbridge and I could sense this would prove to be no exception.

We reach the entrance to Cawdor Castle grounds, whereupon Sam stalls. When the stone gate was built in the fifteenth century I don't think the Thane of Cawdor had accounted for a Fiat Arsepiece passing through it. I can clearly see that it will never fit from 100 yards out. It's wide enough for a couple of horses abreast, at best.

Graham: We're never going to get through that gate.

Sam: Nonsense, loads of space.

Graham: No, really. We won't.

Sam: Stop being such an old woman.

We accelerate towards the opening. Sam's invariable response to any doubt on my part as to the wisdom of a given course of action is to compare me to an elderly female. Sam continues to smile, certain we will shrink to fit at the last moment. And then he rams on the anchors inches from the sides of the stone gate. The laws of physics having finally penetrated his brain cells.

Sam: What if we fold the wing mirrors back?

Graham: What if I just blow up the gate? Or perhaps the camper?

He doesn't laugh.

Sam: I don't think I should reverse.

It is the first thing he has said with which I wholeheartedly agree. To reverse would be madness. The Fiat Colon doesn't handle well in reverse. So instead we sit and stare at the gate, as if our collective gaze might force it to widen. 'Where are you?' crackles line producer Michelle over the walkie-talkie.

Sam: Erm, we can't get through.

I hold my head in my hands. The fatigue and exasperation is too much. Neither of my daughters, Hope, seven, and Honor, thirteen, are this difficult to manage and they have tested me to the limit. As has become customary, I enjoyed the delights of late-night whisky at the hotel before being unceremoniously dumped in the country-side to sleep it off under canvas in the Highland heather. Why do I do it to myself? Sam is showing zero evidence of a hangover as usual. For a fleeting moment I wonder whether he is fully human (I've been watching *Westworld*). No one could drink as much as he puts away with no visible effect. Not even an eye bag. But then he does have Wendy's magic make-up. I bet (hope) first thing he looked like he'd been laid out on Eilean Munde. It's all panstick and Polyfilla . . .

I suddenly notice a sign sticking out of the ground in front of us. Right before our very eyes.

MARATHON, CAWDOR CASTLE, SEPTEMBER 14th 2019

Graham: What's the date, Sam?

Sam: I'm wedged in a gateway and you want to know what day it is . . .

I point at the sign as three men in vests and very short shorts, wearing numbers, literally squeeze past us in the gateway.

I've never run a marathon, citing the fact that the original marathon runner who came from the battle of the same name in 490 BC to deliver news of the victory, dropped dead immediately on arrival. Sam, of course, has run many marathons. He's probably running one as you read this book. Or possibly climbing a Munro carrying a bottle of Sassenach, just in case he can flog it to someone at the top.

Sam speaks 'marathon'. I speak 'latte'. And Sauvignon Blanc and comfy slippers . . .

But even untutored as I am in the world of running ridiculous distances, I am fully cognisant that marathon runners don't appreciate cretinous camper vans blocking their route. I imagine they are a few miles in, settling into their pace, not wanting to push too hard too soon when, lo and behold, some pair of arses have parked their camper van at the only entrance point to the castle grounds. We go neither forward nor back, remaining in stasis as Sam waves encouragingly to the runners who wear expressions ranging from quiet disbelief to naked rage.

It never ceases to amaze me how many people go in for this sort of self-flagellation. Now, I'm all for exercise. I enjoy a hike, cycling (on a modern bike), the gym (sort of), but there are literally hundreds of these marathon people. *[Sam: It's called 'exercise', Graham, you're meant to sweat.]* Some look fit enough, lithe and effortless like Maasai warriors as they run towards us; others look like they are ten strides away from a massive coronary.

And all their hard work is making me hungry. I unwrap a chocolate bar, take a bite and look out of the window just as two runners give me the finger. This is beyond excruciating but I am too tired, hung-over and Heughaned-out to care.

I wonder if King Duncan's arrival was like this?

SAM

Bang! The RV bounces over a kerb. Merlin, the sound guy, launches into the air, somehow never losing control of his fluffy microphone. I've taken a corner too sharply and we are on three wheels for a split second. I strangely hope McT hasn't noticed, but of course he has. He is grinning at me, which is more unnerving than the eye-rolling or the handbag-clutching titters. Yep, he's at it again. Smiling away. All right, Gray? He's not the full ticket today.

And when he's not gurning like a stoner, Graham has been reciting the works of Shakespeare for the entire journey. And I mean the *entire* journey. I have been desperate to answer a call of nature since we set off but we are running late and not stopping for anything. If he does 'Is this a dagger I see before me' I might jump in the back with Merlin and break into the emergency 'daytime whisky'.

Our directions (Graham again) have taken us up a narrow road towards the dramatic castle of Cawdor. It also appears we are on the route of a running race, though I don't let Graham know that. We slalom past various runners of all shapes and sizes on the private drive. As we near a gate in the castle walls I realise (too late) the camper won't fit. Graham is flapping like a popinjay as I wedge the camper in the castle walls, blocking the only entrance, with the runners gaining on us. I look in the wing mirror: the runners are now upon us, bunching behind, squeezing past the camper one at a time. The ones who make it through look seriously pissed off.

There is a break in the flow so I jam the RV into reverse and start to edge back out. The gears crunch and the engine conks out and now I'm in an even worse position than I was before. The sweaty athletes shout at us through our open windows: 'Bloody idiots!' and 'Great timing, lads!'

I wish for the ground to swallow me up and try to slip down beneath the steering wheel, out of sight from the angry horde. Yes, we are 'those guys'. Driving an oversized camper van, disrupting everyone's day, in the most ridiculous way possible. And, to top it all, we are dressed head to toe in *tweed*. We are tweedy wankers, not the dashing and refined fellows we had thought.

I want to shout, 'I'm one of you!' because running is a passion of mine. I've run marathons in Paris, Los Angeles, Edinburgh, Stirling and I hope to run the New York marathon in November 2020, fingers crossed.

Paris (not Hilton) was my first. It was so exciting and nerve-wracking. Twelve weeks of prep, carb-loading the day before, eating *all* the French bread, pasta and croissants. I celebrated afterwards (on my own) with a slap-up meal, bottle of red, steak-frites and yet more bread. I like to do these runs on my own. I enjoy the personal challenge but also the peace when you get to be by yourself. Running somehow is a good way to relax, re-energise and work out problems. The rhythm and tempo enable self-reflection. And the support at marathons is so uplifting, you feel for a day that you are a *real* athlete. My personal best time was three hours eleven minutes at the Edinburgh Marathon. I did a half marathon in London in one hour twenty-four minutes.

Running is a super way to explore cities and the surrounding area; there's nothing quite like seeing the sights of Paris as you run along the Champs-Elysees, past Notre Dame and finish at the Eiffel Tower. In 2014 whilst playing Batman in the immense DC Comics and Universal live stadium production (featuring wire-work, fighting, acrobatics and pyrotechnics) I challenged the cast to run 5km every day for a month. We ran in each city: Berlin, Frankfurt, Prague, Cologne, and on Christmas day we ran together along the Seine in Paris.

After Batman, despite three months of auditioning for TV and film roles in LA, I returned to the UK penniless. I was thirty-four and forced to sign on to pay my rent. Two weeks later, I couldn't face the process – the Job Centre not seeing acting as a legitimate profession – so I gave up and tried to find full-time work as a barman. I had done a variety of jobs to support myself over the years: delivered sandwiches by bicycle, sold perfume in Harrods, drawn up contracts for mental health doctors in the NHS and various other bar/restaurant jobs around London. Moving there after drama school, I had been working as a 'jobbing actor' for almost twelve years and it had been a real roller coaster, some years with great success and others with only a couple of credits to add to my CV. I had just returned from the US, after spending another pilot season there (a busy period in the spring when US networks would commission a large number of pilot TV shows). I had been testing on a number of shows and films (*Agents of Shield, Tron, King Arthur, Beauty and the Beast, Aquaman,* the list of near misses goes on!) that would potentially change my life and I had signed the contracts – spending the money and living the fame – in my head! However, once again I found myself penniless, depressed and back in the UK. I was really beginning to question if I could keep going with no real long-term opportunities in sight. In the past I had had trouble with the Inland Revenue and even seen bailiffs at my front door. Several loans and credit cards were drowning me and I couldn't see a way out. I thought I'd give it another year to see if anything changed and, if not, I knew I was going to have to make drastic changes to my life.

And then out of the blue I was offered a screen test for *Outlander* – a new US TV show – and you know the rest. *Outlander* has given me financial stability and presented me with some amazing opportunities for which I am extremely grateful. More often than not it's about hanging in there to achieve your goal and the harder it gets, sometimes, the nearer you are – just like with marathons. You have to keep on keeping on.

In 2015 I founded My Peak Challenge to help people get out there, achieve goals and become healthier and happier whilst raising money for charity. Members have access to a range of live workouts, yoga sessions, meal plans and a Peakers' forum where people share their successes and failures. There's a whole community across eighty-three countries, 12,000 members who have raised over $5 million for charity. We have supported Blood Cancer UK (fully financing several research projects), Marie Curie hospice care, Testicular Cancer awareness and the Environmental Defense fund.

Initially, I wanted to share my workouts and how I incorporate them into daily life – I need to maintain a high level of fitness and healthy eating (whisky being the exception) on the show because Jamie is a muscular Highland warrior and I am contractually obliged to spend a fair amount of time semi-naked! Part of my training is running and I have a coach who checks in with me each week and sets a plan. I like to run most Sundays between ten and twenty miles, depending at what point I am in my training. I used to run a lot from Glasgow along the West Highland Way. It goes up Connich Hill and past the shores of Loch Lomond. It remains a dream to do the ultra marathon along the West Highland Way, a hundred-mile thrashing over the hills.

I look at Graham who is squirming in his seat dressed in tweed, strangers shouting at him and banging the sides of the camper – he is truly living the dream and I have made that happen. I wonder if I should invite him out for a two-hour training run another day? But the Grey Dog is not a runner. He is, however, very fit. He cycles and hill-walks a lot but I don't think he has the patience to run long distances (and can you imagine the amount of food he would have to eat to sustain himself?). In fact, I don't think I've ever seen him run. He could be *Outlander*'s answer to Roger Moore, who famously never ran on screen. He thought he looked awkward so all running in the James Bond films was performed by body doubles.

During the first year of *Outlander* I asked for a gym at the studio (we got a small room with a weight rack and I bought some other gear). Occasionally he would be seen in there, grunting and sweating profusely. I offered him a slot to workout with my trainer. After one session he never went back, apparently complaining that the exercises were 'dangerous'. However I have seen him work out and have trained with his trainer in LA. High intensity and 100%, the Grey Dog is always willing to give it everything (for a very short time).

A runner shouts up at Graham. 'Twat!'

'Nooo, nooo, oh my goddd,' he squeals. I wave the runners on, hoping the encouragement might make them forgive us. 'Good luck! *Sorry!*' I feebly cheer, until the last of the gang has shuffled past. Then I put the camper into reverse and desperately try to move out of the way. It's a bit like the reversing scene in *Austin Powers* – a forty-seven-point turn.

Graham exhales noisily and his shoulders, which have been up around his ears, drop. A little. 'It couldn't get any worse!' he grumbles.

'Well, I'm afraid it does,' I answer, still trying to get the bloody van out of the gateway. 'We'll have to cycle.' The look of disbelief in his eyes is splendid. We ditch the camper, now completely wedged in the entrance, lift off our two-wheeled steeds from the back of the camper and jump on. 'Race you!' I set off, leaving his ladyship puffing, fuming and generally raging at the world.

GRAHAM

'Ride the bikes up instead,' says Michelle over the walkie-talkie. Ah, the bikes. The kind of bikes a vicar might ride in a tiny country village in the 1930s. A Dutch village with no hills whatsoever. For reasons best known to Sam, all our modes of transport (of which there are many), seem to be chosen for their utter impracticality and general clapped-out-ness.

So Sam and I clamber out of the Fiat Prostate and pull the bikes off a rack at the back. Well, Sam pulled the bikes off. I smile at him encouragingly. I'm not sure how familiar you are with bicycles. Nowadays they can be made from carbon fibre with gossamer brakes, even suspension, and definitely gears – sometimes as many as twenty-one gears just to help you up those awkward inclines. You can even get electric ones. Ours were made of iron, with extra iron attached. If they'd ever had brakes they'd been ruthlessly cut off long ago, so that now they resembled a piece of rusting farmyard machinery with wheels.

We squeeze the bikes through the tiny gap between the camper and the gate, all the while yet more runners struggling to get by.

It was at this point we saw the slope for the first time. Nothing too awful, but when you're about to climb on board something that looks like it was built by Isambard Kingdom Brunel, any slope seems steep. Especially when you're in a tweed suit! The crew is at the top and what they want is a clean shot of us cycling up the hill.

We wait for a gap between panting participants and on 'Action' we set off. Both Sam and I are very competitive, so we go for it. Heughan beats me. I hate him for it.

'That was great. Let's try it again,' said Michelle.

Why?

We return to the gate. More runners. Good grief, how many *are* there? Were they lost? Or running in circles? Take two. 'Action!' More straining against the pedals. Sam beats me again. 'That was good. Definitely better.' (By what criteria, you may wonder.) 'One more time, please.'

Now I've been in the film business long enough to know that, 'One more time' actually means 'Another twenty times.' Peter Jackson (director of *The Hobbit*) would say it just before we did another thirty takes. Minimum.

I feel a cramp coming on.

We do it again. More runners. We wait and then smash our way up the hill for the third time. I am sweating in my tweed. By the time we do another five takes my thighs are screaming and I look like I've been sprayed with a hose. Upon the final take, I begin to compost . . .

Sam as King Duncan
This castle hath a pleasant seat; the air
Nimbly and sweetly recommends itself
Unto our gentle senses

Macbeth, Act I, Scene VI

SAM
This is what Duncan says to Banquo before he's brutally murdered in his bed. Right here. [*Hello, Graham here. Actually, Duncan and Banquo were standing in front of Macbeth's castle in Inverness, not Cawdor, which was built in the fourteenth century, but you get the idea.*] [*Thanks, Professor McTavish.*]

A crimson flag furiously flaps in the wind, high above the battlements of Cawdor Castle. 'Is that a Chinese flag?' Alex the German asks in an even thicker Deutsche accent than usual, possibly owing to last night's 'production meeting' whisky. 'Must have been a recent acquisition, don't get it in shot,' he instructs the cameraman.

Blood red, I think ominously.

After a quick round of photos and pausing to let my Tour-de-Yorkshire friend catch his breath, we cross the drawbridge into the castle. Still unsteady on my feet and slightly delirious due to lack of sleep and multiple takes at the bike race up the hill, I stumble as Graham jokingly pushes me to the edge of the drawbridge. 'Be mindful,' he sarcastically barks, reading the Campbell of Cawdor motto (once the motto of the Calder clan) set in stone above the portcullis. This castle already had a dodgy reputation; I'm going to be on my guard.

The castle's ancient tower house was built in 1454 by William Calder, 6th Thane of Calder, around a legendary holly tree. The Campbells didn't turn up on the scene until the sixteenth century and that's when they added 'of Cawdor' and kidnapped a small child in the process (more on that later . . .).

Steeped in superstition, myth and fable, we are due to meet Lady Cawdor herself who, according to Shakespeare, is not a nice, trustworthy lady. Still, before we die by fatal stabbing or poisoned chalice, we find ourselves awaiting her presence in the courtyard cafe, Graham having sniffed out a latte from a hundred yards away. We order at the counter. 'Would you like anything else?' As I look up from my steaming cup of Joe, I do a double take. The long dark hair, smiling eyes, heaving bosom. Is it . . . ? It can't be. We're almost 200 miles away from Glencoe. Delilah? Delirious. Dagger. My senses are playing tricks on me. But it's not poor, sweet Delilah, I fear, but her mother, Glenn. Because wherever Delilah goes so does Glenn.

'She looks suspiciously like . . .' Graham murmurs out the side of his mouth, a large oatmeal muffin already partially demolished in his hand. Crumbs fall from his beard as he stares at the buxom barista. 'A relative maybe? You know what they're like in small towns,' he backs off to sit in a chair in the far corner. I give the girl a wink and my best smile. 'Let me know if you need anything else. Anything at all,' she says, bouncing off to replenish the cake stand. I take a large gulp of my Americano and wait for the caffeine to hit the back of my eyeballs.

Suddenly a large pair of hands slips around my waist from behind and I spin round ready to fend off the mad matriarch's advances, somehow managing not to spill my precious coffee. Merlin, the sound guy, is attaching a mic belt to my waist. 'Bit jumpy today?' he says as he continues to rummage near my back passage. Perhaps it's an act of revenge for having to spend the morning locked in the toilet of the camper, recording our rambling reminiscences and all of Graham's Shakespearean soliloquies. Not to mention the bumpy ride.

'Lady Cawdor will see you now,' Michelle announces, disappearing as quickly as she had appeared, as if she'd walked through the wall. I take a deep breath, chug the last of my coffee and start to make my way up the spiral staircase. I catch sight of something out of the corner of my eye. Delilah? I turn, but no one is there. I later discover Cawdor Castle is haunted by two ghosts, the 1st Earl Cawdor and a young lady in a blue velvet dress with no hands. It makes me shiver just thinking about it.

The striking chatelaine, Lady Cawdor, is directing the crew as to which priceless antiques they absolutely *should not* touch. She is tall, classy and charismatic; Graham has been reduced to a giggling schoolboy. Absolutely his type, she begins to talk and we are both lost in her spell.

GRAHAM

As we finally pass over the moat beneath the Campbell of Cawdor coat of arms we are greeted by the lady of the house. Not Mrs Macbeth, but the Dowager Countess of Cawdor, Lady Angelika, who has been keeping us waiting because she was washing her hands.

She of the scrupulously clean hands is the perfect hostess. Her husband, the 6th Earl/Thane, is no longer with us and I resist the temptation of asking if there had been a Macduff involved in his demise. She is an actual Bohemian, from Bohemia. A truly beautiful woman. I think both Sam and I, along with every other member of the crew (male and female), all developed a crush on her. Being Dowager Countess of Cawdor, there is, of course, a feud attached. In this case, between her and her stepson, the 7th Earl Cawdor, in an ongoing dispute over the will of her late husband. Her stepdaughter has even written a scandal-laden book about the drama, which Lady Angelika describes as 'fiction'. I told you, that drawbridge had trouble written all over it.

We are led into one of the libraries. The camera crew sets up a large oak table and Lady Cawdor pours us tea. It really is achingly civilised. John, our camera guru, asks if we can put anything on the table to make it look less empty. 'Yes,' says our Bohemian hostess, 'just grab that book'. She points at a huge leather-bound tome – something that could legitimately be described as a doorstop. It definitely looks impressive. The book is placed off centre on the table. Thereupon I casually ask what the book is.

'Oh, it's a second edition of Shakespeare's folio of plays.' I hear ringing in my ears and my heart is thumping. True, I had experienced all of these feelings while Sam was driving, but this is different. I am instantly taken back to my days at Queen Mary College University of London and my Professor of English, Nigel Alexander (a fearsome bearded Scot – much like a small version of Dougal MacKenzie), who had fostered my deep love of Shakespeare by instructing his students to stage eighteen Elizabethan and Jacobean plays in our three years, with me playing leading roles in many of them.

'Can I hold it?' I ask.

'Of course,' came the reply from our elegant hostess. I stand up and pick up the book, published in 1632. The last one sold went for about $178,000. It is a very special moment. To turn the pages of this book is to dive into history. Lady Cawdor goes on to mention in passing that the castle possesses dozens of extraordinary first editions, including the first edition of James I's book on witchcraft. Sam jokes about her poisoning our tea, whilst I drool over her and the books.

SAM

Both Graham and I have a long history with Shakespeare during our careers and the oversized folio is of great interest to me. I'd have liked to examine it – if Graham hadn't been pawing at it so much. I started my early professional experience in Shakespeare productions and was fortunate to play at Glasgow's Citizens Theatre, during Giles Havergal CBE's last season. He had directed over eighty seminal productions in the Gorbals, bringing groundbreaking theatre in the 1970s, to a lesser-known, more deprived area of Glasgow. I was in two productions with Giles at the Citizens, one being *Hamlet*, playing Rosencrantz *and* Guildenstern, and the other *A*

Christmas Carol. More importantly, though, I had returned to the place of many Christmas childhood memories, where I had possibly watched McTavish prance around on stage in the Christmas panto, as an enthralled child eating a bag of dolly mixtures. The most memorable time at 'the Citz', however, was when the role was reversed. During Roald Dahl's *The Twits*, I followed in McTavish's footsteps, dancing on stage to Elvis Presley, wearing a skin-tight sequin pair of flares, corset and full carnival headdress. *[Graham: Even just reading this conjures an image I cannot unsee.]*

Graham closes the book. It is time for tea, and she of the spotless fingers has a large glass teapot next to her steaming from the snout (the pot, not the lady), the liquid yellow and peculiar. Before we continue our chat about Lady Macbeth, the queen responsible for poisoning Duncan's guards, Lady Cawdor picks up a silver strainer and pours the glowing liquid into three china cups. I sniff it suspiciously and look at Graham out of the corner of my eye. He is oblivious, wide-eyed and dutifully smiling. He takes a large swig, never taking his gaze off her. Now in his element, surrounded by historical artefacts and an intriguing woman, I'd lost him. At least if he keels over, I'll know it's poisoned.

'Homemade ginger and lemon tea,' the Lady purrs. Her eyes are witty, intelligent and, like the snake in the *Jungle Book*, hypnotic. 'It's not poisoned,' she laughs, 'I don't think.' I pretend to take a sip and allow myself to relax. I guess if I die, it'll be on camera and we will have evidence. Unless, of course, she takes the whole crew down too.

We ask some questions and she breathily recounts the story of how the Campbells came to Cawdor in the sixteenth century. 'Muriel Calder was a posthumous child, her father had been killed in battle. As an heiress she immediately became ward of the king and Campbell, the Earl of Argyll (later Duke) who was the strong arm of the king – as the Campbells have always been – said to the king, I'd like that heiress for my son, please. Of course the king said yes. The Calders weren't pleased (especially Muriel's two uncles). So old Argyll waited until the child was four years old and, in the autumn of 1499, decided to kidnap her just in case she was 'done away with quietly' by a Calder. Staying with her grandmother in a nearby castle, it became apparent the Campbells were going to burn it down so the grandmother asked a nanny to 'place a key in the fire'. When it was hot they branded the poor little girl on her behind. The nanny is supposed to have pointed out that the mark wouldn't be recognisable by the time she would be of marriageable age at fourteen. 'So, the nanny bit off the tip of her little finger on her left hand.'

Mary Poppins, medieval style.

The Campbells, led by Inverliver, kidnap Muriel. 'They change her into different clothes and dress up a corn stoop in what she had been wearing (as a decoy).' The Calder uncles give chase (with a superior force) pursuing 'the child'. Inverliver sends Muriel off with six men and turns to fight the Calders at Daltullich, close to Strathnairn. The Battle of Daltullich is bloody with many slain, including seven of Inverliver's sons.

'Muriel was brought up at Inveraray Castle (the ancestral seat of Argyll) and married the earl's second son John in 1510. It was a very happy marriage and they came to live at Cawdor, had ten children and Muriel died at the very old age of seventy-five having outlived most of her children. And that is how the Campbells came to Cawdor,' she says, rising regally.

We go down to see the rock upon which the castle is built. Out of this rock grows a holly tree. 'As far as I am aware it's the only castle in Britain that is built around a sacred rock with a tree sprouting from it,' she says. It's quite a *Game of Thrones* sort of moment. There really is something about this lady, her manner, poise and grace. A white witch, or at least a believer in good energies, we discover, she runs the castle business with purpose and strength. Like her husband's ancestors of old, the Campbells were a savvy bunch, but their enemies distrusted them. The surname Campbell originated as a nickname meaning 'crooked mouth' derived from the Gaelic *cam* ('crooked') and *beul* ('mouth').

Standing on the battlements, the wind whipping up around us, the Lady explains the red flag. 'It's a Buddhist prayer flag, sending good energy out into the world,' she explains. Having quietly resisted her powers I too find myself falling for this woman, castle and clan. The manicured grounds, walled gardens, big wood (with the tallest trees in Europe and remnants of the ancient Caledonian forest), replica of the Minotaur's labyrinth in Knossos, Crete, complete with miniature Minotaur – it's a spellbinding place.

I just wish they'd make the gate wider.

CHAPTER NINE

The Circle of Life

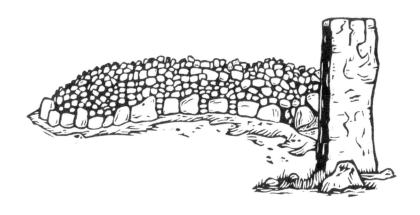

'*For that is the mark of the Scot of all classes . . .
there burns alive in him a sense of identity with the dead,
even to the twentieth generation.*'
Robert Louis Stevenson

SAM

It's now early afternoon and the weather has started to turn. The wind gusts across the Prehistoric Burial Cairns of Bulnuaran of Clava (aka Clava Cairns), a Bronze Age cemetery with ring cairns, kerb cairns and standing stones near Inverness. (A cairn being a man-made pile, or stack, of stones.) Cameron McNeish, our guide, arrives on his electric neon-yellow bike. 'The man of the hills himself,' I greet him warmly. A great storyteller, political writer, author, broadcaster and legendary mountain walker/climber, Cameron knows more about the landscape of Scotland than anyone, having walked every inch of it multiple times. He's bagged all 282

Munros three times round plus many iconic mountains around the world including those in the Alps, the Pyrenees, Spain, Iceland, North America, Norway, Sweden, Pakistan, India, Nepal, Central America, Slovenia, Russia, Guatemala, Corsica, Jordan and Turkey.

I can see Graham eyeing his electric bike with contempt. A stickler for tradition and a confessed technophobe, Graham has even managed to scupper the writing of this book several times, unable to 'share' a simple document. We've tried Word, Pages and finally Google Docs before he set fire to his computer and returned to quill and ink. When we first started Zooming, the time it took for Graham to realise he didn't have to plug in his wireless ear-buds (clue's in the name Graham) was staggering! He is, however, an amazing calligrapher and player of the lute.

I imagine him writing his sections by candlelight, hunched over a rusty typewriter like Scrooge, his pince-nez glasses perched upon the tip of his nose, sipping an excellent Pinot Noir. Mobile phones are an anathema to the balding thespian; the internet, the work of the devil. I wouldn't be surprised if I received a telegram or carrier pigeon from him one of these days, telling me to 'Fu*k off'.

GRAHAM

I wouldn't call myself a Luddite but, let's put it this way, they had a point.

I think J.G. Farrell said it best in *The Siege of Krishnapur*: 'We look on past ages with condescension, as a mere preparation for us . . . but what if we are a mere after-glow of them?'

I often ask people to name a single advantage that the mobile phone has given us. They look affronted, as if I'm telling them the Earth is flat. 'Well we can communicate with each other,' they invariably say. I wonder if these people have any concept of a time before cell phones. Do they imagine people in the 1980s scratching their heads wondering, 'How do I let that person know we need to talk? How can I get a message to them? If only we could communicate!'

But no, amazingly, the world functioned remarkably well. Amazing feats of engineering were accomplished, distant lands were explored, probably the best songs were written before 2000, as were the greatest books (ours excepted of course). And yet, we persist in arrogantly adhering to this notion that new technology is necessarily an improvement.

Even before the coronavirus pandemic of 2020 we were witnessing a kind of zombie apocalypse as people hunched over devices ignoring people inches away from them. In pubs, at dinner, at work: a world of self-isolation before self-isolation. Well done, technology!

So as far as my headphones are concerned, these are, in fact, elaborate ear muffs with no function other than to keep my ears warm. I just have the speaker on full volume.

SAM

I *really* wanna go on Cameron's electric bike. With fat off-road tyres and a 750W geared motor, the bike can help you coast up the hardest of tracks. I doubt Cameron's taken it up the Cullins on Skye (check out the Red Bull cyclist Danny MacAskill, who's done tricks on the inaccessible pinnacle!) but he's always game for a challenge. And so am I.

One weekend in 2018, during shooting of *Outlander*, I agreed to film an episode of the *Adventure Show*, a Scottish TV show Cameron presents, focusing on outdoor sports and activities, which was right up my street! After a late night sitting by his open fire, consuming a generous amount of whisky, the next morning we prepared to head out. His lovely wife Gina cooked a hearty breakfast and ensured we had enough provisions for the adventure ahead. We were climbing the lesser-known Monadhliath Mountains, 'the grey mountain range', situated on the western side of Strathspey, to the west of the Cairngorms. It was winter and the drive through a blizzard the night before had been hairy, to say the least. I wasn't sure if I'd get back to Glasgow the next day to resume working on *Outlander*.

'There's a thick blanket of snowfall from last night but I don't think we need snow shoes,' Cameron mused, sipping on a mug of hot tea. We shouldered our bags and started off down the street, the cars and houses walled in by a few feet of pristine white snow. I'd been experimenting in the hills shortly before this, and had bagged a few peaks, but had never successfully reached a summit in these conditions. A lack of experience and winter equipment had been my downfall. This time I came prepared: winter boots, ski socks, base layers, gaiters, waterproof jacket, fleece, snood, thick gloves and a bonnet, plus a hip flask hidden in my pocket! I felt ready to brave the freezing old hill. 'I doubt we'll need that,' Cameron said pointing at my ice axe poking out the top of my bag, 'probably no ice yet'. Just as the last word left his wind-chilled lips, he turned and was suddenly thrown off his feet, landing on his back, the bag and thick snow cushioning his fall. 'Pretty slippy though, watch out!' he said from the floor. He clambered to his feet and we set out once more, the sky turning grey and threatening to cover us some more, but we made it to the top with me only going once up to my waist in deep snow.

The weather is more pleasant today – cold, but my tweed suit and bonnet are keeping me warm. The thick snowdrifts I fell in whilst climbing with Cameron are nowhere to be seen. At times on that climb I found myself almost waist deep in fresh snow. It didn't feel like the Highlands of Scotland, more like the Arctic.

Cameron tells us to grab the bikes down from the back of the camper. Graham looks at me.

Graham: Sam, get the bikes down whilst I look majestically at the trees.

God, it's like working with Lady Gaga. He regally surveys the skyline, whilst I struggle to take the bikes off. He can see I can't get them down. He gives me a look that could puncture a bicycle tyre. I have arranged the whole trip, have to do *all* of the driving, sort the bikes out, take her ladyship's luggage to her room . . .

Graham: Get on with it.

'I can well see you're experienced cyclists!' And now Cameron's mocking me. The grey bugger is making me look like a chump in front of a Scottish legend. As I haul the vintage steeds down, Cameron admires the sprung saddle ready for Graham's royal bottom. He needs all the cushioning he can get at his age. It won't be long before he brings his own rubber ring along . . . *[Graham: Buns of Steel, I assure you.]*

Graham's certainly not forgotten the almighty thrashing I gave him racing up the hill to Cawdor Castle, so he's away like a streak of grey lightning, pedalling with all his might. Cameron cycles after him, with me struggling to catch up because in my haste to get my leg over I've squished my balls on my non-sprung concrete saddle.

'Argh, my balls!' I squeak.

They film us cycling all of fifty yards, arriving at the gates of Clava Cairns. When it's cut together we can pretend (badly) we've just done a thirty-miler. Still clad in full tweed, we look like lost characters from *Foyle's War*, which given *Outlander* begins in 1942, is not such a leap. The *Outlander* story starts with WWII combat nurse Claire Randall on honeymoon in Inverness with her husband Frank (played by Tobias Menzies.) They visit the fictional Craigh na Dun stones (which we recreated at Kinloch Rannoch). The Styrofoam stones were modelled on the Callanish Stones found on the Isle of Lewis and are similar to the ones found here at Clava Cairns. While searching for wild flowers, Claire accidentally travels back through these megaliths to 1743, coming face to face with Frank's villainous ancestor Captain 'Black Jack' Randall (also played by Tobias). He manhandles Claire and that's where Graham and I come charging in, rescuing the damsel-in-a-ripped-dress and taking her back to Castle Leoch, seat of Clan MacKenzie and the dubious MacKenzie brothers, one played by my current saddle-sore companion.

GRAHAM

For many folk it's only *Outlander* that has introduced them to these stone circles. It is part of Diana Gabaldon's brilliance that she understood the power of such places in the weaving of her stories. Standing amongst these stones reminds one of all the stories that have been lost over millennia, and the even greater importance of telling new ones now. These people recognised that life itself is the quintessential story, with death as the final chapter, and this is a homage to that universal tale.

With this cheery thought in mind Sam and I enter the cemetery built over 4,000 years ago. Because of the association with *Outlander*, Clava Cairns has become a somewhat popular destination on the tourist trail – particularly among fans of the show – so it causes a stir when Dougal MacKenzie and Jamie Fraser cycle past wearing tweeds (Again! Seriously!), riding clapped-out piles of scrap metal. I jealously eye all the top-of-the-range RVs and camper vans, while our f%&s^*! Fiat Farce lies skulking in a corner of the car park, like an overly flatulent uncle at a wedding party. We stop for a few photos. *[Sam: There's no sight of Glenn who's probably out raising a militia right at this moment.]* The Spanish fans are very respectful. Cemeteries do that to people, which is perhaps one of the reasons I love visiting them.

I've always had somewhat of a fascination for cemeteries, which I inherited from my grandfather. I don't find them morbid, they are large-scale memento mori – a reminder of our fleeting time on earth – and it is a destination common to us all, one day. The ultimate shared experience that doesn't differentiate based on your income, where you were born, your race, or your religion. Death, after all, is death, for all of us.

The Bronze Age folk who built Clava Cairns were no different from us in that respect. We try to make sense of death today, much as they did thousands of years ago. It is a challenge that has followed our species through history. Our unique ability to reflect upon our own mortality. While other species can feel fear and pain, we alone are unique in our reflexive mind that allows us to project into a future towards, as Shakespeare put it, the 'undiscovered country'.

The philosopher Ludwig Wittgenstein said, 'For life in the present there is no death. Death is not an event in life. It is not a fact in the world.' We've always known it, and as a result we have always needed to mark it, to have places, sacred places, for the final resting of those who have gone before us. It is still regarded as abhorrent, irrespective of whether one is religious or not, to disturb the dead.

Whenever I am in a place of historical significance, be it Clava, Glencoe or a castle, I always try to place myself in its history. Imagine being in this part of Scotland 4,000 years ago. The burial chambers here only held up to two people, so given the elaborate construction, they must have been for people of status and importance. (Definitely not actors. Up until not that long ago thespians were often buried at crossroads with a stake through their bodies because they were seen as dangerous tricksters – I've definitely worked with a couple who deserved a good staking.)

As for the exquisite ordering of the stones and the building of the burial cairns – imagine the work that went into making them, moving the stones, the precise alignment of them to work best at the midwinter solstice, when Clava is bathed in an ethereal golden light. The dedication and the reverence. It makes for a profound experience whenever you visit. It creates, for me, a gigantic piece of living art: 4,000 years standing as silent sentinels, witness to the world passing around them, as immovable as the death they commemorate.

Julius Caesar, Emperor of Rome, wrote an account of the Celtic Druids in Gaul (modern France):

> 'Beyond all things, they are desirous to inspire a belief that men's souls do not perish, but transmigrate after death from one individual to another; and besides, they hold discourses about the stars, about the size of the world and of various countries, about the nature of things, and about the power and might of the immortal gods.'
>
> **Julius Caesar's *Commentarii de Bello Gallico*,**
> **book VI, written in the 50s or 40s BC**

These stones don't give up their secrets. They offer a tantalising glimpse into an age we can only guess at. Scraps of clothing, jewellery and bones are all we have but one thing has remained and shall remain: these stone guardians, reminders of a time long before the Highlander walked this land.

SAM

A vast tourist coach has pulled up and some people are waving at us as we pass through the gateway. The popularity and success of the show has led to a great number of people looking into their genealogy and history. Tourist numbers to Scotland have increased a great deal, with specific sites seeing a huge rise in numbers, including Clava Cairns and Doune Castle (Castle Leoch), which saw a 227% increase in visitors. The interest has also helped a lot of historic buildings find funding for refurbishment, from the flour mill (where Jamie takes a cold bath) to Geillis's house in the historic town of Cuross, and the traditional sailing boat in which we set sail to France. Culloden battlefield has also seen a huge increase in numbers but there have been concerns over the increased footfall. The Fraser gravestone on the barren field has daily visits from curious tourists and a large number of flowers are laid by the graveside. Historic Scotland has asked fans to be respectful of its significance and the majority are extremely careful. I feel Scotland has been slow to pick up on this increased popularity but is beginning to gear its campaigns towards the new international audience. For the first few years of shooting *Outlander*, the locals were blissfully unaware of the horde of grubby actors running around the local park in Cumbernauld, filming a US TV show. However, a group of Diana's fans (who had read her books some twenty years earlier) were organising and booking trips to Scotland. They knew the prime locations in the story and had even located our inconspicuous studio, hidden inside a derelict warehouse. The number of fans taking photos on the Culloden battlefield or pushing against every ancient stone, hoping to be transported back in time, proved that there was a voracious appetite for this material and that the rest of the world had an interest in and passion for Scotland. This passion has grown extensively in the last few years and I'm pleased that Scotland is now aware and making attempts to engage with the ever-increasing fandom.

Graham: I actually thought you were an 'Ambassador for Scotland'? Still not seen your crown.

Sam: Yours is in the post, Grey Dog.

Graham: Hmm . . . Like the Sassenach whisky.

Many non-official tours and excursions are now available. Graham and I discussed creating our own tour company but I didn't fancy driving a bus around the narrow roads; the camper van is challenging enough. And, besides, I'd have to do *all* of the driving!

We stand silently for a moment surveying the scene before Cameron guides us towards the largest ring of stones. 'There are four cairns here, one outside the wall and three of the cairns have a circle of standing stones, which is quite unusual,' he says.

These cairns identify burial chambers with passageways leading to the prehistoric tombs that once rested here – the stones are a marker or monument to those who have shuffled off this mortal coil. Whilst shooting *Young Alexander* (basically *Buffy the Vampire Slayer* meets Alexander the Great. Don't ask!), I climbed the stairs inside the Great Pyramid of Giza in Cairo. We entered the pitch-black stone burial chamber and I could feel the pressure of the thousands of tonnes of rock above. We are no closer to understanding how the Ancient Egyptians built those structures. Nor are we any closer to knowing how our Scottish ancestors built these cairns or erected the megaliths (vast standing stones) that stand on guard duty outside the tombs.

Journalists ask me the same question, 'If you could travel back in time through the stones where would you go?' It's hard to have a single answer but I would like to watch the pyramids being built. Or see the Khyber Pass as Alexander the Great travels to conquer India and most of the known world. Maybe I would joust in a medieval tournament? I'm sure the reality of all these events is much harder and way more dangerous than they look in the movies, therefore I'm glad I get to 'visit' for the day and then return home at the end of the night. Being an actor means you get to pretend to go backwards or forwards in time and I think it happens to be the best of all worlds.

GRAHAM

I've always been fascinated by history so my destination is constantly changing. Sometimes it's Ancient Rome, sometimes Elizabethan England to see one of Shakespeare's plays performed for the first time. Right now, it's the Dark Ages – the time of Vikings and shield walls (a formation of soldiers overlapped their shields for maximum defence). I suppose the thing that really fascinates me is not so much the period itself but travelling back in time far enough to see a truly alien world. When I travelled to India for work, and to Japan, it's the first time I've been anywhere that *truly* feels like another world – the smells, colours, sounds, the bustle. To stand in a marketplace, at any time in history prior to the mid-nineteenth century, would be a sensory overload.

To be in that marketplace in 879, or 50 AD, or 1599 would be jaw-dropping now but I think many things would seem familiar, too. The facial expressions of a Roman citizen, the laughter of an Elizabethan audience; the things that gave them joy, and pain. To know that our very existence depends on an unbroken line of our ancestors literally stretching back 100,000 years or more is truly awe-inspiring. To think that if one could travel back in time I could encounter a ginger-haired ancestor of Sam's, sporting that exact same grin, wearing the fourteenth-century equivalent of Gore-Tex, is a troubling thought indeed.

SAM

We zone back into what Cameron is saying. 'We don't fully know what the standing stones were for, but it's thought they were burial tombs and the standing stones were for some sort of astronomy. When the mid-winter sun sets on 21st December (a celebration of the Winter Solstice in the pagan calendar known as Yule) the sun will shine right up the corridor of outer cairns and light up the interior chamber. It's extraordinary.'

There are about fifty similar cairns in the area and we can only really guess what they meant to the people who built them. How these stones got here and how they lined them up so precisely is beyond comprehension. 'Later on, the Celtic people living here would have used the stones and burial chamber for their own purposes and would have prayed here. They worshipped the creator goddess of the Celtic world, Cailleach, at Beltane, spring equinox, praying for good crops, and at Samhain (our Halloween), praying for a mild winter.'

My birthday is the day before Beltane on 30th April and I'm a typical Taurus – 'Smart, ambitious, and trustworthy . . . we make amazing friends, colleagues, and partners . . . and personal relationships tend to be drama free.' (Source: Horoscope.com) Also stubborn and loves good food/drink.

Graham's a Capricorn (4th January) and is, 'charming, hardworking with an adaptable personality. Highly adaptable for acting, not so much when faced with camper van, tents, heights, hunger, discomfort, cold water and kayaks . . .' (Source: Heughan.com!)

Given astrology has been around for over 2,400 years and the ancients who built Clava Cairns would have had a great knowledge of the sun, moon and their horoscopes, let's take a wild diversion and see how compatible Graham and I are as friends . . .

I shall consult the modern Oracle: 'Siri, how compatible are Taurus and Capricorn as friends?'

Taurus and Capricorn make fast friends, revelling in each other's dependability. Taurus can count on Capricorn to show up on time to every meeting. Capricorn knows Taurus will pay back a loan or return borrowed items. Taurus encourages the predictable Goat to take a few risks [Sam: ha ha!]. *Best of all, both these signs share a profound appreciation for the great outdoors. Hanging out in forests, gardens, and parks is lots of fun for these nature lovers. Each delights in the other's sense of humour. When times get tough, they make each other laugh. These two have got each other's backs.* (Horoscope.com)

Sam: Ahhh.

Graham: It's true.

In the pagan calendar Beltane marked the end of winter and coming of summer and I remember growing up watching the celebrations of the whirling white witches, painted faces and deer-antlered druids, spinning around the large bonfire on top of Carlton Hill in Edinburgh on the eve of the spring equinox. It felt tribal and primeval. The drums would beat faster and faster and the hair would rise on the back of my neck. My eighteenth birthday felt extra special as my friends insisted we told every White Witch and celestial Virgin I was now 'a Man'. The next day, 1st May, marks the beginning of spring and Jamie Fraser's birthday. I'm one inch shorter and one day off his birthday – ties in pretty neatly, doesn't it?

Cameron says, 'Sam, on your next Beltane birthday you must wash your face in the morning dew, watch the sunrise and dream of your future wife.'

I promise him I will. Cameron has a wonderful, enduring marriage to Gina, two grown-up sons, several grandchildren and, of course, the mountains – a constant presence, his sanctuary and retreat. He is an inspiration to me, and many besides; his inner contentment and sense of belonging are what every restless actor craves.

In *Outlander*, the night Claire watches the druids dancing around the stones occurred on Beltane in the original book; however, in the

TV show it's filmed as Samhain (Halloween) due to the fact we were shooting in the autumn. Strangely, Samhain – Gaelic for 'summer's end' – is possibly more appropriate as it's the time when the veil between life and death is at its most transparent and when pagans honour and connect with their ancestors.

'Mid-winter was a terrifying time for these people so they would pray to Cailleach for a mild winter,' says Cameron. 'It was cold, with snow, not much light, no growth. They didn't know if they'd survive until next spring so it was important for them to have an understanding of nature and of the seasons. We've lost a great deal of that knowledge of and reverence for nature.'

Cameron is right, we have. He is passionate about keeping the connection to the land of Scotland alive. He asks:

'When was the last time you washed your face in the dew? When was the last time you had a skinny dip in a Highland burn? When was the last time you lay on a hillside and watched the stars revolving above?'

Take a moment to ask yourself the same questions.

'It's about allowing nature to touch you in a real way and you can't do that driving through the Highlands in a car,' he says. *However*, you can do it by walking, climbing, running, kayaking, long-distance cycling, anything where you can smell the country as you pass through it. 'And, at a speed you can appreciate the small print of the land,' adds Cameron.

Graham has impressively cycled the Outer Hebrides to Cape Wrath, Mull, Aran, Kintyre and he suggests we do the North Coast 500 together, along an old drovers' route across the Applecross peninsula. I can't wait because the real joy of Scotland is that around every corner is a folktale, legend or landmark that leads us to know a little more of our heritage and in turn gives a greater understanding of who we are now.

The rhythm and deep connection to the land and the knowledge of the seasons that our 'primitive' forebears had gave them 'a sense of belonging'. In Gaelic it's called 'dualchas', which conjures not only the landscape but also past generations. The Scots people were in contact with their ancestors (in battle they'd conjure their relatives to fight alongside them) and it's a word I learnt on

Outlander. It struck me so much, I even got the words engraved on my sword:

Alba n'dualchas: Belonging to Scotland.

The landmarks, stories and mystery of Scotland make the past ever present and Clava Cairns is a monument to our ancestors as well as a stark reminder of our impermanence.

GRAHAM

The pagan world (at least the fictional one) came to life for me whilst filming *The Wicker Tree* in 2010 for Robin Hardy. I had been a huge fan of his 1970s cult horror classic, *The Wicker Man*. Christopher Lee, who plays Lord Summerisle in the movie, regarded it as his greatest film (and this is a man who had made well over a hundred movies, in multiple languages). I had the great pleasure of meeting him. A true renaissance man, he fought in the Russo-Finnish war of the 1930s, was a Commando in WWII and, of course, was Dracula. He spoke many languages fluently and I remember at dinner, when the waitress came to take the order and he realised she was Lithuanian, he immediately began talking to her in her language. It was fabulous.

The movie *The Wicker Man* tells the story of a policeman, Edward Woodward, sent to a remote Scottish island to investigate the disappearance of a young girl. Suffice to say it doesn't go well for him. He has essentially been lured as a virgin sacrifice for the pagan beliefs of the islanders. The climax of the movie is the burning of the policeman inside a giant wicker man. It is one of the most disturbing scenes in cinema. The genius of Hardy's approach was to defy all horror movie tropes and signals. The music is uplifting, cheerful. Christopher Lee is an urbane, charming character in the movie. The islanders are friendly and it is shot almost entirely in warm daylight. There are no jump-frights, just a sustained sense of creeping dread, which is what makes it truly terrifying.

When I got the chance to be in the sequel, *The Wicker Tree*, I jumped at it. It was over thirty years later but had been written by Robin Hardy again (who also directed it), based on his book *Cowboys for Christ* (a much better title in my opinion). Robin was eighty when he made it, but apart from a daily nap at lunchtime (much like Heughan), he had boundless energy. In this story two evangelical Christians are persuaded to visit the small Scottish community where my wife and I run the show. I play Christopher Lee's grandson, and I definitely inherited his taste for the macabre. In this film a similar style was invoked (friendly villagers, innocent victims, paganism). It culminates in the pursuit of the evangelical young man and then him being eaten alive. The girl's fate is to be killed, then stuffed as a trophy, along with all the other May Queens from years before. It was a good movie, but let down by the producers who, against Robin's wishes, overlaid a classic 'horror' score. Big mistake. It broke Robin's heart.

I had a thoroughly good time making it, though, getting the chance to play with dear old Clive Russell who went on to play Simon Fraser, Lord Lovat, in *Outlander*. Jamie Fraser's grandad. We shot it in the Borders of Scotland one summer and it remains one of my happiest experiences. I even got to sing in it . . . which may not have been a happy experience for others!

Sam: What will the sequel be called? *The Wicker Basket*?

Graham: Groan.

Actually, several famous white witches have made a home in the Highlands, including infamous occultist Aleister Crowley who lived at Boleskine House on Loch Ness 1899–1913. According to *Homes & Properties* magazine (a monthly favourite of mine):

'He believed the location was ideal to perform the Sacred Magic of Abramelin the Mage – a spell said to invoke one's Guardian Angel. Unfortunately the spell also involved summoning the 12 Kings and Dukes of Hell. While performing the lengthy ritual, he was called away to Paris. Neglecting to banish the demons he had summoned, it's said they've been loitering around the manor ever since.'

From 1970–1992 Boleskine House was owned by Jimmy Page from Led Zeppelin, who had a deep interest in neo-paganism. (I had a deep interest in Led Zeppelin.) Sadly, Boleskine burned down in 2015, but the ruins are up for sale!

Tempted, Sam?

Sam: I've been on the lookout to find a home in the Highlands for years but I think the bit about Page's caretaker being woken by a 'snorting beast of pure evil' makes it a 'no' from me. There's an actor from *Game of Thrones* who has got a home on an island in a loch. I've always quite fancied living by a loch or, even better, on an island.

I know the exact house on the exact island Sam means because when I was in *Take the Highroad* back in the 1980s (a massively popular soap) the main producer lived there with a teddy bear he used to talk to and take everywhere. 'Teddy did you like that take?'

Then he'd do Teddy's voice, 'No! Do it again.'

'Teddy wants you to do that take again, Graham.'

He was insane.

A bit like my love-interest on *Outlander*, Geillis Duncan, a fervent neo-Jacobite who kills off her husbands (one with poison, the other burned alive), travelling back and forth through the stones until she settles in Jamaica where she seduces and sacrifices virgin boys. A real keeper.

Played by Lotte Verbeek, a wonderful Dutch actress, her character Geillis becomes pregnant by me (presumably by immaculate conception), and goes on to have my bastard son, the descendant of whom he attempts to hang in Season Five of *Outlander* (such are the massively complicated plots and timelines of *Outlander*). I only had one scene with Lotte, where I look at her lasciviously across a crowded room as her poor husband (played by John Sessions) chokes to death in front of her. Perhaps my look alone was enough to impregnate her ... When I signed the contract for *Outlander* it included a nudity clause. In signing it I agreed to perform scenes of nudity. For me, rather than seeing it as allowing for the possibility of nudity, I took it as *a promise* of nudity. (Ever since my days of theatrical nudity I've clearly been itching to get my kit off. Maybe itching isn't the sexiest of words. Dying. Nope. Yearning. I've been yearning to rip it all off.) As it turned out I didn't even get a peck on the cheek.

In the meantime, Sir Ginger of the Nuts barely went a day without dropping his pants on set. However, given the nature of his climactic scenes with 'Black Jack' Randall, on the whole I'm glad I kept my trousers on.

I was naked on stage in 1999 performing *The School of Night* at Chichester Festival Theatre directed by the actor Jack Shepherd. Cut to my parents coming to see the show. I'd briefed them on the nudity but apparently nothing can fully prepare a Glaswegian father seeing his own grown-up son starkers in front of 500 strangers. After the show I met them in the bar. 'You were wonderful, Graham,' gushed my staunchly supportive mother. My father looked at me and merely said, 'There was no need for that, Graham.'

(Incidentally I overheard the outrageously gay landlord of the local pub in Chichester recommending customers the seats where they could get the best view of my 'exposed areas' – charming!) [Sam: The horror.]

In *Dangerous Liaisons* I had to do a scene under the bedclothes with a wonderful young Scottish actress, Gail Watson, who had announced in the read-through that she would do the bed scene nude (not in the script), which I forgot all about until the technical rehearsal. Needless to say I spent the rest of the run apologising for the 'reaction' of a specific body part to this moment. All my lines went out of my head and I felt like some kind of depraved pervert. [Sam: You are!] [Graham: Says the Marquis de Sade himself.] God knows what my dad would have said to that!

Sadly, or fortunately, depending on one's viewpoint, by the time I was getting stabbed to death by Sam and Cait I had come to realise I wouldn't even get so much as a warm cuddle in *Outlander*. And my dad would probably have been grateful.

Geillis, along with Claire (now Fraser, having married Jamie . . . as well) are accused of witchcraft. Scotland proved to be an especially enthusiastic prosecutor of witches. From 1563–1735 a little under 4,000 'witches' were brought to trial, of which it is estimated that around two-thirds were executed. This is four to five times more than in England. In 1563 the first Witchcraft Act basically allowed the hunting, torturing and execution of witches on a grand scale. It ended with the second Witchcraft Act of 1735. In between, Scotland had 170 years of government-sanctioned witch-hunting and killing. For a state with a religious point to make, prosecuting witches was an excellent way to prove its godliness. Some interesting statistics emerge. Half the victims were under forty years old, most were middle-class, and only 4% practised 'folk' medicine. 15% were men.

Janet Horne was the last person to be executed in Scotland and, indeed, in the whole British Isles. Janet, who showed signs of senility, and her daughter, who suffered from deformities in her hands and feet, were turned in to the authorities by their neighbours. One can only imagine what her neighbours were like. They accused Janet of riding her daughter to the Devil to have her shod like a pony. Seems reasonable. The authorities certainly thought so. Needless to say this was quite enough to find them both guilty of witchcraft, and sentenced to be burned at the stake. The daughter managed to escape (a particularly impressive feat with deformed hands and feet I'd say!), but her poor mother was stripped, tarred, paraded through the town, and then burnt alive. Religion doesn't muck about with witches. It brings new meaning to the term 'Neighbourhood Watch'. The witchstone, found in the private garden of a house in Carnaig Street in Dornoch, Sutherland, marks the spot of her execution.

And the same hysteria surrounding witchcraft was going on simultaneously in France (in Season Two, Claire is feared as *La Dame Blanche* – The White Woman) and over the pond in Massachusetts, USA, the famous Salem witch trials took place in 1692, later inspiring Arthur Miller's masterpiece *The Crucible* (1953) based on the McCarthy witch-hunts over 250 years later. Witch-hunts never go away. Just like a pandemic, we're sort of due one . . .

Geillis actually saves Claire at the witch trial (with some help from her ginger friend) but Dougal believes Claire to be a witch (he's had doubts about her all along), probably because she so stoutly resisted his sexual advances . . . by breaking a wooden stool over my head.

Claire: 'Stop trying to convince people of your patriotism. It's tedious. I'm not sure you'll grasp the meaning of this, but fuck yourself.'
Dougal: 'All right then. Perhaps you're right about me. I do love my own reflection. But make no mistake, lass. I love Scotland more.'

But Dougal loves a strong woman; we never meet his actual wife but I suspect she has a fearsome left hook. And like all femme fatales Claire finishes me off in the end. Well, her *and* Heughan (bastard). I think he's still trying to kill me on this road trip.

Sam's grinning at me now. He's plotting something . . .

Sam: I'm not. But two more busloads of tourists have pulled up with passengers eager to try their luck at time travel by touching the stones.

Time to vanish.

CHAPTER TEN

Castle Leod

Bless a' the Mackenzies an' a' the Mackenzie childer; their sons an' son's childer and their dochters for a thousan' years to come.

Be Ye gracious an' send doon mountains o' snuff, an rivers of whisky.

An' oh Lord send doon swords an' pistels an' daggers as monie as the sands on the seashore to kill the MacDonalds, the Clan Ranalds, and the Campbells.

An oh Lord, bless the wee coo, an' make it a big coo.

An oh Lord bless the sucklin' and make it a grand boar.

An oh Lord, bless the wee bairns, yon Angus, Alex an' Bessie an' Maggie an' Florrie.

An oh Lord, build up a great wall between us an' the Irish, an' put broken bottles on the top, so they cannae come over.

An' oh Lord, if ye hae anything gude to gie, dunna gie it to the Irish, but gie it to your chosen people, the Scots, especially to the Clan Mackenzie an' a' their friends.

Glorious ye are for ever more.

Anonymous

SAM

As we walk up the impressive tree-lined driveway to Castle Leod (pronounced 'loud'), seat of the MacKenzies, Graham puffs out his chest and takes in the view of the Highland fortress.

Graham: Ach, home at last! I used to hang out here a lot with Colum. And, we let you stay here for a while. (The fictional seat of the MacKenzies in *Outlander*, Castle Leoch, was actually filmed at Doune Castle in Stirling.)

I'm feeling a wee bit peely-wally after another evening of whisky and a long drive over the bridge across the Great Glen Loch to the Eilean Dubh (the Black Isle) where we are this morning, an isthmus ten miles wide and twenty miles long, north of Inverness within Ross and Cromarty. Scotland is so much bigger than people think. There's a whole other world above Glasgow and Edinburgh.

John MacKenzie, 5th Earl of Cromartie, chief of Clan MacKenzie, has agreed to meet us thanks to an email from Cameron McNeish.

Sam,

Just a thought and I don't know if it's helpful but I'll tell you anyway.

The present Chief of Clan Mackenzie, John Mackenzie, the Earl of Cromartie, is a good pal of mine. He's a mad keen rock climber, and a bloody good one in his day. He's written rock-climbing guides. I made a television programme with him years ago. He lives in Castle Leod at Strathpeffer. He's also a bit of a nutter, and really good fun. In a previous life he was an explosives expert – loves blowing things up . . .

I'll see if I can find a YouTube of the show I did with him . . .

Cheers

Cameron

Staunch Jacobites, this branch of the MacKenzies has followed the House of Stuart since the Battle of Flodden in 1513, when James IV of Scotland declared war on England to divert Henry VIII's troops from France, honouring 'The Auld Alliance' (1295–1560) between the French and Scots in an attempt to curb the numerous English invasions. James IV died at Flodden, the last British king to die in battle. (The English won. Again. Groan.)

John MacKenzie walks with purpose to greet us in the grounds of his stunning fifteenth-century castle. Well spoken, unassuming and nothing like Gary Lewis who plays Colum (no hug! More on that later . . .), it's great to meet another man of the mountains. Hill walker and climber extraordinaire, he's climbed the Old Man of Hoy, a towering stack of rock over 400 feet high off the north coast of Scotland. 'I started rock climbing at twelve,' he says. 'I don't know how old I am now – the birthday candles fall off because the cake isn't big enough but I'm still climbing! It's a fantastic thing to do – I see it as a celebration of life.'

The gardens at Castle Leod are vast, with a number of enormous ancient trees, the ground covered in bluebells in the spring. He shows us a grove of lime trees with a secret tree house in the centre and then guides us to a stone commemorating the fallen MacKenzies on both sides of the Jacobite Risings. As we've discovered, nothing was clear-cut during that period with husbands and wives dividing their allegiances between opposing forces – 'wisely sitting on the fence' as John says – so they wouldn't lose everything.

The MacKenzies are an enormous clan so many were pro-Hanoverian (aka British) but this branch was pro-Stuart (Jacobite – Latin for followers of James, specifically James II). 'It was disastrous for the MacKenzies after the 1745 Risings but we're still here. It was a lost cause with the benefit of hindsight,' he says.

As we make our way into the medieval tower house that dates from 1400, he shows us the Marriage Stone over the original medieval oak door. 'It was for Sir Rorie MacKenzie, the Tutor of Kintail, who married Dame Margaret McLeod of Lewis – bringing unity. They lived at Leod and her money made this place more comfortable! Sir Rory was a formidable character who was given the 'Patent of Fire and Sword' by James VI to 'civilise' the north and west. I love the word civilise – more ethnic cleansing – which was done effectively.'

Sir Rorie certainly had a fearsome reputation, inspiring sayings such as, 'There are only two things worse than the Tutor of Kintail, frost in spring and mist in the dog-days'. And there is an apocryphal story of him riding alone near Blair Castle, when he was asked what he was doing by the Duke of Atholl's men. He said nothing, dismounted and began sharpening his sword on a rock. They watched him as he finally told them his mission. 'I am about to make a road between your master's head and his shoulders.' The men rushed to tell the Duke who replied, 'It can only be two people, it is either the Devil or The Tutor of Kintail, let him pass safely!'

Sam: Graham – leave the door alone!

He won't stop touching the door. I think he's fallen in love with it. A huge, thick wooden studded door, reinforced with steel and bolts. No enemy would be able to gain access without permission. I think Graham wants it for the home he's building in New Zealand which, he says, has '270 degree views of the harbour and the hills.' I love how specific he is.

GRAHAM

It is a truly splendid studded oak door. They don't make those in Ikea, I can tell you. 'It dates from 1605,' says Chief MacKenzie. 'So relatively modern,' he smiles. Over 400 years old and, yes, Sam is right, I can't stop stroking it.

But whoa! Then there's the key, an enormous iron thing that could also be used as a club, or possibly a doorstop. MacKenzie hands it to me; it's the weight of a brick and doubles as – I kid you not – a firearm. '.45 calibre,' he grins. 'Just as well we're not in America.' I bet he's fired it given his former penchant for blowing things up. I wonder if he's got any cannons we could play with? On second thoughts, Sam's here, maybe not.

The walls of the castle are 2.4 metres thick in places – I mean this really is a proper castle – and one to which Mary Queen of Scots aka Mary Stuart (who reigned 1542–1587) had a lot of ties.

We make our way up a winding spiral staircase and enter a room oozing history with portraits of the Chief's forebears lining the walls like a rogues', gallery and, there it is, Mary Queen of Scots' prayer stool (*prie-dieu*), one of several belonging to Mary and her mother before, Marie de Guise, who ruled Scotland as Regent from 1554–1560. In the grounds there still stands a sweet chestnut planted for Marie de Guise's visit all those centuries ago.

There are two beautiful high-backed chairs with gently curving arms from 1701 owned by the 1st Earl of Cromartie. It's wonderful to speculate who has sat on these chairs and what was discussed and plotted. 'The 1st Earl was six foot two or three, a polymath, Secretary of State for Scotland, Lord Justice General, Founder Member of the Royal Society of Scotland, friend of Sir Isaac Newton, spoke eight languages, including Gaelic, and strongly disagreed with extreme religions and the burning of witches, which he considered to be idle superstition,' says John. What a guy.

A modern thinker, he was instrumental in the union of the crowns (uniting Scotland and England). 'However, on the principle that both countries would be considered *equal trading partners*. But guess what happened? (England feathered its own nest? Surely not?) And, that's one of the reasons this family became Jacobite,' explains MacKenzie.

We look at a portrait of the 2nd Earl who was involved in the plot to oust George I. A good swordsman, he ran a Frenchman (who was a government spy) through in a tavern before cleverly covering up the murder with a drunken bar brawl. 'The 3rd Earl of Cromartie was an out and out Jacobite who supported Bonnie Prince Charlie and after Culloden was sentenced to death with other Jacobite Lords,' says Chief John showing us a surviving bedpost owned by Simon 'The Fox' Fraser, aka Lord Lovat, who was executed in 1747 at the age of eighty. The 3rd Earl was sentenced to suffer the same fate but was saved by his wife who petitioned the King, fainting at his feet. George II commuted his sentence from death to 'life in exile south of the River Trent'. Never to see Scotland again he lived in Honiton in Devon, all titles, lands and money confiscated.

However, the MacKenzies got it all back in one generation. The son, Lord McCleod, still only nineteen when released from the Tower, went to Sweden and became a legendary soldier, given the honorary title by the Swedes of Count of Crowmarty. He returned to Scotland and raised a 'regiment of foot' (unmounted foot soldiers), which was later to become the Highland Light Infantry. After serving in the British Army in India he was allowed to buy back the Leod estate for £19,000 – a vast sum in those days.

But let's get back to the Old Fox, Simon Fraser – now there was a Highland character! I think having played Dougal MacKenzie, I have an affinity with rogues like Lord Lovat, played brilliantly by Clive Russell in *Outlander*, Season Two. There is a sketch of Fraser by Hogarth. It is the drawing of a man who clearly enjoyed life to the full. His saturnine face, full mouth, and twinkling eyes make him look like he is plotting mischief, which he undoubtedly was.

He was a famous double agent, spying for the Jacobites and the Hanoverians – think Lord Sandringham in *Outlander* (portrayed magnificently by Simon Callow) who played politics for his own ends, revelling in the mischief and sadistic outcomes he created. Our host, John MacKenzie, tells us it was none other than The Fox who persuaded his ancestor to 'come out' for Charles Stuart by handing George, the 3rd Earl, his great-great-grandfather's sword named 'The Triumphing Sword of the Clan MacKenzie'. I mean how could you say no?

After Culloden, the Bonnie Prince headed for the hills and Lovat rowed across Loch Ness where gout and arthritis hampered his escape and he had to be carried 'on a litter' (think enclosed sedan chair!). If Hogarth's depiction is correct he was vastly overweight so it would have been slow-going. It was rumoured he went 'to ground' at several local castles including Leod and Cawdor (in a secret turret) until he was eventually discovered hiding in the Isles of Loch Morar.

He finally met his end on the scaffold at Tower Hill on Thursday 9th April 1747. It was a public holiday. Tens of thousands turned out to witness it. On the day itself Fraser was very particular about how he looked, the stylish clan chief till the end. He sent his wig back because there was too little powder on it. He said that if he had a suit of velvet he would wear it to the executioner's block. This was MacShimidh Mor, 'The son of the Great Simon'. They had fought their way onto the beaches of England with William the Conqueror; one of Lovat's forebears was Robert the Bruce's chamberlain. Another had been William Wallace's compatriot, who shared the same punishment of hanging, drawing and quartering. This was to be Simon's fate but it was commuted to simple beheading.

In the build-up to the execution a timber terrace built for the occasion collapsed under the weight of spectators, crushing and impaling dozens, killing nine of them.

When told of this, Lord Lovat laughed. 'Good, the more mischief the better the sport.' What a wag! He is supposed to have found it so funny that the phrase 'laughing your head off' comes from his execution.

Finally a message was sent to the prisoner – 'The axe demands your body.' (Not a message you ever want delivered. It's a bit unequivocal.) He walked with a straight back, smiling and joking, as he climbed the steps to the scaffold. He shook off the supporters who tried to help him. He paused at the top to test the edge of the axe, and looked at the casket waiting for him, as if he were browsing in a particularly macabre shop. He had left instruction in his will that his funeral should have pipers from John O'Groats to Edinburgh playing before his corpse and the women of the country should sing a 'coronach' for him (a Celtic keening song involving clapping of palms, howling, rocking and tearing of hair – weirdly exactly the same instructions as I have whenever I'm working with MacGinger).

He spoke to the axeman and knelt down while two supporters stretched a scarlet sheet in front of him to catch the head as it fell from his shoulders. The executioner adjusted Lovat's position and they spoke again. He would raise his handkerchief to pray; when he dropped it the executioner should strike. Among his last words was a line from the Roman poet Horace: *Dulce et decorum est pro patria mori*. (It is sweet and seemly to die for one's country.) He died, in his own eyes, as a Scottish patriot.

He stretched out his short, thick neck and less than a minute later dropped the handkerchief. His head was severed in one blow and he had the grim honour of being the last person to be beheaded in Britain. It was commanded that his remains be buried at the Tower of London but legend has it that his body was spirited away to the family mausoleum in Wardlaw, Kirkhill, near Inverness. However, in 2019, forensic scientists found that the headless corpse in The Fox's coffin was actually that of an eighteenth-century well-to-do woman, which means wily Lord Lovat continues to fox us even from the grave!

To examine Lovat's story gives a wonderful glimpse into the life of a Highland chieftain in the late seventeenth and early eighteenth centuries. He once said of his kin that, 'The Highland clans did not consider themselves as bound by the letter of the law, like the inhabitants of the low country around Inverness, but to a man would regard it as their honour and their boast to cut the throat, or blow out the brains of anyone who should dare to disturb the repose of their laird.'

It's the descendants of folk such as this who went on to colonise the world, and help build the British Empire. In a famous feud between the Murrays and the Frasers, Simon didn't muck about. It started with him trying to marry Amelia, the Murray heiress (she'd only just reached puberty). Rather than let this happen, the mother of the unfortunate Amelia along with the Marquis of Atholl contrived to have the teenage object of Lovat's affections whisked away. In return for being spared on one occasion the Murrays went to court to declare the Frasers had risen in 'open and manifest rebellion'. This was a capital charge.

They asked for a 'Commission of Fire and Sword' like John MacKenzie's ancestor the Tutor of Kintail was given. This was effectively DEFCON 5 – the nuclear option – which would allow soldiers to go into the Fraser lands and kill anyone of the clan, and destroy their homes. However, the Crown was not inclined to give this power to the Murrays for what they considered a private feud. But good old Simon wasn't done yet. He went with his men to Castle Dounie. If he couldn't have the daughter, he'd have the mum. Then he'd have them *both*! He proposed marriage. 'Come on, doll, we've known each other all our lives, let's get it on.' Or words to that effect.

She refused.

He urged, 'If you don't marry me the Atholl Murrays are going to come and burn and pillage my homeland, and kill everyone I know!' Somehow she managed to resist this outpouring of romance!

Not to be deterred, he thought for a moment then sent two of his men to kidnap a drunken priest. (Reminiscent of how Dougal gets a priest to marry Jamie and Claire.)

What followed is summarised by one of Fraser's kinsmen, Fraser of Castleleathers:

'The Lady not yielding willingly, there were some harsh measures taken, a parson sent for, and a bagpipe blown up.'

She was dragged in next to Simon, in front of the priest and was declared married while the sound of deafening bagpipes bounced off the walls. It's like an episode of *Love Island*.

The 'wedding night' involved some of Lovat's men forcibly undressing her and lifting her onto the bed. They placed her face down and cut the stays of her corset with a dirk, and then left the happy couple alone. The sound of her subsequent screaming was drowned by the faithful piper playing for his life outside the room. In the morning she was found speechless and out of her senses. Diana Gabaldon would have been proud. Indeed when I told one of the showrunners of *Outlander* this, he desperately wanted to put a version of it in the show. However, given that a rape occurs in *Outlander* so often you could set your watch by it, there probably wasn't room in the schedule for yet another ravishing to occur.

I could write a whole book about Simon Fraser alone (in fact people have), such is the extent of his extraordinary life. But hopefully this gives a glimpse into the character of the old fox. A man who would even make warlord Dougal MacKenzie blush.

SAM

Up the spiral staircase in Castle Leod, past suits of armour, crossbow bolt holes, and various pieces of centuries-old furniture, we stop to admire a rather new addition on the wall: a wooden plaque, thanking everyone who has donated money to help restore and maintain the upkeep of the castle. Diana Gabaldon is the latest donor and the interest that has been created in her books is generating revenue for these ancient fortifications. Graham and I are added to the list, happy to donate to the Trust in return for the personal tour. The castle holds so many secrets; many characters have walked through that thick wooden door and up the same spiral staircase. We hope many more people in the future get to follow those same footsteps and be warmed by the MacKenzie hearth.

A fireplace, large enough to stand in, is situated at the end of an oak-panelled room; a smaller fire crackles and warms the room. We set up a good spot to shoot and sit in three chairs, all over 200 years old. I couldn't help imagining the amount of arses that had sat there before. Mary Queen of Scots' prayer stool, a priceless dining table, the room was filled with history and John patiently took us through it all. Various lords and ladies had done the same for centuries, entertained, played music, admired the paintings and sat where we were. These included a notorious eighteenth-century guest who, after drinking with the MacKenzies for five days straight, had to be revived by a doctor.

There is also a ghost protecting the castle – possibly from other binge-drinking guests – called the Night Watchman, a haunting figure that has been seen in this very room, a lantern in his hand. He apparently loves music and during a recital some years ago, he appeared suddenly, walking through the wall, much to the distress of some Spanish tourists. Now covered by a large grandfather clock, the old passage leads to the guardroom, which is bricked up. John told us he hears the Watchman some nights, walking up the spiral staircase, past his bedroom, with very distinct footsteps. Just as he was speaking and we joked about the panicked tourists, the door behind us slowly opened, then slammed shut. Clearly the Watchman wasn't interested in our conversation, or lack of musical ability.

John told us about another experience in which he was hanging three pictures, one of a man and the other two of ladies. The first couple was up and he was happy with his handiwork. As he placed the second lady next to the couple, he felt a pair of hands firmly push him directly off the ladder. Lying on the ground, unscathed, he looked up and the picture he was trying to hang now had a large diagonal tear right through it. Clearly the couple didn't want her near them – some ancient love triangle or love tiff?

We admired many of the pictures and history involved. The last one was a painting by George Watson (1767–1837) of a young man (John Hay MacKenzie, aged thirteen) with impressive calves, wielding a shinty stick – the earliest painting of someone playing a sport in Britain. I can see Graham stiffen, his sporting loss still raw after our fictional uncle/nephew battle on the shinty field in *Outlander* (Season 1, Episode 5). Never one to miss an opportunity to wind the weary codger up, I have arranged with Michelle's help a surprise for Graham in the castle grounds.

★★★

On the empty playing field, in sight of Castle Leod, we are joined by a group of polite, quiet, yet fearsome-looking girls – the Local Inverness Shinty Club. The game of shinty is a cross between field hockey and lacrosse, with some barely contained fighting thrown in. Half our height and my age (a quarter of Graham's), the Inverness lasses seemed shy of our cameras. Graham isn't happy at all. He asks them the question of the year . . .

Graham: Is it called shinty because they used to smash each other in the shins with sticks?

Scots are good at two kinds of sport. Either the type they can do drunk/in the pub – snooker, darts, curling, golf *[Graham: You can't curl or play golf in a pub!]* – or sport that requires the participant to be fearless, e.g. rugby, shinty, fighting. Back in the day, Highland clans would get together in a mass chaotic frenzy. Entire villages would gather to play hundred-a-side games. Wooden sticks in hand, they'd battle for the ball (bit of wood, sheep vertebrae or even cow pat, whatever they could find). The game has progressed a little since then and possibly become even more dangerous with the addition of a solid leather ball. Many current players have lost teeth, eyes and been knocked out. Players can hit the ball into the air, volley it, smack it up the field and you can shoulder into people to try and push them off the ball. The only thing you can't do is kick it.

In *Outlander*, we recreated a shinty game with Jamie and his Uncle D playing on opposite sides. Apparently, Dougal taught Jamie to play; no doubt he cheated a bit, and Jamie was ready to teach his uncle a lesson. I too wanted to see if Graham would keep up. During shooting, Graham was ruthless, aggressive and dominant. For a take. Then he pulled a hamstring or was it a tendon? Maybe a migraine? He then sat and watched from the comfort of his chair, latte in hand, snack bag discarded as he finished the last cereal bar, as his stunt-double ran, wrestled, fell and played ball, over and over. I even had to pick him up and throw him over my shoulder and onto the hard ground. So today, after visiting Castle Leod, I was looking forward to really putting him through his paces.

As the ladies take to the field the beast is unleashed. They charge at us, stealing a ball (I brought another just in case), and fire a rocket shot at the poor goalie. She doesn't flinch and fires it straight back at Graham and me. We duck and begin to realise we are out of our depth. This isn't acting; the Inverness Shinty Girls are the real deal. 'Maybe I should feign an injury?' Graham pants, but I am determined to win.

I charge the pack. A third ball appears at Graham's feet, definitely safer to attack him than these crazed teenagers. We grapple for the ball, much like the scene in *Outlander*, and it's exhausting. After only ten minutes of running around we are done and, while the girls are distracted taking pieces out of each other, we sneak off to the camper for a coffee (and Graham's mid morning snack).

SHINTY FACT FILE

* An ancient Scottish Sport brought over from Ireland in St Columba's times.
* It was used as a way of practising sword-play.
* The 'caman' (stick) is traditionally made of ash (now a mix of ash and hickory). Any piece of wood could be used if it had a bend or was crooked ('cam' – Scottish Gaelic for crooked).
* A game was said to have been played the night before the Glencoe massacre.
* An annual game is played between Scotland and Ireland (slightly

different sticks are used by both sides, the Irish playing a game called 'hurling'; the rules are changed for the game).
* The game can be mixed gender – women in Scotland are hard.
* The 'Ronaldo of the glens', Ronald Ross, scored 1,000 goals and played for Kingussie Camanachd, the most successful sporting team *of all time*, winning twenty consecutive league titles.

GRAHAM

Sam: I want to win. Come On!

He is so pathetically competitive, running around like a sugar-spiked six-year-old.

Sam: Come on, Graham!

The ginger Duracell bunny is roaring up and down the pitch, barging into me, pushing me, roughing me up.

Sam: Come on, girls, I'll show you how it's *not* done!

He's like Lord Flashheart on speed.

Shinty is – by the standards of most sports – exceptionally violent. When we were training for the shinty scene in *Outlander*, Sam and I were tutored by a Highland shinty player who confided that hacking ankles and shins was completely normal. Historically, there were *no* rules for shinty until 1848. Every community had their own team. Some games were friendly, but some between communities with a long-standing enmity would descend into mass brawls often resulting in severe injuries (as there was no protective padding for players). Back in the day there were no rules on numbers either.

So while today we are restricted to twelve on each side and a regulation-sized pitch, it used to be that up to fifty people would play *on each team*.

One rule was that no hands could be used (apart from the goal-keeper, but they weren't allowed to catch the ball). They were also not allowed to hit the ball with their head. Considering the ball used to be made of solid wood (not the leather-covered cork of today), you would think this rule would be redundant and unnecessary, but clearly some particularly violent players thought nothing about heading a solid wooden ball travelling at speed towards them.

I suspect Sam Heughan would have been such a man. Any opportunity for rolling around, shoving, grappling and general brawling is welcomed by the head of ginger. When we filmed the shinty game, I made sure I tried to act as well as I could with the violence and fighting. However, I couldn't help suspecting that if the director had uttered the immortal words 'Just go for it' (words that I have heard uttered more than once before a fight scene), Sam would have gone completely berserk and attacked everyone, including the camera department, catering, and costume girls. You could see him barely struggling to contain his rising rage during each take.

As for shinty today . . . I'm out of puff, Heughan's thwacked my ankle bone and I have groin strain. I've always preferred tennis myself.

SAM

After shinty, we drive up to the Prickly Thistle pop-up mill, just outside Inverness, and walk inside. Not a single comment about my driving. Suspicious. He asks if he is kickboxing this afternoon. No. He is surprisingly chatty, I expect him to moan about 'shinty aches' but he is positively happy. There is even a hint of a smile under that proud beard. It has a character of its own, bristling when angry, drooping when tired. I suspect he uses beard oil and combs it every night. Maybe the opportunity to let out some aggression and fight some teenagers on the pitch has perked him and his beard up.

A former accountant, Clare (owner of the Prickly Thistle pop-up mill) had no idea how to make tartan, let alone assemble the vastly complex ancient machines she had just purchased. Some months before, I had promoted her appeal to help fund the refurbishment and creation of a traditional woollen mill. *Outlander* fans are so generous and passionate, they could see what she was doing was preserving an ancient craft. Within a matter of days they helped finance her project and the Prickly Thistle mill was in business. Clare and I spoke about creating a tartan, the real challenge being not the weaving of wool or the design and colour of the plaid, but the official registry of tartans. We wanted to call it, you guessed it, the Sassenach. The officials thought it a derogatory name; we convinced them otherwise. Due to *Outlander* and Scotland's

Day trip out
on Loch Ken in my
favourite wellies.

My first Perch. I loved the
experience of fishing, but not
killing a fish. After this one I
tried not to catch any, at times
fishing without any bait.

Playing Malcom in *Macbeth*, with
Christopher Brand as Macduff,
1998 at the Royal Lyceum Theatre,
Edinburgh. My first time on the
Lyceum stage I had been an extra in
another production of *Macbeth*.

Starring as Roderick in *The Pearlfisher* by Iain F. MacLeod at Traverse Theatre, Edinburgh, 2007. Directed by Philip Howard who gave me my first break as an actor, in my second year at drama school he cast me in *Outlying Islands* at Traverse Theatre.

Playing Dickie Greenleaf in *The Talented Mr. Ripley* at Royal & Derngate, Northampton, 2010. The scene where Tom kills Dickie was performed on a boat suspended above the stage. The fight scene was terrifying!

Touring with 'Batman Live'. This time at the O2 World in Berlin, Germany, 2012. We toured around the world and a highlight was flying over the audience, trying not to drip sweat on them, as I fought Catwoman in mid-air.

Me and my favourite horse, Sleepy, on the set of *Outlander*. He loves mints and hates goats.

Being an MI-6 agent in *The Spy Who Dumped Me* in 2018. Filmed in Budapest, Amsterdam and Berlin. Kate McKinnon and Mila Kunis – what a comedy duo!

Meeting The Prince of Wales (known as the Duke of Rothesay while in Scotland) during his visit to the Royal Conservatoire of Scotland in Glasgow in 2019. Later I would present an evening of music from the RCS at Buckingham Palace to HRH and the patrons of his charity.

Crossing the finish line at the Stirling marathon – not quite a PB (I've run three hours eleven minutes at Edinburgh), but marathons are a big passion of mine.

Receiving my honorary doctorate from the University of Stirling, in recognition of outstanding contribution to acting and charitable endeavours. Later that year I received a second doctorate from the University of Glasgow. Just call me 'Doctor, Doctor Heughan'.

The Spy Who Dumped Me Los Angeles premiere in July 2018. The red carpet was filled with *Outlander* fans who came to support, it made me so proud and thankful that they were there.

With Richard Rankin and Sophie Skelton for PaleyFest NY, 2018. We really are a big family and I feel so lucky to work with such lovely, talented people.

Outlander Season 5. The Frasers have settled in NC, America. This was a really strong season, with the loss of Murtagh being my favourite storyline.

The Los Angeles premiere of Sony Pictures' *Bloodshot*. The film was delayed in other countries due to the 2020 pandemic yet went on to do extremely well online.

(Left) Vin Diesel and I at the Columbia Pictures after-party for *Bloodshot*, and (below) in character as Corporal Jimmy Dalton. I loved working on this movie. The main shoot was in South Africa, one of my favourite places having shot there before for *Outlander* Season 3. Jimmy Dalton: half man, half dinosaur.

Triumphant having lifted the Puterach Lifting Stone at Balquhidder. It weighs around 100kg but is very slippery to hold. Graham didn't want to do his back in . . .

McTavish and I hurtling around the Highlands in one of our many modes of transport. Try getting him in a kayak though . . . impossible!

A lesser known Scottish battle. Graham and I about to take on the Local Inverness Shinty Club. They're a terrifying bunch, softly spoken but hard as nails. Don't let the sweet smiles fool you.

Tweed-clad and proud while filming for *Men in Kilts*. We shot over three weekends initially, whilst I was shooting *Outlander* Season 5. We returned for a three-week shoot in August 2020.

It always starts with whisky… and usually ends with it too.

Rowing on the iconic Loch Ness – no sign of the monster, yet. Except the bearded one in the boat.

Learning how to make tartan at the Prickly Thistle pop-up mill. Did I mention I released my own limited-edition tartan collection called . . . yes, you guessed, the Sassenach Tartan.

progressive nature, the word had taken on a new meaning. It was a term of endearment, 'the Outsider', of which we are all one. We wanted to create something using ancient skills, crafted with natural fibres, sustainable and which would provide employment for the community in the Highlands. Clare was very excited and we set out to make a new tartan.

Clare gives us a tour of the mill and looms as we nod politely and pretend to understand what is going on. 'Yarns we use all start off their life on a very large cone,' she says. 'Depending on the design of tartan we've created for clients we break cones down into a particular order and number of threads.' Using two looms from the 1920s and 1950s Clare and her team prepare yarns into perfect order building chains that are the 'computer programme' of the looms. It takes up to a week to prepare those elements alone before we even start to weave. One half of a tartan comes from a back beam of the loom called the 'warp'. The strands of warp are held in tension by the back beam as the 'weft' is then drawn through and inserted over and under by the loom. Traditionally done by hand or foot pedal until 1745 when powered looms were invented, the engineering is amazing, so much happening at high speed. The shuttle flies back and forth almost invisibly and becomes a dangerous projectile if something goes wrong. Many early factory workers were injured and some even lost their lives. As we watch the cloth being made, I could see Graham's eyes wander. He is looking at my scarf, my Sassenach tartan. I could tell we weren't going to leave until he got one. He marches off to the storeroom to find the most expensive freebie he can. He still doesn't realise I charged it to his room. [*Graham: Fortunately, knowing Sam's 'Mr Gradgrind' grasp on money, I had taken the precaution of charging my room . . . to his room.*]

On *Outlander* we also had a tartan created for us. Most current tartans and their colours are actually quite modern, a creation of the Victorians, fashionable and segregated into their separate clans and colours. In the past there would have been little or no unity. The only consistency or variation would have come from the various plants and berries used to dye the wool. Using the local vegetation or animal dyes surrounding Inverness, they created a brown and grey/blue pattern for the MacKenzie clan. Men would have lived in their kilts, exposed to all weather and conditions. So the colours were probably faded and less stark, with softer shades and hues. Obviously Jamie only had access to his MacKenzie colours but when he returned to his home at Lallybroch, we then were able to use his Fraser tartan (he is married to Claire wearing his family's colours; I know Graham was secretly jealous of my glam threads and terrific hair). [Graham: If you've watched the episode, he resembles Liberace in a kilt.] [Sam: No one under fifty will get that reference, Grey Goat.] Nowadays, tartan manufacture is more regulated and many clans have a unique, formal pattern, also possibly a 'hunting tartan' used to blend into the woods.

GRAHAM

'Tartan was a form of identity where people used native raw materials from the land to create distinct colourways and fashion,' says Clare.

After the Battle of Culloden, the Act of Proscription (1746) was introduced to cut off the head of Jacobitism and neutralise the clans by the forced removal of weapons – a key part of a Highlander's identity and a way of defending clan or property – and by banning the Highland dress or plaid, a symbol of Highland identity and clanship. Kilts were replaced by trousers and because people could no longer wear plaid, many traditional skills used in dyeing and weaving were lost in a generation, including various ancient patterns.

Abolition and Proscription of the Highland Dress 19 George II, Chap. 39, Sec. 17, 1746:

That from and after the first day of August, One thousand, seven hundred and forty-six, no man or boy within that part of Britain called Scotland, other than such as shall be employed as Officers and Soldiers in His Majesty's Forces, shall, on any pretext whatever, wear or put on the clothes commonly called Highland clothes (that is to say) the Plaid, Philabeg, or little Kilt, Trowse, Shoulderbelts, or any part whatever of what peculiarly belongs to the

Highland Garb; and that no tartan or party-coloured plaid of stuff shall be used for Great Coats or upper coats, and if any such person shall presume after the said first day of August, to wear or put on the aforesaid garment or any part of them, every such person so offending . . . For the first offence, shall be liable to be imprisoned for 6 months, and on the second offence, to be transported to any of His Majesty's plantations beyond the seas, there to remain for the space of seven years.

The law was repealed on 1 July 1782. After the repeal, tartan and clans, as we now know them, flourished and, even today, we are creating new tartans, such as the 'First Love' collection from Sassenach Inc. Sam is modelling yet another scarf. Lucky world.

SAM

It's time to meet the Badenoch Waulking Group, a charmingly devilish bunch of ladies assembled around a table at the back of the mill. They first appeared in Season One, Episode Five of *Outlander* when Claire goes on the road with Dougal to collect taxes and joins in with some villagers 'waulking the wool', listening to their gossip and song. In the episode they ask her to pee on the cloth, a traditional technique to soften it up. She politely declines but downs a few drams of whisky, which probably made them all better singers!

The ladies get waulkin' the wool whilst singing a burst of the beautiful waulking song they sang on the show (Mo Nighean Donn – 'my brown-haired girl' – is one of Jamie Fraser's pet names for Claire, alongside 'Sassenach'):

'S Mithich Duinn Eirigh, Mo Nighean Donn
(Time That We Awaken, My Brown-Haired Girl)

'S mo nighean donn,
Bheir mi ó ro bha hó
'S mithich duinn éirigh,
Mo nighean donn.
'S misde dhomhs' bhith dol dhachaigh;
Tha mi fad air mo chéilidh.
'S misde dhomhsa bhith gluasad

Seachad buaile na spréidheadh.
Bheir mi m'aghaidh air Muile
Ged a's duilich leam-fhéin e.
Ged a's duilich an-diugh e
Bu ro-dhuilich an-dé e.
A Dhòmhnaill 'ic Lachlainn bhon Bhràighe
Chuirinn fàilte roimh cheud ort.

Sheila Mackay explains to us that waulking is an ancient and traditional way of working the wool, shrinking the fibre and felting it. 'When the cloth comes off the loom it's a very loose weave and to render it wind and waterproof it has to be tightened and shrunk.' (This can be done with sweaters at home on any cycle over thirty degrees in a third of the time!) It's a laborious task, so to pass the time they sang. 'There's a lot of rhythm in the songs to match the task; as the wool got lighter and drier the songs got faster!' There were work songs for most things back then: sweeping songs, milking songs, you name it. Helping to pass the time and make life a bit more enjoyable. The traditional songs were handed down orally, with some going back to the 1700s. Many are about love, sailing, going to war and local gossip.

GRAHAM

'Prickly' Clare is a delight, the machines are indeed impressive and *very loud*, but when all is said and done, this 'visit' to the mill is simply the chance for an extended advert for yet another Heughan enterprise into which he's stuck his murky corporate fingers. On a side note my great-great-great-grandfather came from the Highlands to Edinburgh in 1830 to find work. His occupation during the census of 1841 was listed as 'basket weaver'. He had arrived, probably with Gaelic as his first language, bringing the only skill he could use in this urban environment. I try and imagine what Edinburgh would have seemed like to Alexander McTavish. Coming from the village of Achahoish in Argyll it would have seemed like another world. I've no doubt he was discriminated against because of his Highland origins, mocked for his accent and his rough ways. And yet he married and established a family in that city. They were illiterate up to 1870 for sure, as the 'X' for their signatures proves on marriage certificates. Only fifty-two years later my father was born, who then went on to be an airline pilot. Such is the journey of the Highland family over a period of less than a hundred years, which would be echoed by countless displaced Highlanders from across the country.

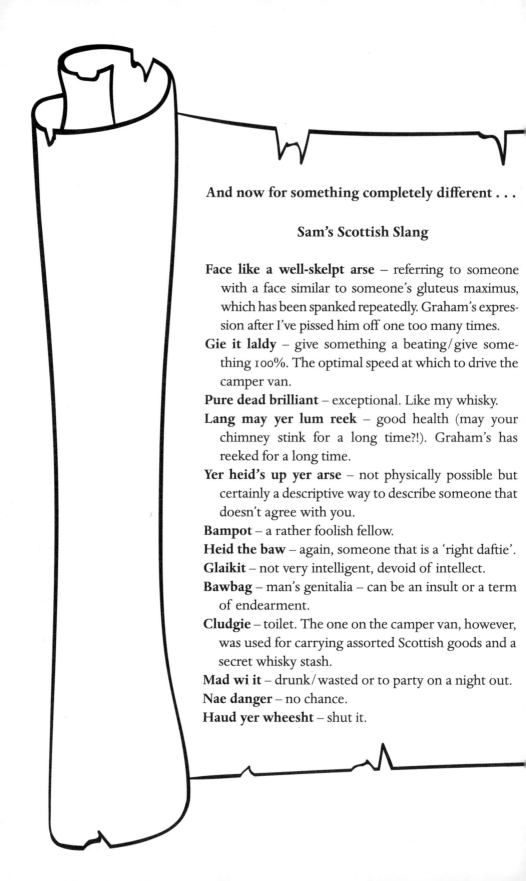

And now for something completely different . . .

Sam's Scottish Slang

Face like a well-skelpt arse – referring to someone with a face similar to someone's gluteus maximus, which has been spanked repeatedly. Graham's expression after I've pissed him off one too many times.

Gie it laldy – give something a beating/give something 100%. The optimal speed at which to drive the camper van.

Pure dead brilliant – exceptional. Like my whisky.

Lang may yer lum reek – good health (may your chimney stink for a long time?!). Graham's has reeked for a long time.

Yer heid's up yer arse – not physically possible but certainly a descriptive way to describe someone that doesn't agree with you.

Bampot – a rather foolish fellow.

Heid the baw – again, someone that is a 'right daftie'.

Glaikit – not very intelligent, devoid of intellect.

Bawbag – man's genitalia – can be an insult or a term of endearment.

Cludgie – toilet. The one on the camper van, however, was used for carrying assorted Scottish goods and a secret whisky stash.

Mad wi it – drunk/wasted or to party on a night out.

Nae danger – no chance.

Haud yer wheesht – shut it.

Yer a chancer – you're pretty dodgy but I like you.

Taps aff – take off your clothing and burn as much as possible in the sun, similar to 'suns out, guns out' (rare in Scotland, usually a week or two in summer).

Can o juice/can o ginger – juice is anything non alcoholic and fizzy, 'ginger' is Scotland's other national drink: IRN BRU – impossible to describe the taste but the Scots swear by it for a hangover. When they tried to change the recipe and make it more healthy with less sugar, there was a national outcry.

Ya fanny – you are a rather ridiculous fool.

Scunnered – very confused.

THE WISDOM OF WENDY

Face like a careless beekeeper
If yer maw had baws she'd be yer da
Bigger bum than ten arses
Keep the heid or you'll lose the baw
Banging away like a Salvation Army drum
You rip ma knittin'
That's enough tae gie yer arse the toothache
Kick the eyes oot a spider wi' they stilettos

Overheard comment from Johnny Beattie whilst a woman was telling a long story:

Do you get a pie wi' that story, hen?

CHAPTER ELEVEN

Rocking the Boat

SAM

It's now late afternoon and Graham is holding on tightly as the camper van gathers speed down the Great Glen. Essentially we are driving down a massive ice age cliff to our destination below: the iconic Loch Ness. The camper's brakes are under pressure and I pump them to avoid locking up. Graham, however, is on 'full lock', his body stiffened, his jaw clenched (and probably his buttocks too). I let the camper run a little downhill – maybe we'll end up in the water? I wonder if our margarine tub can float? It would be like an episode of *Top Gear*, I muse. Graham looks at me with pleading eyes. I brake hard and we arrive safely by the water's edge. After allowing a little time for Graham's breathing to return to a normal rate, we stand silently looking out across the glimmering water, enjoying the uninterrupted peace of Loch Ness. Waiting for it to be rudely interrupted by our friend and *Outlander* alumnus Gary 'McHugger' Lewis's arrival in a rowing boat.

But for now there is just peace. The Great Glen is a truly iconic landscape, formed by a glacier cutting a huge scar across the centre of Scotland. Much of the sixty-two-mile glen is taken up with a series of lochs and connecting rivers, including Loch Ness, made famous by the folklore surrounding the creature that lies beneath the surface – the Loch Ness Monster or Nessie for short. The 'legend' of a strange creature living there goes back to the time of Irish monk St Columba in the sixth century, when a local man, swimming in the water, was attacked by a 'water beast' that mauled him and dragged him under. Columba sent one of his men into the water and the beast approached. Columba made a sign of the cross and commanded him to go back; the beast turned tail and torpedoed away and all the Picts cheered at this perceived miracle. And that's how they converted the Picts to Christianity. Well, sort of.

Loch Ness is one of those iconic places that carries with it a wonderful sense of myth and mystery. And it's just *so* big. It overwhelms you with its grandeur, and even though your rational mind tells you that there can't be a Loch Ness Monster, part of my brain is thinking, *Maybe today . . . maybe today I will see it*. I think this actually is my first real view of Loch Ness and will be my first time on it but it's all coming back to me now . . . *Family Ness*, the 1980s kids' cartoon which I used to watch with my mum and brother when I was little.

I don't generally speak about my family too much. I try to protect them from any sort of spotlight. We are a small family and my mother, Chrissie, raised me and my older brother, Cirdan, as a single parent in the south of Scotland in Dumfries and Galloway. Chrissie is a very creative woman and had been working in a local clog-maker's workshop (run by a friend) for several years when we were growing up. However, she had always yearned to pursue a career as an artist. When the time was right, she applied to the Edinburgh School of Art and was offered a place on the printmaking course. That's when, aged twelve, we moved to Scotland's capital.

Edinburgh was a whole new experience for me and after attending Gillespie's Primary, a state school, we applied for and were lucky to receive an assisted place (not being able to afford the fees) to attend the Edinburgh Steiner School, which is probably one of the reasons I became an actor. Rudolph Steiner schools focus on a rich, creative environment to inspire learning rather than taking a conventional academic approach. It was a good time for me and the teachers covered many subjects, including philosophy, astronomy and medieval history, that were 'off-syllabus'. Graham sent his kids there, so too did Gary Lewis; and Tobias Menzies, who plays 'Black Jack' Randall, went to a Steiner school in Canterbury, Kent. I recently did a really rewarding interview with the school and they posted a video online (including some class photos that I'm not so proud of!).

Despite being a single mother to two teenage sons, Chrissie completed her course at art school and went on to create her own studio, where she continues to make various pieces for exhibition or commission. She has collaborated with many interesting artists and travelled the world, learning the skills used in papermaking and bronze casting in Japan and India, to name a few. Growing up I was always aware how hard it was for her financially and also creatively. Like all artists, it was feast or famine, shuttling from success to inertia and back again, but my mother worked extremely hard to support us whilst never discarding her creative aspirations.

When my time came to choose what I wanted to do she encouraged me, whilst underlining the reality that it would be hard to be a self-employed actor. But she never discouraged me and attended all of my early performances. In one of my first productions I had to play a character losing his virginity, and having your mum sitting only metres away was mildly off-putting, to say the least! Add to that your agent and the majority of London's theatrical critics. Chrissie has always been very proud of me and still sends me newspaper clippings of my achievements – (never articles from the *Hollywood Reporter*, *Los Angeles Times* or *New York Times*) but usually the local newspaper or the annual school newsletter. At first a little scathing of an American TV show portraying Scottish history, she is now very proud of *Outlander* and watches it (when it's on DVD or terrestrial TV). I dream about being able to take her to a premiere in LA or New York and give her a glimpse into the world I sometimes get to explore. But like all children, I fear she will embarrass me when a journalist asks her to reveal some personal facts about me on the red carpet!

My uncle is creative, too. He lived on the Isle of Eigg for many years where he looked after several properties and grounds – he was basically a glorified gamekeeper. That's where we used to go on holiday growing up. He plays the fiddle and has a ceilidh band, touring around Scotland playing at events and weddings. However, his main business is basket weaving and he makes all manner of things, doing a booming trade in wicker coffins! Biodegradable and sustainable, I think it's a great idea. And you can 'try before you buy' – test your coffin, see if you like it and pre-order! He also makes enormous wicker figures used at festivals such as Burning Man and Wickerman festivals. He made the Stag (Season Two) and the Fiery Cross for *Outlander* in Season Five. I think they got the idea for the stag from when I asked him to make one for our showrunner Ronald Moore's birthday.

Ron was the original showrunner on *Outlander* – a great writer and *Star Trek Next Generation/Voyager* alumni. He's created and worked on many iconic TV shows including the *Battlestar Galactica* remake, *Carnivale*, *Electric Dreams* and *For All Mankind*. He also loves good sushi and fine Scottish malt whisky. It was he, alongside Maril Davis and Ron's genius wife Terry Dresbach (the *Outlander* costume designer) that convinced Diana Gabaldon to let them produce her novel series as a TV show.

The stag was transported up from the south of Scotland to the Highlands and looked remarkable in the grounds of Ron Moore's ancient lodgings. Ron loved the whole evening of festivities, with guests being able to experience falconry and blend their own bottle of whisky, and we all ate some delicious local food from the Mhor restaurant group. As it got dark we set the wicker stag alight. I think the Americans were bemused and slightly terrified that these mad Scots were burning something so beautiful.

There was another important person in my life during my formative years, my grandfather, 'Ginge'. Strangely it's Graham's fond nickname for me (not used as yet on this trip!) among others that are not so fond and can be expressed only in %s&£@%* symbols. Formerly a redhead, by the time I knew Ginge he was partially bald with a shock of white hair in a gentlemanly combover. I come from a family of flame-haired relatives, my mother's side being proper gingers! I only worked out Ginge wasn't my granddad's real name one day when I was in his garden (in the south of England) and his next-door neighbour kept calling for someone called Stan. 'Stan? Who's Stan?' I said, looking at the neighbour dumbly through my thick NHS spectacles. An insecure, awkward teenager, embarrassed by my glasses, I didn't really like to engage with people I didn't know. In fact, I'm still wary, though I guess I have become better at hiding my fears or have at least found a way to approach people. Acting does that; it gives you social skills and an ability to interact, at times lead a conversation or adapt to another person's energy. I always wondered why actors were considered strange or too outgoing and gregarious. Perhaps these skills we've learnt allow us to navigate the social boundaries with more ease. I certainly think my sensitivity and early insecurities gave me the ability to judge a situation or 'sense' the atmosphere in a room.

'Is your granddad in?' the neighbour asked again in her estuary English accent, arms crossed, thinking me slow-witted. Scottish kids clearly were very slow. 'Oh, you mean Ginge! Yes, he's in the tool shed.'

I used to spend many summer holidays with my granddad; coming from a small family and not knowing my relatives on my father's side, he was probably the closest member of my family. I loved to be with him. Quiet and good-natured, he had a great laugh and a warm smile. I'd like to think I see him in my own smile. I'd sit in his kitchen eating cereal and we would listen to the 'wireless'. *The Goon Show* was a revelation; it was a ridiculous radio sketch show with hilarious characters and Ginge had a large collection of them on cassette. Written by Spike Milligan and performed by Milligan, Harry Secombe and Peter Sellers, the actors would perform live on stage in front of an audience. My favourite character was Eccles (the rather slow but lovable character who was best friends with a young boy scout called Bluebottle, who would invariably accidentally blow himself up!). We also listened to *Hancock's Half Hour*, another weekly sketch show, much like the current-day *Saturday Night Live* or other modern TV sketch shows. The humour and comedy was from Ginge's time, the

1950s and 60s, and they would touch on World War II and at times would be considered slightly inappropriate in today's climate. I think this humour is similar to *Monty Python* (also a great love of mine) and quite possibly the basis for my friendship with Graham. Anarchic, silly, at times inappropriate and most definitely not for broadcasting, we tend to create ridiculous scenarios in our heads and then laugh about them for days, building on the characters and situation until it becomes utterly absurd.

My grandfather had been in the war but was injured in training operations and was ultimately dismissed back into civilian life. He then worked for the Post Office until his retirement. He always had a bad limp and would try to keep up with me as we walked to the shops for an ice cream, the loose change jangling in his pocket as he quick-marched beside me. Beginning my career as an actor, I featured in many WWII period dramas and always thought of him. I only wished he'd seen them. I wonder if he'd have approved or thought them to be accurate? When I met, and later played, Battle of Britain pilot Geoffrey Wellum in the film *First Light*, I saw much of my grandfather in him, the chipper personality and can-do attitude covering up the traumatic daily experiences of the Second World War.

First Light was the true story of the youngest Spitfire pilot in WWII and it was where I first met Gary 'Hugger' Lewis in 2010, who played Sergeant Mac, my superior officer. Sporting a well-manicured moustache, he was a father figure and sad witness to the tragic destiny of these young fighter pilots. I was honoured to play Geoffrey Wellum, whose book the film was based on, and I met him some weeks before. Full of energy and great respect for his fellow pilots, he never considered himself a hero but believed he just did what was required of him. He bore the scars internally and the loss of his friends was a deep sadness. He was gracious and forthcoming and I studied him a lot. My greatest thrill was going up in a plane, performing evasive manoeuvres and learning how to start a Spitfire, just as he had, with the use of a basic manual and little experience. These young men were left to figure it out for themselves; if they came back alive, they'd graduate to pilot. As the Rolls-Royce Merlin engine exploded into life, with its unmistakable deep throaty sound, I felt the thrill of being behind such a powerful machine. Like a

Formula One sports car, these were the height of technology and speed. It was easy to put myself in Geoffrey's place among 92 Squadron, feeling his sense of duty dispel any fear. He took part in the Battle of Britain and flew multiple missions, the stress and loss of his friends causing a near breakdown towards the end.

Ginge didn't talk about the war much, but he was always game for an adventure and would take me to various theme parks. I, of course, wanted to go on the biggest roller coaster (though pirate ships and log flumes were my favourites) and reluctantly he'd sit beside me and grimace the whole time. Yet he still took me back each summer. Back at his house, I'd escape the heat of a proper English summer, hanging out in his tool shed with its cool air and smell of wood. His various tools and equipment were a throwback to the post-war effort, encouraging British citizens to be industrious and fix things themselves. I'd hammer away at bits of wood, rather ineffectually, generally making an interpretation of a new sword or axe that I could use to fight off the invading English army.

Years later, I was in Eastern Europe at the age of eighteen doing some backpacking before I committed to University. I had just returned from Estonia, with a brief visit to Latvia, Lithuania and St Petersburg. I remember the border into Russia was like a James Bond movie. At three in the morning, my sleeper train was ushered into a compound and surrounded by various Russian forces with search-lights, guard dogs and Kalashnikovs. Each carriage was searched; even the roof and walls of the train were pulled apart to look for contraband. When it was my turn, a burly soldier pointed to my large rucksack; I pulled it off the shelf and my hiking boot struck him in the face. He didn't flinch but signalled for me to open it. I undid the top and a penknife fell out. As he reached down to pick it up he noticed a stuffed lion, perched on top of my belongings. The soldier shook his head and spat the word 'Americanas' in disgust.

Upon finally arriving back in Scotland I learned my grandfather had passed away. As I drifted off to sleep that night, I thought about Ginge; the coins jingling in his pocket, his shed, the Goons, his smile. 'Tick tick tick tick.' The sound of a metronome, at a walking pace, woke me from my sleep. On my shelf, still covered in dust, was the metronome he had bought me, along with the trombone I no longer played. I watched the pendulum rock back and forth, keeping military time. *That's Ginge*, I thought, *no doubt about it!* The window and door were closed and there had been no breeze or other reason for the device to start moving. It gave me chills but also a sense he was still with me. I often think of him during the summer months, when sitting on the grass or listening to the birds – little reminders of those balmy summer evenings of childhood, Ginge contentedly pottering in his tool shed.

Of course, being with Graham is like having a new grandfather in my life. I think that's why I'm so drawn to him. And, I'm the son he never had (he has two beautiful daughters, Honor and Hope). But now I have stiff competition for the old dog's attention because his on-screen brother, Gary 'McHugger' Lewis, is on the scene and they have their own elderly bromance going on. I love Gary. Everyone loves Gary but Graham *really* loves Gary.

GRAHAM

My dad was a passionate communist. He even converted the man who became the leader of the British Communist Party to communism. For my dad, politics was everything. He was self-educated, having left school at fourteen (same for my mum), and a voracious reader. Always non-fiction; I don't think I ever saw my dad read a novel.

Growing up in 1930s Glasgow, it was regarded as the next most likely next place in Europe, after Russia, to have a communist revolution. Tanks were deployed in George Square to suppress such a revolution, like an early Tiananmen Square. Dad read everything he could. I still have his copy of Karl Marx's *Das Kapital*, and his copy of Chairman Mao's *Little Red Book*. It led, I later learned, to physical fights between my dad and my granddad. The latter was a staunch socialist but, for him, communism was going too far.

The fall of communism in the 1980s, along with glasnost and perestroika, was a crippling blow to my dad's long-held beliefs. It was like watching someone who was a Christian being definitively shown God does *not* exist. (Incidentally, I grew up in a completely secular household. My mum was a lapsed Catholic; I never even went into a church until I was twenty-five and only because I was curious to see what they were like).

My dad's war diary as an RAF pilot is littered with references to 'our comrades in the Soviet Union', never to American troops. I grew up having *Soviet Weekly* delivered to our door. I thought this was completely normal until I learned that *no other child* had a dad who had *Soviet Weekly* delivered. Apart from Gary Lewis, who plays my brother, Colum, in *Outlander*. His dad was a Glaswegian communist too. One of many things I found in common with him.

Inviting Gary on our *Clanlands* journey was a stroke of genius, which I grudgingly credit to Heughan. *[Sam: I think you'll find I invited all the guests.]* Gary's hugs are the stuff of legend. A normal hug is a steady two to three seconds. The first two to three seconds of a Gary Lewis hug is merely a warm-up, a testing of the waters. He then devotes the next eight to ten seconds tightening his bear-like grip, holding on to you for dear life as if he has just returned as the sole survivor of Scott's expedition to the Antarctic. Just as you think this must surely be it, he begins a warm and steady rub of your back, sometimes accompanied by extra squeezes, all the while murmuring 'Brother, brother,' if you're a man, or 'Darlin', darlin',' if you are of the feminine persuasion. Finally, after what is now perhaps close to thirty seconds, he releases you from his vice-like embrace. It is entirely possible that you could have passed from day to night while receiving the attention of one of these hugs. But, far from objecting to this, everyone, me included, feels much better afterwards. That's a proper hug.

Gary is not a tall man. He does not have the Viking gene coursing through his veins, or if he does it was the midget Viking from the village that snuck onto the longboat and stayed behind after everyone had left. He possesses the classic Scottish physique. Short legs, a longer trunk (good for traversing the heather like a kilted goat), surprisingly strong arms for strong hugs. I love Gary. I'd go so far as to say I don't know anyone who doesn't love Gary. Originally a school teacher, he came to acting late. Gary has all the necessary talents for an actor: wonderful truthfulness, passion, and an access to emotion. He is also completely filthy.

I remember filming the great hall scenes in Castle Leoch sitting at the big table with Gary and the lovely Aislín McGuckin, who played Gary's wife, whom Dougal impregnated because Gary's character was too enfeebled. When we were in the background of a scene Gary took great pleasure in trying to make us laugh. He always succeeded. I won't go into all the coarse detail but suffice to say it involved comparing my character to a rabid stoat, and me regularly defiling the poor cook, Mrs Fitz, by, as he so charmingly put it . . . actually, I cannot write it down, it is simply too depraved! We were often helplessly crying with laughter.

I first met Gary in, of course, a pub.

We were both jobbing Glasgow-based theatre actors. He was part of Peter Mullan's acting crew, and I would see them at the Victoria Bar near the Citizens Theatre in Glasgow. It was an Irish pub, and the landlord (Sean) would *always* remember what you drank even if you'd not been in for months! Mine was Guinness. I used to sit with Gary, Peter and Davey McKay watching live music, getting pissed on Guinness and generally putting the world to rights. When I learned he was playing Colum I was delighted. Firstly because Gary is a first-rate actor, secondly because we actually could be brothers (apart from the height), as without a beard we bear a striking resemblance. When it came to Colum's wizened legs, Gary was given these harlequin-like stockings to wear (for the digital effects people to use). He had to wear shoes with inserts in them to make his legs curve outwards. They must have been bloody painful but he never complained. I always tried to make Gary laugh before a take. This invariably involved graphic descriptions of depraved sexual imaginings involving him and some farmyard animal in the castle. But Gary never flinched.

When it came to the Gaelic, Gary was not a fan. In rehearsals, rather than do the actual Gaelic lines, he would simply recite a list of whisky brands. But doing scenes with him was a joy. His death scene and the scene in which he exiles me were among my favourite scenes to shoot. We shared our very last shoot day together: his death scene. There was lots of emotion, focus, and truth-pumping. On one's last day on a job, especially one you've been on for years, it's traditional for the 1st AD (Assistant Director) to announce that this is your last scene ever, and then lead the applause from crew and cast alike. Producers tend to come on set to join in with this. It's actually quite touching. But this time, as 'cut' was called, the plugs on the lights were pulled, leaving Gary and me in darkness. The 1st AD announced the scene was complete and they started to move to another set. I think the cameraman mentioned, 'Isn't this your last day, guys?' Gary and I muttered an affirmative. To which there was a smattering of half-hearted applause as the crew moved away in the darkness leaving Gary and myself alone next to the empty space where the series producers should have been standing.

It fair brings a tear to your eye.

SAM

Michelle and I had persuaded an unsuspecting fisherman to hand over his livelihood for the day and we decided the least responsible of us would be Gary, so therefore the most fun if he arrived by water. A couple of years earlier I'd helped him get a short film crowd-funded, where he played a Lewis fisherman. He jumped in and instantly looked the part, complete with woollen bonnet and plastic fish.

Graham and I continue standing on the harbour waiting for a lift. Our terrific photographer says this would be a great time for a shoot. A couple of large rocks situated next to the shore are an ideal setting. We make our way down and I jump up onto a rock and start to pose. Graham remains firmly on shore. 'Come on!' I shout. Gary is gathering speed, he'll be with us in minutes. 'Nope, not doing it,' says the landlubber. 'Too dangerous.' Graham crosses his arms. The photographer and I encourage him, 'It's only a rock!' Begrudgingly, Graham gingerly puts one foot on the rock. Then, crab-like, he climbs up on all fours, as if it's the side of a cliff. The stone couldn't have been higher than a bench!

GRAHAM

Old Russet-Top is meanwhile posing like a Barbour model for a country lifestyle magazine (yes, he's done that too), jutting his jaw like Keira Knightley, chest out, turning and adjusting his pose as the camera clicks. It's utterly nauseating. And then he actually goes and does it – he puts one leg up onto a higher rock and, resting his elbow on his knee, looks into the distance to create his signature 'Full Nash' pose. Lacroix and I used to take bets on when Sam would go

'Full Nash' (short for the full National Theatre) on *Outlander* to bring brooding thoughtfulness or a sense of foreboding to a situation – one wonderful example is in Season Two, Episode Ten, timecode: 11:44 at Prestonpans!

We all have our 'signature looks'. Sam's is a tightening of the eyes as he focuses on a distant object, leg cocked. Cait's is a small smile, a misty eye, an arching of the eyebrows and the faintest of head shakes. Mine is probably a three-quarter turn of the head, followed by an expression that wouldn't look out of place whilst having a prostate examination.

SAM

Luckily for McCrab, still clinging to a foot-high rock for dear life, rump to the stars, Gary hoves into view in a rowing boat.

Gary: Lads! What you've got in the way of beverages?

We take our hip flasks out. 'Whisky.'

Gary: Get in, yer pair of reprobates.

Graham is helped off his rock by Michelle before he cautiously climbs aboard the boat looking nervous. I bound aboard like a Labrador, rocking madly. Graham is clinging to the sides like a fallen pensioner so I make sure to rock it a little more before we set off. 'Just trying to balance it,' I say, giving Grey Goat a slap on the back.

Gary hands me an oar to help him row. Graham is positively frightened that I shall be sharing the rowing duties. I have to move into position, which means rocking the boat again, which I'm really trying not to do this time. 'Please stop rocking the boat you ginger tw . . .' He doesn't finish the sentence. I offer to row on my own but Graham is having none of it. Gary and I are to row together and he will be the self-appointed cox.

Graham: Stroke, stroke.

Gary & Sam: Stroke who?!

Graham: I'm going to have one!

We all explode with laughter. It's good to have some of the gang back together. Today it feels like we are on a Viking galley ship, the oarsmen pulling in unison, the blades cutting through the water, the oppressive Viking King (complete with his safety belt) commanding us to row harder. 'Stroke, stroke,' he bellows, slipping into the role of cox with ease.

GRAHAM

Loch Ness is a place that everyone has heard of. Even people who don't know where Scotland is, or think it's just part of England, have heard of Loch Ness. It's the monster, of course. That creature that is rumoured to lurk in the depths of this enormous loch that runs the length of the Glen Mor (Great Glen). I definitely want to believe a plesiosaur is alive and well, living at the bottom of this body of water, the largest volume of fresh water in Britain. Given that it's 240 metres deep, if a monster is going to live anywhere, it's here.

Our doughty crew are all assembled, bristling with drones, lenses and sound equipment. Michelle is barking instructions, having set up a shot whereby 'Hugger Mor' Gary would magically appear in a row boat, and invite us aboard to row across the loch. The crew would be on a separate boat that would follow us. (The magic of filming.)

It is taking a long time to set up, so in the meantime, Sam suggests we do some still photos. For some reason this involved us clambering across rocks at the loch side, which have been coated in ice in order to make them as treacherous as possible. Clambering like a drunken goat across the rocks I dutifully stand for the photos, with Sam, no doubt, doing bunny ears behind me. Finally Gary makes his appearance. The first take Gary decides to do with a rubber fish in his mouth. (For the love of God, now there are two of these maniacs!). He finally ditches the fish so that he can actually speak coherently and we climb aboard. Sam and Gary take up oars, so I decide to fulfil the role of that guy in Spartacus who beats out the rhythm for the galley slaves.

Out on the water, Gary tells us some fascinating stuff about the history of Scotland, which I'm relying on Sam to remember because I was concentrating on not being tipped out of the boat. It's times like this that I am reminded of Samuel Johnson's quote, 'Boats are prisons with the possibility of drowning.' It's almost as if Johnson knew Sam Heughan personally.

Although I will tell you about Urquhart Castle, which definitely has huge bragging rights as a 'romantic' castle. Other romantic castles must be sick with jealousy of its undeniable beauty and location. Perched on a stubby peninsula it is consistently one of the top ten most popular attractions in Scotland. The fact that visitors might possibly glimpse the waters of the loch frothing with Nessie bursting to life in front of them only adds to its popularity. Its role as a strategic castle goes back to the thirteenth century, with occupation by Edward I and Robert the Bruce, among others, culminating in it being the scene of a siege by Jacobites in 1689 against a garrison of supporters of the Protestant monarchs William and Mary. When they finally left they blew it up, which goes a long way to explaining why the castle is the romantic ruin it is now.

We are blessed with stunning weather, with just enough cloud to contribute to a truly spectacular sunset. It really is a special moment as we drift on the water, looking across this majestic loch. At times like this I like to stop to appreciate how lucky I am to be here with Sam experiencing Scotland like this. And at that moment the Ginger Merkin tries to tip me out by rocking it. I had been totally lost in my thoughts and meditation, actually considering his friendship with sentimental affection, until the nine-year-old lunatic is back to practical joking. I grip the gunwale with both hands and say a stern 'Nooo, Sam!' Chiding him like a parent.

SAM

In spite of the laughter and uneven technique, we make it to the centre of the loch. It's magnificent; the sun is blazing, the water deep and sky blue. Urquhart Castle stands defiant, its ruins silhouetted by the sun. We are silent, caught by the beauty of the land and 'dualchas' – a sense of belonging. We all feel it and Graham and I both feel we were born with a connection to the land. It's a sense and understanding of the rhythm of nature, just as Cameron McNeish talked about at Clava Cairns. The druids and pagans felt it and they, and clansmen who followed them, would have known much more besides, reading the seasons, the birds, trees and their crops, understanding the mighty mountains, rivers and lochs all around them.

Gary has a great knowledge of Scottish history and culture so it's great to get his take on what happened to the Highlands and their people. 'When you're out on the water it's a good place to get perspective,' he says wisely. 'This is a landscape that tells a story of its people. The key thing for the Gaels was relationship to the land; it wasn't about who owned the land, it was that the land owned them. They lived in the land so the whole idea of ownership was something altogether different. The Gaels would have been bewildered by this modern abandonment of dualchas.'

He tells us there is a great book called *Soil and Soul* by Alastair McIntosh, full of love, wisdom and beautifully written stories about the changing use and ownership of the landscape. It's one I'm sure Cameron will have read, being so instrumental in protesting against the Land Reform Act and championing the right to roam. I look forward to reading it.

We are lucky to have this moment of peace and sense of belonging but it doesn't last long. As we try to make our way back, Graham is now hungry again and I'm desperate for the toilet (and more whisky). Gary is smashed in the eye by a camera lens as the crew are setting up for our sunset shot. Which only serves to prove the truth of that old saying, 'It's all fun and games until someone loses an eye.' Fortunately Gary's eye was fine but it was bloody sore, I'm sure.

Back at the Lochardil Hotel that night, Gary's infectious laughter lifts everyone's spirits. 'Och, my man! Come heeeeere!' Short in stature but large in life, I am enveloped in the Mighty Hugger's arms with little chance of escape. After a good ten-minuter he moves to give Graham – who, having changed out of his kilt, is now 'dressed for dinner' – another massive squeeze. I still have my muddy boots on, having had a quick meeting with Michelle to plan the next day. Mussels, Cullen skink, beef blade and lamb shoulder, the crew digs into the hearty Scottish food. I make do with some form of butternut squash and a large Oban. Oh to be a vegan. We order wine for the table and discuss the day's events. Gary brightens the room with his booming voice, managing to hug *everyone* at least twice over again!

I want to hug Graham but he's still not happy with me having 'rocked the boat' earlier. He doesn't look at me the way he looks at

Gary. He emotes love at the wee man but when he looks at me it's more with pleading eyes and a face slapped by fear. I need to go easier on him. I know I do.

Emboldened by my third dram I take a leaf out of McHugger's book, walk over to Graham and give him a long embrace. He hugs me back. Gary, moved by our bromance and fired up by whisky, opens his arms wide and cuddles us both. It feels warm and life-affirming, like brotherly dualchas.

CHAPTER TWELVE

A Bicycle Made For Two

When the spirits are low, when the day appears dark, when work becomes monotonous, when hope hardly seems worth having, just mount a bicycle and go out for a spin down the road, without thought on anything but the ride you are taking.
Sir Arthur Conan Doyle

I thought of that while riding my bike.
Albert Einstein on the Theory of Relativity

INT. JAMIE FRASER & CLAIRE BEAUCHAMP RANDALL'S ROOM – LALLYBROCH – DAY (1746)
Outlander, Season Two, Episode Thirteen, 'Dragonfly in Amber'
Writing Credit: Toni Graphia & Matthew B. Roberts
Based on the novels by Diana Gabaldon

SAM

The sharp dagger is inches from Dougal MacKenzie's chest, blood runs down the blade from my hand that he'd bitten seconds before. It drips onto his chest as he strains to push the knife back at me. Using all my strength I twist the blade around so it's pointing towards Dougal's heart and, using every ounce of strength and my weight, I slowly drive the blade into my uncle's chest. There is a terrible sound from the MacKenzie war chief, the sound of terror, stifled breath, shaking and then stillness. (He's practised that scream in front of the mirror, I'm sure.)

Moments earlier Dougal had discovered his nephew Jamie (me) and his time-travelling wife Claire were plotting to murder Bonnie Prince Charlie. We were filming a scene from the last episode of Season Two and Graham's character was about to die by my hand. It would be Graham's last day on set after two years of filming together (or so we thought) and although I was feeling sad about not working together anymore – he'd become a great friend and integral member of the *Outlander* cast – I secretly loved the idea of messing with him, one last time.

We were shooting the close-up of the dagger (or Scottish dirk) as we grappled to kill each other. Discussions with the director brought us to the idea that Claire should assist the stalemate and lend her strength and weight to the fight by leaning down on the dirk as well and forcing the blade deep into Dougal's chest. This was not in the book and I'm not sure Diana Gabaldon approved. It's ironic that Claire – a healer – actually kills most of the people in the books! We joke that she may actually be a serial killer and not a healer at all . . . For this close-up, Claire's stand-in, or double, was used as you'd only see our hands.

'Action!'

We push the blade towards Graham, who is pretending to struggle, coughs a mist of fake blood from his mouth. After a few moments I decide to push slightly harder, just to see his reaction . . .

'Oh! No! No! Maeve, not so hard!'

The poor stand-in, Maeve, was barely touching the knife handle. She was resting her hand on mine at best.

'Nooo, not so *hard, Maeve!*' Graham bellows.

I snort and try to stifle a giggle from behind the camera.

I admit, I have a childish obsession with tormenting Graham. The moment he feels uncomfortable, the hard-man, all-action, brutish exterior crumbles and he sounds like a caricature. Blustering and cautious, this hardened warrior metamorphoses into Lady McTavish, whose catchphrase is, 'No, I'm not doing it!' when asked to ride a horse, kayak or do anything remotely exciting ('dangerous'). It is a great source of amusement to me.

During the fight that led up to this moment, I proposed putting some knees into his groin. I'd been recently training in Muay Thai (kick-boxing) and knew how to use the knobbly part of my knee. Graham wasn't happy and I could see the distrust in his eyes. It spurred me on. You can even see in the close-up on Caitriona's (Claire's) face as we begin to kill him, she tries to hide her face and look away. Being a notorious corpser, this is the first sign she's about to go. Graham moaned and increased his protestation, which set us off again . . .

The knife slams into Graham's chest and Dougal MacKenzie takes his last breath on *Outlander*. I fall by his side and apologise to my uncle in Gaelic, our first language. It's the first time I've killed him but won't be the last time I try to put him in danger . . . I know, I know, I'm meant to go easy on him but it's like an addiction, I just can't stop myself.

GRAHAM

My death was actually my favourite scene because it placed the characters in a fascinating dilemma. On the one hand Claire and Jamie believed killing the Bonnie Prince would save Scotland (because Claire from the future knows what happens to the Highlanders after Culloden). On the other hand, Dougal, a faithful Jacobite, saw only treachery, as he had no understanding of Claire's secret origins. For me, playing that scene was heartbreaking as it represented the collapse of Dougal's world and his nephew, whom he loved, was revealed to him as a viper. So here were two people, neither *wanting* to kill the other but feeling that they *had* to.

The fight was great. Originally it culminated in Jamie killing me on his own, with Claire standing and watching. We even filmed that version but I argued it was unrealistic that Claire wouldn't get involved, being a strong woman who wanted to protect and help the man she loved. Having her involved also, importantly, made her complicit and active in the killing. Thankfully, that's the one they went with. It also gives me the bragging rights of being able to say it took both of them to kill me! I have a photo, taken as I was lying on my back ready to be stabbed by these two latter-day Lord and Lady Macbeths, looking into their grinning faces.

But I think before Sam gets carried away with his charming view of my relationship with danger, we should put this into some sort of context. Sam and Cait's murder of me is only one of the many, many times I've been killed during my career. I've been stabbed (loads), shot, burned alive, had a fire poker driven through my chest with my throat cut (Kiefer Sutherland on 24), drowned, strangled, poisoned, speared, bayoneted, beaten with sticks, and had a stake driven through my heart. It's not surprising, given such a large and varied number of encounters with death, that quite a few have resulted in actual injury. Stabbed twice (once by a stuntman), speared in the ribs, punched in the face (four stitches), hit with a camera (another four stitches), kicked in the balls, and nearly set on fire (during my first job, a horror movie called *Lifeforce* with Tobe Hooper).

AND, THAT'S WHY I DO NOT WANT TO GO BLOODY KAYAKING!!

[Sam: Never been hurt, just saying.]

I've been told by the producers that on my arrival at our next location, kayaking is what I'm expected to do, but I have already told Sam I'm *not* doing it. As if getting Michelle to tell me is going to change my mind. I'm fine with kayaks. I've been in many kayaks before: on my own, with my kids, with friends, on rivers and on the ocean. I even used to train by capsizing in my school swimming pool at Kayak Club. Kayaks are not the problem, Sam Heughan is the problem.

Why, I hear you ask?

It's the same as saying you love to swim but draw the line at swimming with a tiger shark. I have known Sam for a while now. I love him as a dear friend. I admire his work ethic, his passion for charity work, climbing, his enthusiasm, and his ability at lifting heavy things, but the key thing you have to understand about Sam is that he is a nine-year-old masquerading in adult clothes. I have no doubt whatsoever that if I had agreed to climb into a kayak with him he would have done his very best to tip me out of the kayak. Probably more than once. He wouldn't have been able to help himself. He would have seen it as his duty.

'Don't fire that catapult at that window, Samwise,' I can hear his mother saying.

But guess what? He'd have fired it just to see what would happen.

As adults we learn about actions and consequences. For Sam 'consequences' are just fun things that haven't happened yet.

I manage to dodge a bullet with the kayak but there are only so many bullets you can dodge from 'He of the Russet locks'. Sooner or later, his catapult will find its mark . . .

SAM

Speaking of tiger sharks, I need to take you surfing, my follically challenged friend. Scotland boasts some of the best surf in the world because of the Atlantic and North swells. Come on, Big Man – imagine the sand in your beard, the seawater in your eyes and up your nose, trying to stand up on a board for the twentieth time in freezing water . . . We'd win an Emmy for all the drama you'd create! I am yet to surf Thurso East, Tiree and Pease Bay (all epic surfing spots in Scotland) because I only got my first taste of the action when I was in lockdown in Hawaii in March 2020. It was my 40th birthday so I decided to book a lesson with a pro-surfer as restrictions began to ease. While he was teaching me the basics I casually asked my instructor if he had ever seen a shark. 'Two,' he replied. 'One a long time ago and the other was the biggest tiger shark I've ever seen.'

'Where was that?' I asked, trying not to let my imagination run away with me.

'Right outside your house [a rental on the ocean],' he said nonchalantly.

'When?!'

'Yesterday,' he smiled, pulling up the YouTube video to prove it.

Let's just say the first surfing lesson was a lot harder with the *Jaws* theme tune on repeat in my head!

I think this is the moment I should tell you about the time Graham 'saved' my life. Being hyper-cautious has its merits, he would say. We were on our second night-shoot, filming a battle sequence for Season One of *Outlander*. The rain was coming down hard on our side of a mountain, overlooking a small town called Muthill (pronounced 'Mew-thill' by the locals). I sheltered in the green 'easy-up' – a small tent offering minimal protection from the wildest of Scottish weather. We were shooting the second half of a battle, with the local Grant Clan attacking our travelling company of MacKenzies.

The day before, the small hilltop and glen had been verdant and covered in fresh grass; however, after two nights of constant rain and a horde of grips, assistant directors, actors, props, horses, extras, stuntmen and a single reluctant coffee man, it now resembled a muddy bog. Our boots sank deep into the clag and we slipped and fell owing to the leather soles of our boots, left without grips for historical accuracy. Having no grip on your boots during a fight scene in the dark in a bog is far from ideal.

Curled up in a foldaway chair in our grimy tent, Dougal MacKenzie, Clan War Chief, tried to stay warm, with only the occasional grumble or heavy sigh to show me he was still awake. We had both been involved in filming the fight sequence over two nights, a night-time raid and battle, and were fitted into camera rigs which we could operate ourselves, capturing our reactions as we cut and thrust our way through a throng of enemy clansmen. The rain started to fall harder as the crew set up and lit the next shot. Night shoots are notoriously hard to light – a large fire had been made and was kept alight by a hidden gas canister – another hazard we had to remember as we slid and sank in the mud. The other light source was an enormous fluorescent globe, hoisted high above our heads on a crane that acted as the moon, flooding the entire muddy swamp with a cold, natural light.

By now silence had fallen upon the easy-up and Graham's latte had no doubt grown cold. We had been making light conversation for some time, peppered with occasional outbursts of 'What the f**k is taking them so long?', but now all mutterings had ceased. I pushed my chin deeper into the woollen folds of my coat and folded my arms and, as my eyes started to close . . . I noticed Graham's large figure shifting around in his chair. I closed my eyes again.

'Oh! OH! OH!'

I opened them and saw Graham leaning forward in his chair, tense and staring over my shoulder. 'What?' I asked. His head bobbed from side to side, as he tried to look over my shoulder through a clear plastic side of the tent.

'Is that bloody great thing coming towards us?'

I turned to look and made out the vague silhouette of the moon-crane, a tractor-like machine, travelling in our direction.

Graham was now on high alert. I'd seen him like this before (in the presence of a shaggy Highland cow) and knew his propensity for personal safety. 'It'll be fine,' I yawned and dug deeper into the folds of my kilt.

However, I couldn't help but watch with some amusement as the Great War chief, fearsome warrior of the MacKenzie clan, gripped his chair tighter, straining ever further forward . . .

'Uh . . . uuuuuh . . . uhhhhhhhh . . . RUN!' yelled Graham, off like a flash through the canvas and into the night. As I turned the crane was suddenly upon us, a large piece of steel pipe from the scaffolding perilously close to my head. I ducked and hurled myself out, crashing into Graham as we watched the entire tent, apparatus and chairs mown down by the runaway tractor.

The machine stopped and the driver – yes, it had a driver – looked out. Not uttering a single word he merely shrugged his shoulders.

'You see,' whispered Graham in my ear. 'I saved your life.'

★★★

Kayaks, however, are much safer than tractor-cranes, but this time Graham has firmly dug his size eleven heels in, also adding camper vans to his 'banned list'! After five days 'off' from the trip (so I could keep doing the *Outlander* day job and Graham could swan around on holiday) the Old Duchess has decided to travel by *car*, citing my 'terrible driving' and his 'serious back problem' as reasons. I honestly don't know what mode of transport to expect when he arrives – a Bentley, a Bugatti Royale, a Limo? But certainly a cavalcade of chiropractors in procession . . .

Meanwhile, I am alone behind the wheel of the fecking Fiat negotiating narrow country lanes and a potholed track to our new lodgings. The Taychreggan Hotel is a remote seventeenth-century cattle drovers' inn on the shores of Loch Awe not far from Oban in Argyllshire and, to be honest, I'm loath to tell anyone about this place because it is so special. Converted into a superb hotel, I know the high-maintenance history buff will be in his element . . .

I arrive at the inn as the day is drawing to a close. There's no sign of Graham and, even as the sun begins to set, he still hasn't materialised, undoubtedly lost between here and Inverness, his poor driver bombarded by his helpful 'directions'. Michelle and the team are eager to capture the sunset and an evening kayak across Loch Awe but as time continues to pass I realise my *compadre* won't be here any time soon because he is being late on purpose.

We need to crack on with the kayaking so I quickly get changed in my hotel room. The view from the window is stunning, the blood-orange hues of the setting sun illuminating the appropriately named Loch Awe. The inn, situated on the narrowest part of the loch, was where cattle drovers would persuade their cows to swim the stretch of water to Portsonachan on the other side. It's a fair distance, so would have been quite a swim.

I pull on my wetsuit. Part of me wants to kayak but most of me can't be arsed – I'm dog-tired tonight. I take a breath and march through the bar in neoprene as some of the camera boys are ordering stiff drinks. Oh, for a libation of whisky! But we have work to do. John, the director of photography and drone operator, always ready to shoot, whips out his remote control and we head out.

Wendy is hanging out of her window clutching the free bottle of sherry supplied by the hotel as a 'welcome' treat. 'Go oan, an gies it a whirl, big man!' she waves and disappears from sight, no doubt falling back onto her four-poster bed. It has been quite a journey so far for all of us and, with many of the team having a full week's work on the set of *Outlander* every week, we are ready to crash.

I push the red kayak out into the still waters and begin to paddle across the golden lake. Then I see the headlights of Graham's car enter the car park. Nice timing, McTavish.

GRAHAM

I was actually parked around the corner with a pair of high-powered binoculars. As soon as I saw Sam zipped into his Action-Man scuba outfit (you know the one? The one you used to put in the bath and have your other Action Man drown on purpose), we waited, lights off until he put the kayak in the water and pushed off. Then I knew it was safe to drive in and make my way to the restaurant for a chilled Chablis and a delicious dinner of poached fish and steamed vegetables. *[Sam: Or the bread basket and two desserts.]*

I begin with a little heart-starter – a crisp Sancerre and a selection of olives and half a dozen Loch Fyne oysters on the side. Then I tuck into the venison terrine appetiser and ask the waiter to keep the wine chilled. My dinner is accompanied by the gentle turning of the pages of my book (Sam is somewhat of a stranger to literature. His idea of a cracking read is a book showing pictures of mountains, or perhaps a collection of dumb-bells), and the ticking of the clock. He makes it there and back from his Willard Price Kayaking Adventure without incident; I'm glad to report my meal passed in similar fashion. *[Sam: Until the waiter presented the bill?]* *[Graham: I forge Sam's signature having made a point of checking on his room number when I arrived.]*

SAM

As I look back towards the drover's inn I can see Graham's *driver* slowly pulling in. Knowing he is now safe, he booms at me across the loch. 'See you at dinner!' I shout back that he is missing out. And he really is. As I start to paddle I truly am sad he's not sharing this sunset with me. The peace on the loch, the distant chatter of the crew 'getting on it' in the bar and the lights from the hotel, a warm inviting glow in the falling darkness. The longest freshwater loch in Scotland, many clans lived near to these shores, in particular the MacGregors, Stewarts and Campbells. Tomorrow we will visit Kilchurn Castle, home of the Campbells of Glenorchy, just north of here. There are actually four castles on the loch: Kilchurn, Fraoch Eilean, Innisconnel and Fincharn. They were once served by galley ships. The island near Innisconnel is called Innis-Sea-Rhamach – the island of the six-oared galleys. My kayak is not quite the fearsome galley, but it certainly will do.

As I round the headland the current picks up; a wind is driving from the northern end. I can make out Ben Lui, one of Scotland's most striking peaks, in the distance. I'd taken the cast of *Outlander* up there some months before, whilst preparing to shoot the beginning of Season Five. Duncan Lacroix was with us, surprisingly sober, at least until we got back down!

I make my way westward, the waves and splash of water are exhilarating. St Conan's Kirk is hidden from view, complete with Gothic flying buttress, Celtic cross and Saxon tower, but we will pass it tomorrow on our way to Kilchurn. I paddle onwards. It is getting dark; the drone hovers overhead, its green and red lights blinking through the enveloping veil of night. I turn the kayak around and power back towards the inn. Graham will be doing a turn for the locals in the bar by now and Wendy will be fast asleep throwing out some zeds.

GRAHAM

I feel it's only fair to mention that I have rowed a Viking longboat out of a fjord in Norway, 250 miles north of the Arctic Circle, and navigated a barrel down a white-water river in New Zealand filming

The Hobbit. But I'm sure paddling a kayak on Loch Awe is very impressive, too.

Sam: I've *swum* in the water north of the Arctic Circle!

Graham: Note to editor: cut line above.

GRAHAM

The next morning after a proper breakfast and a latte grande, Sam finally lets me into the surprise he has in store for me today. We shall be taking a tandem to Kilchurn.

No one has mentioned a tandem. Not a hint or a whisper of this ridiculous contraption in the contract or anecdotally.

In the tradition of our filming for *Clanlands*, the equipment was sourced with maximum discomfort and danger in mind. If the bikes we cycled up to Cawdor Castle were reminiscent of rusting farm machinery, the tandem which they present to me outside the inn looks like it was buried, perhaps at sea, in the late nineteenth century and then resurrected for the sole purpose of wreaking havoc with my arse.

To say it had a saddle is like saying I have a full head of hair. The Spanish Inquisition had lost a valuable asset. I once visited the Museum of Torture in Prague (yes, there really is one) – I was there playing a torturer in a TV show, just to be clear. It wasn't a casual drop-in on a rainy day. *[Sam: Dressed in a full-length flasher's mac.]* I'm pretty sure I saw the saddle of our tandem there on display. In fact I'm doubly certain Samwise Heughan spent many an hour there researching what he'd do to me on *Clanlands*.

I give it a once-over. The bike has wheels, check, and primitive versions of brakes. I believe Sam has some false memory of our soundman riding the tandem to reassure me the brakes work. Rather like the belief the Earth is flat, or that Elvis lives *[Sam: he does]*, this is a figment of Sam's imagination. *[Sam: I have a photo.]* Now I'm not saying the brake cables had been cut but they had a tenuous relationship with the brake pads. I might as well have used my feet to slow down. In fact, I did. The tandem bike may have actually weighed more than the camper van. If not, it certainly was made of a metal hitherto unknown to man. Think lead, with added lead. 'Okay,' says Michelle, 'we're going to drive in front with the camera. You guys pedal behind, keeping a safe distance.'

The key words in this sentence are 'guys' (plural) and 'safe'. Needless to say, neither word is acted upon. It's time to decide who should be in which position on the bike and there are advantages and disadvantages to both. The individual at the front obviously has access to the brakes (however in this case this was like having access to prayer). The other advantage is that you aren't inches from the arse of the man in front of you. Now, I like Sam, I really do, but I've seen enough of Episode Sixteen of Season One of *Outlander* not to need a view of his arse ever again. The disadvantage is that the one at the front can't see what the one at the back is doing (or not doing). I choose the front. We climb aboard and I swear I can *hear* Sam grinning like a schoolboy.

It's time for a practice run. I push on the pedals and immediately stop. I have cycled the length of Britain, all through Ireland, the Outer Hebrides, from Arran to Cape Wrath, and across the Welsh Mountains but this . . . this was like wrestling an old drunk down an alleyway. (Come to think of it, Sam had been on the sauce again last night.) *[Sam: Er, and so had you – Mr bottle of Chablis to myself and two double whiskies. On my bill as usual.]*

I look behind to check with Sam.

The smirking ginger attempts a look of innocence.

'Let's try again,' he says.

We try again.

The handlebars have a life of their own and I dredge my brain for a reason. Somewhere from the recesses of time I remember a physics lesson talking about loads and weight distribution. I realise that Sam *is* the weight. He *is* the load . . .

Third attempt.

This time we get twenty feet before nearly sliding into a ditch.

By this point Sam isn't even attempting innocence. The bastard is up to something.

We finally get going enough for the camera car to film me complaining vociferously to Sam about yet another attempt to cause me serious injury. It's only later on I discover (when I watch the footage) that Sam's feet never make contact with the pedals!

Like some deranged, booze-soaked uncle, legs splayed either side, Sam is literally a dead weight at the back. He even has his arms crossed. Piss-taking bastard.

Meanwhile I am straining like a galley slave at the front desperately trying to pedal fast enough so as not to topple over. Finally, on attempt four, we start to get some speed up as Sam begins to join in with the pedalling, but only because he can see we are about to go downhill. Now he's forcing the pedals round faster than my legs want to go and we are gathering speed at pace. Faster and faster, because he is like a bowling ball of weight at the back and we are getting nearer and nearer the crew car. And now, Mr DeMille, I'm ready for my close-up. With your exhaust pipe.

I squeeze the brakes.

They work!

Sam is indignant.

Sam: Are you braking?

Graham: Yes, I am, because we're going downhill.

Sam: Don't brake! Come on! Let's *go!*

He pedals even harder like Chris Boardman.

Graham: It's like being with my seven-year-old! You're such a *tit!*

He ignores me and we press on until suddenly, out of nowhere, he decides he's 'done' with the tandem thing. The film crew have what they have. He's over it. And, without telling me, he drops his feet to the ground, stopping the back of the bike dead and causing the front wheel to almost jack-knife, which very nearly sends me flying over the handlebars. I somehow manage to save myself, sliding off my concrete saddle and castrating myself on the crossbar instead. *[Sam: Hmm, I somehow don't remember this . . .]*

Yeeeeooooooooooowiiiiiiiiiiie!!

I dismount and hobble off, raging at the sky and nature and god, if there is a god, and take my aching walnuts and arse – which feels as though it's had a week-long visit from 'Black Jack' Randall – as far away from Sam as I can.

SAM

Graham never wanted to go behind me because he wanted me to look at his arse. FACT.

Ach, I have never heard a grown man complaining so much. Claiming to have cycled the length of Britain, circumnavigated the globe in a barrel, rowed an entire fleet of Viking longships and climbed Everest dressed as a dwarf, I thought getting Graham on a tandem, before his mid-morning snack, would be relatively easy. He is about as old as the bicycle in question and just as rickety. Point blank refusing to sit behind me – the rear passenger really does get a 'bum-deal' – I thought we could at least complete the eighteen miles to Kilchurn Castle, before he demanded a nap, so I agreed to let him steer.

Now, I have no idea of Graham's manhood, prowess or general condition (although I have heard some peculiar, rather unsettling sounds emitted from his adjacent room at night. A lady friend or the nightly terror of piles? It's hard to tell . . .) but the tandem bicycle is apparently close to 'castrating' him. Anyway, after a great deal of moaning and gasps, he finally manages to get his leg over (clearly never a problem before!) as I sit at the back of the bike to stabilise it. [*Graham: Perhaps we should have got an elephant to sit on the back to 'stabilise' it still further. At least it might have done some pedalling.*]

As soon as his ample arse lands on the ancient leather sprung saddle, I give us a push. 'Hold On!' I shout as we swerve all over the place, Graham's driving a little disturbing. Perhaps he's forgotten what side of the road we are supposed to be on? He spends a great deal of time swanning around in a posh Porsche in Santa Monica, LA.

'Nooo, stop pushing! The brakes don't work!' he whines. I have actually tested the bike on my own earlier and stopping is not a problem. 'It's fine,' I say, egging him on, hoping the camera crew are recording all of this. The views are splendid – Loch Awe, the mountains and another blue sky – I decide to let McTandem do the work and sit back, legs dangling down, enjoying the scenery. A mile or so later, Graham is panting loudly and has totally run of out steam.

I let him take a little break to get his puff back and, this time with me helping to pedal, we start to get some speed up – fantastic stuff. Round a bend there is a slight downhill stretch which the Grey Dog wants to 'freewheel' down (i.e. take a break). I pedal with all my might but he starts braking and calls me a twit. *[Graham: A tit.]*

We come to a standstill. 'No, that's it. I'm exhausted. Bloody bike doesn't work. I mean, who in their right mind would bring this? It's rubbish. Utterly useless.' He is on a rant and we all wait for the steam coming from his ears to subside.

I hide my smile and try not to catch Wendy's eye and crack up – she's seen his diva antics on the set of *Outlander* and it's the shot in the arm that a tired band of crew and actors need sometimes – the wonderful sight of someone 'going off the deep end'. We live for the meltdowns because we are all pushed to the point of having the odd moment from tiredness and a relentless filming schedule. Wendy and the camera team give me the thumbs up. We have got what we wanted: Mr Shouty's comedy gold.

Just then Merlin (the sound guy who gets thrown around by my driving in the back of the camper) decides he needs to get the sound of the bike wheels turning. He jumps on the back of the bike, and using no hands, he pedals away, complete with a sound box and holding the telescopic microphone. And that, Grey Dog, is how it is done.

Graham: These are the ravings of a man on hallucinogenic drugs.

'The bike seems to work fine, Graham,' I smirk. But Graham has gone, already snacking on a protein bar in the camper van, grumbling about the pain in his arse. I think he may be finally realising that the pain is in fact me!

Grey Dog's morale is only restored at the sight of a 'big breakfast' burger truck in a layby on the horizon. The grumpy oversized dwarf stiffly marches towards it, still wearing his cycling clips. He orders something large, covered in pastry. Is it lunch? Elevenses? It can't have been more than an hour and a half since breakfast. He bites hungrily into his beige delight, spraying crumbs. The food trucks in Scotland are not like the ones in America. Or even the rest of the world. There's no ceviche, fish tacos, pulled pork buns or ubiquitous Corgi truck, the Scottish ones are more basic – think buffet carriage on an InterCity Express train or greasy roadside cafe.

In Seasons One and Two of *Outlander* there was no proper craft service (the catering department for the cast and crew). In America, the catering is amazing: omelette stations, pizza, candy, latte stalls for Graham and snacks brought all day. However, it's easy to put on a lot of weight and find yourself struggling to fit into your previously already snug costume! On *Outlander*, however, the producers thought the crew worked better on less . . . The tradition was that the only snack was at 5pm when a plate of white bread sandwiches would arrive, which had usually been sitting on a table in the rain for a few hours, attacked by the odd hungry lighting guy. Only the even less appealing soggy sandwiches would remain.

The other 'highlight' was a family-size tin of biscuits, to be shared among the hundred or so crew. Now I'm not saying we expected more or thought ourselves hard done by, but the crew worked long hours, usually outdoors in all conditions. 'Four seasons in one day', is the expression used for filming in Scotland, however, in reality it's mainly winter with a few moments of spring/summer/autumn. Torrential rain, mud and wind were the meteorological backdrop to Season One and during the first week I remember going to get our breakfast from the catering van with Caitriona. It was still dark and windy, with a spattering of rain. Newly arrived from Los Angeles and a former model, I started to think she may not be ready to face a 'Full Scottish' of fried eggs, square sausage, bacon, tattie scone (yum!), baked beans, toast and haggis at 5am.

'Whatyawantin?' the pasty-white gruff chef barked in his authentic Glaswegian burr.

'Erm . . . what do you have?' asked Caitriona, nursing a Styrofoam cup of black thick liquid that bore no resemblance to coffee. It was tepid, rancid but at this hour, on the shore of Loch Long in the pitch dark and rain, we weren't going to complain to the overworked chef.

He looked at Caitriona in disbelief. Who in their right mind doesn't know what is on the menu at breakfast!?

'We got beans, sausage, haggis, bacon, egg . . .' he was about to reel off the full list of artery-stopping breakfast ingredients.

'I'll have an egg,' Caitriona replied, and I got the feeling she'd rather go hungry but didn't want to appear ungrateful.

'Fried, scrambled, hard boiled . . .' he began again, one hand stirring a pot of thick porridge.

'Can I have poached?' Cait enquired.

The chef stopped stirring momentarily, raising his eyebrows and giving his young, slightly spotty teenage apprentice a look.

'Eeeeh, aye,' he reluctantly agreed.

'And do you have any avocado?' Cait asked hopefully.

There was silence, broken only by the burr of the generator supplying the energy to the bright neon light. The wind swirled and the teenage apprentice turned his back and leaned further into his task of buttering slices of bright white bread.

'Avowhat?' The chef finally leaned over the counter to look Caitriona deep in the eyes, leaving his vat of porridge to bubble and spit in disgust.

'Avocado . . . you know . . . it's . . .'

'Oh aye . . . I'll see what ah can do.' Without a hint of belief in his voice, the chef turned away and I gave Caitriona a tug.

'We will get you some,' I tried to reassure her, not hopeful the chef either knew what it was or could find an avocado at 5am in a layby outside the remote town of Arrocher on the shores of Loch Long. Apparently Cait actually did receive her egg and half an avocado in its skin, and received the same meal for almost a year, not wanting to upset the catering crew or ask for anything different, lest they thought her difficult or struggled to comprehend her.

So the craft services weren't looking good: Graham was going to go hungry and we were *all* feeling the brunt of his disdain. Something had to be done, and done it was! After much complaining, a small wet carrier bag from the local Tesco store was produced with an assortment of Kit Kats, Penguin bars and the occasional, supposedly slightly healthier yoghurt-coated muesli bar. This was carried around in the wet jacket pocket of a small, caring, yet sarcastic, ginger-haired Assistant Director. Whenever the time arose, Graham would be fed! However, it would take a few more years before we managed to progress to something slightly healthier and by this point, Graham would be dead.

But he's still very much alive on *Clanlands* and now McPasty has refuelled, we need to press on. The clouds are gathering and the sky, like Graham's testes, is beginning to bruise. On one last ride, with excess calories to draw upon, Graham digs deep and we cycle the couple of hundred yards to the foot of the castle.

GRAHAM

I did indeed stop at the food van. I think I gave them a hurried message written on a torn piece of paper begging for help. Like something smuggled out of Colditz Castle in the war.

The food is surprisingly good. There are only so many protein bars a man can eat (unless they're Sam), and it gives me a chance for the throbbing in my nether regions to die down. I endure another few miles on the tandem with Sam just before the heavens open upon reaching Kilchurn. Sheltering indoors is our guide, Kenny. The ever-prepared Michelle magics some umbrellas into our hands and we stand outside in the seasonally appropriate dreich Scottish weather bombarding Kenny with questions. At least the rain is too heavy for the midges.

The castle itself is wonderfully dramatic, sitting broodingly at the end of a peninsula. Originally it was on an island and, at its height, must have been a formidable fortress. They knew how to build castles that basically looked like a massive 'F**K OFF' to anyone for miles around. Built in the 1440s by Sir Colin Campbell of Glenorchy, you could see from its position it was a powerful strong-hold at the head of Loch Awe, the peak of Ben Cruachan visible in the mist.

Sam: I actually shot a commercial here a few months ago and thought it so striking that we had included it in the show . . .

Graham: Whoring yourself again for a few shekels. Were you wearing a kilt touting your Highland haemorrhoid cream?

The lands were originally owned by the MacGregors but were 'acquired' by the Campbells of Glenorchy (the same Campbells of Glenorchy whose descendant presided over the massacre at Glencoe). At the end of the sixteenth century the castle was strengthened and improved by the extravagantly named 'Black Duncan of the Seven Castles' (7th laird of Glenorchy). I've always wondered if he was addressed like this to his face? 'Excuse me, but can you direct me to where Black Duncan of the Seven Castles lives?' Did he start out as Black Duncan of the One Castle, and then slowly his name changed as he 'acquired' six more? Did his friends call him 'Duncan' or perhaps 'Black D'? Is it a bit like Puff Daddy? [Sam: It's P. Diddy, granddad!] Did he start as Black Duncan and then just shortened it to B. Duncan? What about his wife? 'Oh Black Duncan, youse are a one, put down that axe and gi'e us a kiss!' Was she known as Mrs Black Duncan of the Seven Castles? If only we knew!

I think Black Duncan might be my new name for Duncan Lacroix – 'I'm off oot cuttin' aboot the toon, gettin' tanked up wi Black Duncan – don't wait up.'

Sam: Black D and Mr McCampy T!

The Campbells famously sided with the Commonwealth in the aftermath of the War of the Three Kingdoms (also known as the British Civil Wars 1639–51, when Charles I famously lost his head). During the Interregnum rule of Oliver Cromwell, who became Lord Protector (1653–58), Kilchurn Castle withstood a two-day siege from General Middleton in 1654 before Cromwell's forces drove him back. To withstand a two-day siege is no mean feat.

Sir John Campbell of Glenorchy did some more 'acquiring' in the late seventeenth century from George Sinclair, Earl of Caithness by foreclosing on his vast debts. That is one of the things we learned more and more about the Campbells as we progressed on this journey. They often didn't need to resort to violence, as they were very good at getting people indebted to them (like a particularly adept Monopoly player who owns Mayfair and Park Lane with two hotels and sits back smirking while he watches all the other players bankrupt themselves).

On this occasion, though, Sir John combined pecuniary shenanigans with good old-fashioned slaughter. He apparently killed so many Sinclairs in this campaign that the Campbells were able to cross the River Wick without getting their feet wet (it's not a narrow river . . .). It was this that gave rise to that jaunty pipe tune, 'The Campbells are Coming', and I don't think the 'coming' was ever a welcome one. Sir John, not to be outdone by Black Duncan, went by the name of 'Slippery John'. Again, one wonders if and when this name was ever used.

'How was Christmas, Slippery John? Slay many men, women, and children? Many evictions?'

Apparently this nomenclature came from being involved with both the Jacobites and the government. Slippery indeed. But it also made him one of the most powerful men in Scotland. Towards the end he lived in Kilchurn and it is his initials along with those of his wife Mary that are carved into the lintel that Sam and I passed beneath to shelter from the rain. He went to his death in 1717 suspected of being a Jacobite, but it was never proved. Slippery to the end.

Kilchurn was eventually converted into a barracks that garrisoned 200 Hanoverian troops during the Jacobite rising of 1745. As we stood in the open courtyard in the rain I imagined the scenes when the Redcoats came to stay. I wonder what Slippery John would have made of it all. No doubt he would have given them cake with one hand, while poisoning their ale with the other.

In commemoration of this visit and the medieval nature of the tandem debacle, Sam will forever become known in my mind as simply . . . 'Slippery Sam'.

'Shovellin' Coal' by Tony Pranses (It's about a tandem!)
There are those who think the tandem is the instrument sublime
For the serious cycle-tourist, and the man concerned with time.
It has drive and rolls much faster as it gobbles up the track,
But it's quite another matter to the guy who sits in back . . .
*   shovellin' coal.*

But just look at the advantages with twice the power at hand,
And half the wind resistance as it travels o'er the land.
The weight is less than double. This alone gives peace of mind.
But it's still another matter to the guy who sits behind . . .
*   shovellin' coal.*

Yes, the man up front is master. It is he who shifts the gears.
He decides when brakes are needed, and on top of this he steers.
He can go the wrong direction and wind up in Timbuktu;
But refuses any protest from the guy who's number two . . .
  shovellin' coal

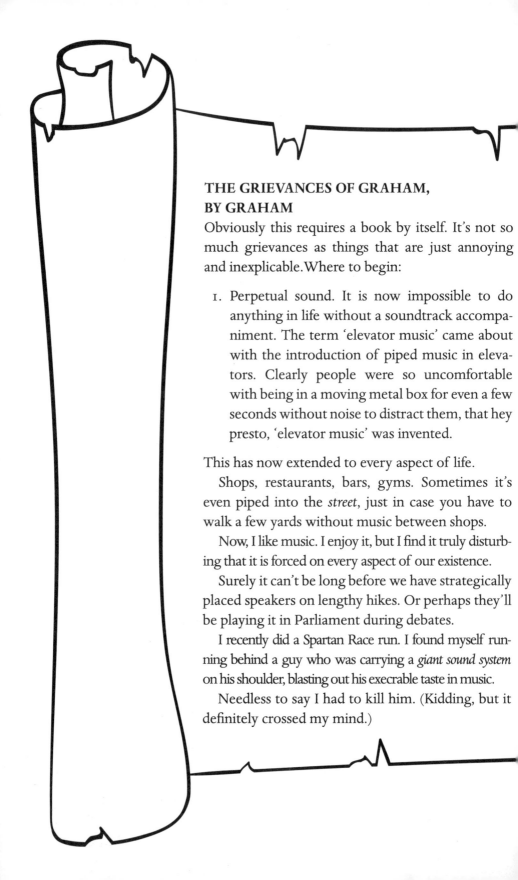

THE GRIEVANCES OF GRAHAM, BY GRAHAM

Obviously this requires a book by itself. It's not so much grievances as things that are just annoying and inexplicable. Where to begin:

1. Perpetual sound. It is now impossible to do anything in life without a soundtrack accompaniment. The term 'elevator music' came about with the introduction of piped music in elevators. Clearly people were so uncomfortable with being in a moving metal box for even a few seconds without noise to distract them, that hey presto, 'elevator music' was invented.

This has now extended to every aspect of life.

Shops, restaurants, bars, gyms. Sometimes it's even piped into the *street*, just in case you have to walk a few yards without music between shops.

Now, I like music. I enjoy it, but I find it truly disturbing that it is forced on every aspect of our existence.

Surely it can't be long before we have strategically placed speakers on lengthy hikes. Or perhaps they'll be playing it in Parliament during debates.

I recently did a Spartan Race run. I found myself running behind a guy who was carrying a *giant sound system* on his shoulder, blasting out his execrable taste in music.

Needless to say I had to kill him. (Kidding, but it definitely crossed my mind.)

(I've realised that if I write this much about everything that annoys me, I'll be here all day.)

So I will just list.

[Sam: Oh . . . I just happened to do a Spartan Race? Graham probably thought it was an opportunity to 'actually' fight people. Or Spartans. Or dress as one?]

2. A lack of honour among politicians. (The last time a politician resigned as a matter of honour was Lord Carrington in 1982 – and this is a man who fought at Arnhem in WWII!)
3. Mobile phones.
4. The celebration of mediocrity.
5. Hand sanitiser.
6. Cyclists who wear lycra (you're not in the Tour de France!).

[Sam: MAMILs (Middle Aged Men in Lycra) is what we call men in Lycra in the UK.]

[Graham: I call them c***s.]

[Sam: Hmmm does that include Lycra underpants? I feel I've seen you wear those, Mr Shouty?]

7. Adults wearing onesies.

[Sam: Tick.]

8. Emojis.
9. People who can't laugh at themselves. I'm glad to say Sam can, which is a prerequisite of a decent human being and not being a 'see you next Tuesday'.

10. Any corporation that says, 'Your safety is our number one priority.' They're lying.
11. Staff who begin their conversation with you with the words, 'How's your day going so far?' Sometimes at 6am (a little early to say, I would venture).
12. People who play videos on their phone at full volume. I once suggested to one such cretin that perhaps they'd like me to read aloud from the book I was enjoying. (They didn't get it.)
13. Bad manners.

[Sam: Thank you.]

14. The high five and the fist bump. (The loss of the handshake is a terrible thing. There is something powerful and meaningful about taking the hand of another human being as a mark of respect and connection. What is meaningful about a fist bump?)

[Sam: *A huge argument I had on* Outlander *was that 'apparently' human beings didn't shake hands until after the 1700s. It's a pet peeve of mine. What absolute utter tripe. There are images of Romans/Greeks/Egyptians . . . dammit, children naturally take you by the hand, monkeys do . . . don't get me started!*]

15. Stores that say, 'What's your email address?' when you buy deodorant, or indeed anything at all. Stamps, paperclips. '*No!* I don't want to be on your fucking mailing list. Who in their right mind *would?*'

16. People who wear T-shirts saying 'VEGAN'. I once worked with an actor (in 1988) who wore a T-shirt with 'LEAVE ME ALONE' written on it. *That* was funny.

Lacroix and I both bought business cards (independently of each other!) that read, in very small writing, 'Please shut up.'

Ahem . . .

17. *Any* kind of bullying. A real trigger for me. I became a kind of vigilante in the mid 2000s. I was like Charles Bronson.

18. Weak handshakes (*make an effort!*). (See No.14.)

19. People who queue-jump and when I point out their selfish and colossal error, pretend they hadn't noticed you. I'm a 6'2" bald, bearded man of 200 pounds. I'm not inconspicuous. This trait is sadly particularly prevalent among the French. Even my French girlfriend admits this.

20. The ubiquity of the phrase 'No worries' to accompany every transaction.

    'I'm worried I might have a terminal illness.'
    'No worries.'

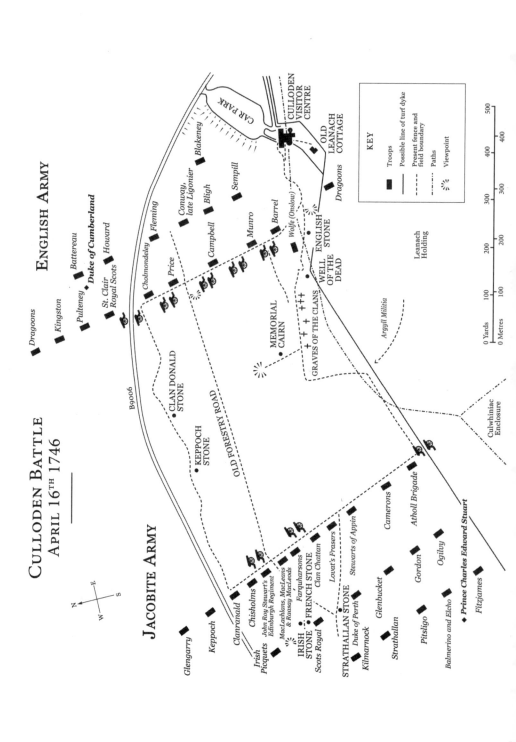

CULLODEN BATTLE
APRIL 16TH 1746

ENGLISH ARMY

JACOBITE ARMY

KEY

Troops

Possible line of turf dyke

Present fence and
field boundary

Paths

Viewpoint

0 Yards   100   200   300   400   500
0 Metres   100   200   300   400

CHAPTER THIRTEEN

Culloden

Skye Boat

Chorus:
Speed bonnie boat like a bird on the wing
Onward the sailors cry.
Carry the lad that's born to be king
Over the sea to Skye

1. Loud the wind howls
Loud the waves roar
Thunderclaps rend the air
Baffled our foes
Stand by the shore
Follow they will not dare

Chorus

2. Many's the lad fought on that day
Well the claymore did wield
When the night came
Silently lain
Dead on Colloden field

Chorus

3. Though the waves heave
Soft will ye sleep
Ocean's a royal bed
Rocked in the deep
Flora will keep
Watch by your weary head

Chorus

GRAHAM

The day has finally dawned and we are travelling to Drumossie Moor, site of the Battle of Culloden, which, on 16th April 1746, signalled the end of Highland culture and the decimation of the clan system. This is the part of the journey I have been looking forward to the most. I visited Culloden over thirty years ago and, although I remember it well, this time will be undoubtedly different because the jigsaw pieces of our road trip, the people we have met along the way, my wider reading of history and the Jacobite story recreated in *Outlander* will come together in one picture of understanding.

However, after all that tandem nonsense, I haven't slept well and am as stiff as a post. I'm currently sitting on the edge of my hotel bed unable to put my socks on without sounding like my dad in the twilight of his years.

Urghhh-eeearr-yuhhhuuupp!

[Sam: Very similar to the noises I hear most evenings, emanating from his hotel room.]

Damn that flamed-haired bawbag! He ruined Culloden for me in *Outlander*, too. Killing me off just before the battle started. Not going to Culloden was like a knife to the heart. No, it literally was. Fighting in the battle scene would have felt like honouring my ancestors as well as being a bloody great day at the office, but instead I got Prestonpans. Which was a lot of fun – we shot it inside a gigantic inflatable tent so that they could control the atmosphere inside, with horses charging, explosions, sword fights – a child's playground, *but* it wasn't Culloden.

Instead, I had to die at the hands of Clytemnestra (Claire) and her ginger hubbie. I mean, filming Dougal's death scene was fabulous but I wish it could have happened *after* Culloden. Culloden – the very name has a bite to it. The sound it makes in one's mouth. There is a finality in the name. It certainly echoes throughout history since that day in April 1746 and the battlefield has become a sacred shrine to the memory of the Highlands. For countless *Outlander* fans it has become a place of pilgrimage.

So whilst I try and get my other bloody sock on – my thighs are throbbing like Black Jack's crotch – let's get some context to the last battle fought on British soil. The Jacobite Rising of 1745 was a brief episode in British history, only nine months, from the raising of Bonnie Prince Charlie's standard at Glenfinnan to the battle that ended his hopes at Culloden. In an age when the army was a gentleman's occupation, there were few who really knew what they were doing in the Jacobite camp. Lord George Murray was one. MacDonald of Keppoch was another, along with Cluny MacPherson (who had practically been pressed into service by Cameron of Lochiel) and yet they took control of Scotland. It is tempting to imagine that this was because of their strength, their courage, their strategy.

Murray did his best to create a decent army, but on the eve of the Battle of Prestonpans (17th September 1745) no one knew how they'd perform. It's extraordinary to think that when they charged out of the mist and caught the raw British troops unawares, for most of the 2,500 Highlanders this was their first battle. Victorious at Prestonpans, no one can doubt the Jacobites' courage, but we also shouldn't doubt their luck. At Prestonpans they didn't face disciplined artillery fire using canister shot (similar to a giant shotgun being fired at close range).

The victory swelled numbers in Charles's army to 5,500 men

intent on marching to London and crowning their 'true king' but the rebels' artillery was rubbish and they didn't have enough cavalry to mount a single charge. The Highland Charge made up for this to a great extent. Who needs cavalry when you have hundreds of screaming Highlanders brandishing their fearsome broadswords and targes? They were the 'shock' troops of their age, especially trained to carry out sudden assaults.

By the time they reached Falkirk on 17th January 1746, they had learned how to fire a withering volley of musket fire into the charging horsemen of General Hawley, adding the Battle of Falkirk Muir to their battle honours. When they crossed the border into England they were met by much support – the ringing of bells, lighting of bonfires and people illuminating their houses to welcome them at Manchester. The Jacobite numbers continued to swell (although not in the numbers they had hoped) so why did Charles turn back at Derby? Why not push on to London as per the original plan? The Bonnie Prince certainly wanted to but his generals, in particular, Lord George Murray, persuaded him that without French support (which had been at best a dream and at worst downright lies) the rebel army was no match for the British army they would face in London. On 6th December 1745, known as 'Black Friday', they turned around and marched north from Derby.

The British had blockaded the Scottish coast (depriving Charles of French gold to keep his army fed and paid) and the only port the Jacobites still controlled was Inverness. It was defending the port (and the main roads up to it) that led them to make camp at Culloden Moor where they stayed for six long weeks before the eponymous battle took place.

In the end it wasn't Culloden that killed Highland Jacobitism. Even long after Culloden, Cumberland's successor as Commander in Chief, the Earl of Albemarle, still found plenty of willingness to fight against the Crown. No, what finished it was a growing realisation that the French could not be relied upon. Without them, they knew it was a lost cause.

[Sam: So we can blame the French for this? Is blaming the French still allowed?!]

[Graham: Absolutely!]

SAM

There's much less banter between us today because we are both thinking about Culloden and the visit ahead. It's the apex of our journey and poignant to us as Scotsmen (and members of the *Outlander* cast) because we know how incredibly significant this point in history was to our land of birth.

I first visited Culloden before starting work on *Outlander* and it coincided with my first fan experience. The Eden Court Theatre was screening a small independent movie I had shot in Brighton, England, and I had played the theatre some years before, in *Outlying Island*. I remember Inverness being a picturesque place, with the theatre sitting on the banks of the River Ness. However, that night the quiet city was to be besieged by one particular type of tourist: Heughligans – an *Outlander* fan group devoted to supporting anything to do with me! These ladies had been fans of Diana Gabaldon's books for twenty years and everyone and everything to do with the forthcoming show was a passion for them now, too.

I entered the theatre foyer and was greeted by a large cheer and an abundance of tartan. The Heughligans had organised a couple of coaches to ferry them from Edinburgh Airport (most travelling from the US or Europe) and were spending the weekend visiting *Outlander* sites and enjoying the Scottish food and culture. This was before the *Outlander* show was well known so the staff of the theatre looked on bemused as I was surrounded by a sea of excited women. Little did I know that this was only the start of things to come! I was flattered and rather surprised to see so many people there and, after sharing various hip flasks (whisky kills all germs and actually boosts your immune system: FACT), I made my excuses and set out to find my lodgings. The Heughligans, however, found a local ceilidh and danced the night away.

I was up early to visit the battlefield on a particularly grey and dreich morning. A melancholy mist covered the field so I could barely make out the flags marking the battle lines. The Culloden Experience Museum was closed and there wasn't a soul to be seen so I wandered aimlessly, looking for a rough guide or clue to the history of this place. Damp and cold to the bone, I stood alone on the moor. As the mist parted, the Fraser headstone, like the one

Claire visited, stood solemnly ahead of me, marking the mass grave of the renowned Scottish clan. I took a moment to reflect on my fictional character, Jamie – men like him were buried here, younger than me because they believed in a cause and fought for their way of life. A slow walk revealed more graves: Cameron, Campbell, MacDonald and MacLeod. Many rivals now joined together in death. The wind picked up and chilled me to the bone, driving me hurriedly from the battlefield.

That night, in a warm hotel, I planned a climb up neighbouring Ben Wyvis (try getting my business partner, Alex the German, to say that!), a brooding Munro near Dingwall.

Nearing the top, slipping in the snow and ice, I could see a dark storm was approaching over Culloden. A local climber in full mountaineering equipment passed me and stopped in shock. 'It's a bit blowy up the top, might want to think twice!' He set off down the mountain, his ropes and crampons a sure sign I was dreadfully underprepared in only my training shoes and leather jacket. I took a moment to admire the view, Culloden battlefield and the River Ness far off in the distance and vowed to return to conquer both the Munro and battlefield. Apparently Munro himself also didn't make it to the top of Wyvis.

So I find myself here years later, looking up Graham's kilt, which is not quite the return visit I had imagined. Eeewwwiiiee! It's a sight that would make a Highlander warrior wince; however, it's the girl-friends I feel sorry for (and there have been a few . . . !). I am showing the Grey Dog how to put on a great kilt, and after years of practice wearing one on *Outlander*, it's like second nature to me.

'This is the last time I ever help you get dressed!' I lie, thinking that squeezing him into a wetsuit and flippers would make TV gold! (Starz's *Men in Kilts* Season Two?) 'Scotland the Brave' is blasting from the next room as the Inverness Youth Pipe Band warm up, the base drum reverberating off the walls. The kids have swapped PlayStations for bagpipes and bravely agreed to play some tunes on the battlefield. Unfortunately, it's blowing a hooley on the moor, even windier than my last visit. Lady McT is ready, the kilt hanging off his hips, twinned with a scarf and fleece combo he's insisting on wearing but which is doing little to uphold his 'macho image'!

Wendy applies some make-up shaking her head disapprovingly at his 'old man fleecy'.

Outside the Pipe Band forms a human wall against the wind. A few are blown sideways and instantly scolded by the pipe master for being weak. 'My kind of man,' Graham enthuses.

Catriona, not Balfe, but McIntosh, is the visitor services supervisor at the Culloden Museum. One of our most engaging cameos, she leads us from the British side of the battlefield across no-man's-land to the Highlanders' side, where the Frasers stood alongside Bonnie Prince Charlie, facing down the enemy. 'On the day of the battle it was blowing a gale like today. They were standing here for twenty minutes, a volley of sustained cannon fire overhead, rain and sleet in their faces, waiting and waiting for the order to charge,' says Catriona. 'There's loud bangs, shouting, pipes playing in the Jacobite lines, pipes sounding from the government troops, smoke from cannons and muskets – it was sensory overload.'

The Jacobites rally themselves with battle cries. Graham and I push our chests out, walk forward towards the British surrounded by our pipers and beat our chests, shouting the Cameron clan war cry:

> *Oh sons of dogs, oh dogs of the breed,*
> *Come, come here, on flesh to feed!*

As we roar the words against the howling wind and rain like the Camerons had done some 200 years before, something dormant stirs inside us, creating an energy urging us to move forwards. We are ready! Our hardy pipe band answers our call and plays 'Scotland the Brave' – the shouting, war cries and pipe music are all significant in raising our mood levels to murderous intent.

Come on, Graham! Let's goooo!

GRAHAM

Standing on the bleak moor in the cold and rain with Sam, I conjure the brooding atmosphere that hangs over this national monument. I have stood on many historic battlefields, but none has affected me so deeply. To look out to where the British lines would have stood, today marked by fluttering flags two kilometres across, is to truly understand the scale of what the Jacobites faced that day.

The night before the battle (15th April) the rebels set off on a disastrous night march (attempting a pre-emptive strike on the Duke of Cumberland's camp at Nairn). 'If the night march had been successful they wouldn't have been fighting here,' explains Catriona.

However, they were forced to turn around after one of the two columns of men got disorientated in the dark (easily done without GPS and flashlights; don't forget, those were still the days of natural navigation). At 2am they marched twelve miles back but were seen by the British, who set off to Culloden at 5am, knowing the rebels would be now severely weakened. (And they really were. Over a thousand men slept through the battle due to exhaustion and malnutrition.)

In order to get the full experience, let's observe the battle through one of its participants: Alexander Campbell (yes, a Campbell, which goes some way towards dispelling the pervading myth about clan loyalties), a drover from Lochaber, thirty years of age. Alex fought with Cameron of Lochiel's Regiment, led by Colonel Donald Cameron of Lochiel, Chief of Clan Cameron, who bore the sobriquet 'Gentle Lochiel' (and lived at Achnacarry Castle).

Some 700 men in the regiment stood on the right of the Highland line, a position of honour, and it was from here they would charge first towards the British lines. Alexander had marched the night before to attack Cumberland's camp, and had returned dog-tired and dispirited amidst the monumental cock-up before the impending slaughter.

Five hundred feet above sea level, between the Moray Firth and the valley of the River Nairn, the land stretches twelve miles in a descending gradient from Loch Ness to the town of Nairn. It's bleak and treeless. Standing there on that April morning Alexander would have felt as if he were hanging between sea and mountain, and yet with quagmire under foot – the worst of all worlds. The sleet, carried by a biting wind blowing off the North Sea, stung the faces of men who had barely slept or eaten for days. To the south-east was a ragged group of beggars, men, women and children, ready to loot the dead like crows.

The words of Psalm 20, being sung by the Jacobites, floated across the lines of men.

The Lord hear thee in the day of trouble; The name of the God of Jacob defend thee;

Send thee help from the sanctuary, And strengthen thee out of Zion;

Remember all thy offerings, And accept thy burnt sacrifice; Selah.

Grant thee according to thine own heart, And fulfil all thy counsel.

We will rejoice in thy salvation, and in the name of our God we will set up our banners: The Lord fulfil all thy petitions.

Now know I that the Lord saveth his anointed; He will hear him from his holy heaven With the saving strength of his right hand.

Some trust in chariots, and some in horses: But we will remember the name of the Lord our God.

They are brought down and fallen: But we are risen, and stand upright.

Save, Lord: Let the king hear us when we call.

King James Bible

They would have used the 1611 King James Bible, the English translation of the biblical text sanctioned by Bonnie Prince Charlie's great-great-grandfather, King James I (VI Scotland), who essentially took a writing credit for the religious text. When you think of this religious history and the fervent belief that a monarch is 'chosen by God', it's little wonder Charles Edward Louis John Casimir Sylvester Severino Maria Stuart is propelled by blind faith and religious imperative to fight and take back what is rightly his.

[Sam: The man had a name longer than Jamie Fraser; incredible!]

And, a closer inspection of the House of Stuart family tree reveals *who* the Bonnie Prince is actually fighting. King George II is Charlie's third cousin (sharing James I as a great-grandfather), which makes George II's youngest son, Prince William, Duke of Cumberland, Charlie-boy's third cousin once removed. Okay, they're not brothers, or first cousins – William of Orange and Mary (both Stuarts) were first cousins who married each other! *But* the Hanoverians and Stuarts *are* all related to one another, descended from James I (VI of Scotland), which arguably makes Culloden a clan feud over power and religion (Protestantism vs. Catholicism) played out on a national scale. It is the clan feud to end all feuds and, indeed, the clans themselves.

THE HOUSE OF STUART
RULED ENGLAND AND SCOTLAND 1603-1714

JAMES VI
King of Scotland
(b. 1566 r. 1567-1625)
and JAMES I,
King of England and
Ireland (r. 1603-25)

= Anne, dau. of
FREDERICK II,
King of Denmark

Henry Frederick
Prince of Wales
(d. 1612)

Elizabeth = Frederick V,
(d. 1662)   Elector Palatine
            (d. 1632)

CHARLES I
King of England,
Scotland and Ireland
(b. 1600, r. 1625-49)

= Henriette Marie
dau. of HENRY IV,
King of France

Charles Louis
Elector Palatine
(d. 1680)

Rupert
(d. 1682)

Sophia = Ernest
(d. 1714 before   Augustus
ANNE)   Elector of
                  Hanover
                  (d. 1698)

Mary = WILLIAM II
(d. 1660)   of Orange
            (d. 1650)

CHARLES II
King of England,
Scotland and Ireland
(b. 1630, r. 1660-85)
m. Catherine dau.
of John, dau. of
Braganza, dau. of John,
King of Portugal

JAMES II
King of England, Scotland
and Ireland
(as JAMES VII),
(b. 1633, r. 1685-88, d. 1701)

= (1) Anne Hyde
dau. of Earl of
Clarendon

= (2) Mary
dau. of Duke
of Modena

Elizabeth   Anne   Henry   Henrietta = Philippe, Duke
                           Anne   of Orléans

WILLIAM III
King of England,
Scotland (as WILLIAM II),
and Ireland, Prince of Orange,
Stadtholder of Holland
(b. 1650, r. 1689-1702)

MARY II
Queen of England,
Scotland and Ireland
(b. 1662, r. 1689-94)

ANNE
Queen of England,
Scotland (Great
Britain from 1707),
and Ireland (b. 1665
r. 1702-14)

= George
son of
Frederick
III King of
Denmark
(d. 1708)

James Francis Edward = Maria Clementina
(The Old Pretender)   Sobieska
(1688-1766)   granddaughter
                        of JOHN III,
                        King of Poland

William
Duke of Gloucester
(1689-1700)

Joint sovereigns

Charles Edward
(The Young Pretender)
(1720-88) m. Louise,
dau. of Gustav
Prince of Stolberg-Gedern

Henry, Cardinal
of York
(d. 1807)
Last of the Royal
House of Stuart

GEORGE I = Sophia Dorothea
King of Great Britain   dau. of Duke of
and Ireland, Elector   Brunswick and
of Hanover (b. 1660,   Celle (div. under
r. 1714-27)   Hanoverian Law) 1694)

GEORGE II = Caroline
King of Great   dau. of Margrave of
Britain and Ireland,   Brandenburg-Ansbach
Elector of Hanover
(b. 1683, r. 1727-60)

Frederick Lewis
Prince of Wales
(1707-51)

William
Duke of Cumberland
(1721-65)

Other Children
-Anne, Princess Royal, m. WILLIAM IV, Prince of Orange
-Amelia
-Caroline
-Mary
-Louisa, m. FREDERICK V, King of Denmark

Augusta =
dau. of Frederick
of Saxe-Gotha
(d. 1772)

And, just as the leaders at the top are all related, so too we need an understanding of who the enemy on the ground was – and, you've guessed it, many were related. The Battle of Culloden was won by a British army and not an English one. The same British army that went on to win celebrated victories throughout the second half of the eighteenth century and right through the early nineteenth century, culminating in Waterloo. No fewer than four of the sixteen infantry battalions were Scottish, and there were plenty of Scottish officers as well as rank and file standing in the notionally English battalions too. Alexander would have seen men with his own surname standing 450 metres across the moor, shouting their war cry of 'Cruachan' (the Scottish Munro/Mountain near Loch Awe) as they killed for George II.

Of the 5,500 men of the rebel army gathered that day, many had been *forced* there, under the clan system, threatened with death, or at least the burning of their homes. Alexander was probably one of these men.

An example of 'recruitment' comes from a government intelligence report of the time:

> *Upon Thursday 15th August 1745 Cameron of Kinlochlyon, Cameron of Blairchierr, Cameron of Blairmachult, Cameron of Glenevis, and Cameron of Strone . . . came from Lochiel's country and entered Rannoch with a party of servants and followers to the number of about 24 and went from house to house on both sides of Loch Rannoch . . . and intimated to all the Camerons, which are pretty numerous on both sides of the loch, that, if they did not forthwith go with them, that they would that instant proceed to burn all of their houses and hough their cattle; whereupon they carried off the Rannoch men, mostly about one hundred, mostly of the name of Cameron.*

It's fair to assume that Alexander Campbell was one of those who was dragged along who was not a Cameron; hardly the romantic notion of the Highlander keen to get to grips with the evil English. The men who stood next to Alexander were a mix of all those types: men like himself, threatened into service, alongside romantic adventurers, diehard Catholics, deserters from the English army, French sympathisers, Lowlanders and proud clansmen. Some were undoubtedly drunk. Many broadswords were inscribed with the words 'Scotland' or 'No Union' so, in one sense, the fight that day was between those who longed for independence and those who wanted a union. (Although the Bonnie Prince would have ruled Scotland, England and Ireland should he have seized the throne.) It also marked a fork in the road for Scottish independence, the struggle for a different Scotland passionately rekindled in recent years, with Sam and I both publicly advocating and campaigning for an independent Scotland.

At the front stood the clan chief, his deputy, his piper and two of the best clansmen to form a bodyguard. Those in the first rank carried long firelocks, broadswords, dirks, and targes. Some would have had land, others none, but nevertheless they were deemed to be gentlemen. The second line carried the lesser gentry, and so with the third line. Some were six lines deep. Those at the back were bare-chested men, their beards and hair making them look more like savages from another age than soldiers. Some of these men barely carried any weapons at all.

Alexander is in the fourth line armed with his broadsword, dirk and targe, his plaid (kilt) tied high between his thighs so he can run more freely. In his bonnet, the white cockade of the Stuarts, a large knot of five bows in linen or silk with a laurel wreath containing the words: 'With Charles our brave and merciful P.R. [Prince Regent] we'll greatly fall or nobly save our country.' An oak leaf badge marks him as a Cameron.

Catriona points at the blue flags that identify where the Jacobite front line was, and 450 metres across the field, the government side is marked by red flags. 'The 8,000-strong British army line up in a straight formation, two kilometres across. The 5,500-strong Jacobite army tries to mirror the British line but, at the northern end, there is a deep bog so the Highlanders are forced to stand several hundred metres further back, breaking the line. This is to have a devastating impact on the Highland Charge,' she explains.

Lord George Murray was also worried about a protruding low enclosure to the right. He wanted those men to be able to negoti- ate the obstacle quickly when the charge began so, without advising anyone else, he moved the section of the line forwards. Already affronted by not being given the honour of standing on the right of the line (as had been their reward from the time of Bannockburn), the MacDonalds simply refused to move up to make the line straight. So we have something resembling a playground squabble developing down the line. The pipes of each clan compete with one another, the wind lifting the music across the moor until, suddenly, a rebel cannon is fired high across the British lines, missing the first and second lines before cutting a soldier in half at the rear.

The battle of Culloden has begun.

Alexander stands as cannonballs sweep through the lines: a rolling fire like the sound of a dozen iron doors slamming. The balls of iron seem to hang in the sky, arcing lazily towards the waiting rebels. He watches one bounce and smash into Malcolm Cameron as he screams his defiance, his head exploding into mist, the body collapsing like a felled tree.

Alexander turns his head to the right: Clan Chattan (the Mackintoshes, MacBeans and MacGillivrays) yell their battle cries of 'Loch Moy' and 'Dunmaglass' and begin to charge. Donald Cameron screams 'Claymore' and now he too must rush forwards, drawing his sword. He quickens his pace towards 2,623 bayonets under 461 British 'Redcoat' officers and non-commissioned officers (NCOs) drilled in the art of platoon volleys, each battalion divided into groups of twenty to thirty men, who have been trained to fire in a sequence of murderous shots, up and down the line, like a deadly Mexican wave.

However, at Culloden, the tactic has been changed. They have been taught the art of battalion volleys, ranks of three deep firing diagonally towards the centre, with the rear rank not firing until the screaming rebel army was only twelve paces away. *That* takes nerve! Imagine, a man sprinting towards you, glittering steel raised, his mouth open, howling a war cry in a language you probably don't understand. To the English private soldier these men were as terrifying as Zulu warriors. At Prestonpans, just the sight of them caused the raw recruits to break and run. At Culloden, however, the seasoned army held its nerve.

Alexander is unaware of what is happening to the left side of the Highland line. The MacDonalds have to cover 700 metres to reach the British, 250 metres more than on the right. Add to this, these men weren't just going over boggy ground; the water went halfway up their legs.

If you've ever run 700 metres you know what that feels like. Now imagine running it carrying a shield and a broadsword. Hungry. Cold. Sleep-deprived. Now imagine doing it while being shelled with round shot, peppered with grape shot and musket fire. The grape shot, 3cm in diameter, is tearing into the advancing clansmen at about 100 metres. The muskets wait for the order at fifty feet. Such is the pall of smoke and mist, Alexander and his brothers-at-arms collide into men of Clan Chattan: Camerons and Mackintoshes, long-standing feudal enemies, disorientated by the fog. Alexander and Clan Cameron lurch to the left to get a clear line of attack. At twenty yards the smoke lifts and he is confronted by a long line of white-gaitered legs and Redcoats, like a crimson wall. Waiting.

SAM

The rebel front line is in disarray. 'You want a Highland Charge to be released at the same time so it impacts at the same time,' explains Catriona. 'So the north needed to charge first, with the south waiting to accommodate the north's position further back. What actually happens is after twenty minutes of sustained cannon fire, the men at the southern end want to go so they run and the line is broken.'

Once they start the charge it takes them only a couple of minutes to cover the 450-metre distance. I'm tempted to recreate this charge to see if McTavish and I can make it. To test who arrives first, without needing a snack break. Starting at a gentle jog, about halfway they fire their muskets creating a smoke screen, then they scream war cries at the top of their lungs as they sprint the last fifty metres hell for leather, sword aloft, running straight into three-rounds-a-minute musket fire in formations. The front line fires first, then there's a six-second gap and the second line fires, then the third line, and it repeats, aimed at the legs to stop the Highlanders running.

The southern end of the charge gets to the government lines and 700 men break through Barrell and Munro's regiment, but the Duke of Cumberland has studied the Highland Charge and knows how it works. Cumberland is up front at the northern end. Bonnie Prince Charlie is up front amidst the action too. Catriona tells us many people think he was at the back but in fact he's right behind his front line. Both leaders are young men, Charles is twenty-six and Cumberland is ten days off his twenty-fifth birthday. Some of the 'men' fighting in the battle are as young as thirteen or fourteen.

The 700 rebels who break through soon find themselves encircled by soldiers led by General 'Hangman' Hawley and James Wolfe (of Quebec fame, of which more later!) and within two or three minutes all are dead or injured, including Frasers, McTavishes and McIntoshes (from Catriona's family).

At that precise moment the battle is over. The Jacobite retreat is sounded and the government army chases the rebels all the way to Inverness. In the sixty-minute battle, and the three days that follow, at least 1,500 Jacobites die. British government casualties are only counted as those that arose from the sixty minutes of battle and number fifty, but the mass grave discovered at the battlefield suggests the number is more like seventy-five.

GRAHAM

The Highlanders 'came running upon our front line like hungry wolves.' Alexander hears an Englishman bark, 'Make ready!' The British front rank drop as one to their right knee. He watches the muskets rise to face him. They wait until Alexander and his men are fifty feet from them . . . 'Fire!' Then the second rank, 'Fire!' and the third, 'Fire!', decimating the men around him. Some throw up their plaids to shield themselves. A .75 calibre lead ball from a brown bess musket is accurate at fifty feet and the recovered bullets found by archaeologists tell a horrifying story. Many bullets show only slight traces of impact, having passed into, and often straight through the fleshy parts of the body. When the same bullet hits a bone it is flattened by the impact. At close range the red-hot lead bullet will actually take on the warp and weft of the fabric worn by the victim. Some bullets turned into the shape of a clamshell, almost split in two as they hit the hard edge of an upraised broadsword.

Despite the sustained battalion volleys, some break through the first rank, only to be cut down by the bayonets behind. But still the British lines stand firm. Big John MacGillivray of Clan Chattan smashes through, his sword arm swinging in bloody arcs, killing twelve soldiers single-handedly; he is on his way to the next battalion at the rear when he is finally cut down. Alexander can hear the sound of broadswords smashing on muskets. He ploughs through the line and encounters Colonel Rich of the Barrell's regiment, standing on foot. The Colonel holds out his slender sword to parry Alexander but the Campbell broadsword takes off the man's sword hand at the wrist. Alexander can only see what is in front of him, the tunnel vision of battle gripping his senses. Behind him, 'the heather writhed with the injured and dying.'

When the collapse comes most of the Highlanders are forced to flee along the Inverness road where they received no quarter from the British cavalry pursuing them. Our hero is taken prisoner; his fate, 'transportation' to the colonies, common for many of the 154 rebel prisoners and 222 'French officers and soldiers'. Many of the rebels are hanged; those who escaped were hunted down, and their properties were burned or taken.

Much has been made of the behaviour of the British troops after the battle. It was undoubtedly a vengeful, gruesome affair. However, those British troops had learned lessons the hard way when it came to facing these particular 'men in kilts'. From their experience at the Battle of Falkirk they knew that they were in a brutal stand-up fight against a ruthless enemy that was guilty of murdering men in cold blood. They had seen their own Colonel Munro wounded and finished off as his brother was bandaging him. His brother was also killed on the spot.

This, and the butchery at Prestonpans, all contributed to the belief that they were not fighting chivalrous-minded professionals, but murderous thugs, and should respond accordingly. Dougal MacKenzie's actions at the end of Prestonpans, deliberately murdering the wounded, appalled at good treatment of British prisoners, speak of this brutality.

However, in spite of the slaughter and men shot for cowardice, it is the bravery and the courage I want to think about most deeply as

I stand on the battlefield side by side with Sam. And, about my own ancestors, fourteen of whom are listed in the muster rolls.

The McTavishes fought as part of the Fraser of Lovat's group (yes, Simon the Fox Fraser, whom we met earlier). Even then my ancestors couldn't escape the Frasers! I like to imagine one of my ancestors – bald, bearded, perhaps drinking the equivalent of an eighteenth-century latte – looking across at the man next to him, a tall ginger-haired, energetic lunatic who was probably doing one-armed press-ups just before we charged, and then afterward was there at the 'exits' trying to flog his branded Culloden memorabilia! *[Sam: Yours were definitely wearing scarves.]*

The Frasers (and McTavishes) charged with the right wing of the Highlanders along with the Camerons (those sons of dogs, dogs of the breed!), Clan Chattan, and the Stewarts of Appin. Casualties were severe with as many as 250 killed. Their colonel, Charles Fraser, was injured and then shot in cold blood either on the orders of the Duke of Cumberland, or General 'Hangman' Hawley (I wonder if his friends called him that to his face!). The future General Wolfe, of Quebec fame, refused to act as executioner.

SAM

There were three James Frasers killed at Culloden but no James Alexander Malcolm MacKenzie Fraser. It's extraordinary to think that on that freezing day of 16th April 1746 you even had a 'Dougal McTavish' (a hybrid of Graham and his *Outlander* character), a 'Jamie Fraser' and a cohort of MacKenzies all charging into battle together. One wonders how well they knew each other (after all, they'd been together for a while). Had they already fought along-side one another? Perhaps they had shared the meagre amount of food together. But one thing is for certain: they would have run towards those British lines together, screaming their clan war cries, and were among the very few who made it to the British lines.

GRAHAM

The muster roll does not contain the names of all present at the battle, only those for whom records were kept. It is entirely possible that at the close of battle, McTavishes, Frasers and MacKenzies lay dead, side by side, on the cold ground of Culloden Moor.

The McTavishes are listed as finally surrendering in Inverness on 17th May 1746, almost exactly a month after the battle. One can only imagine what they went through for those thirty-one days. Evading government troops, hiding where they could, until, like so many others, starvation forced them to surrender.

SAM

You can only hope the McTavishes who fought at Culloden had more grit than the latte-loving ladyship that stands before me, because imagine poor James Fraser standing next to someone who looked the part until, after standing around for too long on the moor, wanted to put his wee scarf and fleecy on and needed a snack . . . and then a coffee . . . moaning, 'Urgh, will they just get on with it?! We've been here twenty minutes, lumps of metal falling out of the sky, freezing our man nipples off. I want to go and cleave some heads in!' And then finally the signal to charge comes but Graham – 'is not ready yet!' – and is spilling his latte on his brand new fleece, and he hasn't tucked his plaid into his thermals!

However, when he's ditched the coffee and is properly tucked in, he charges through the enemy lines raging with anger and battle cries, wielding his broadsword like a scythe through butter. His eyes are wild, he's splattered in blood, he has a six-pack drawn on with mud, snarling and shouting: 'Come on your bastards. Come *on!*'

Brave and savage, he is the epitome of a warrior . . . for a full five minutes. Before needing a little sit-down because – ah – cramp! I've got cramp! But there is no director shouting 'Cut' in this scene. And Jamie's already lying in the heather, his mortal enemy on top of him.

For two seasons, with the backdrop of the Battle of Culloden fast approaching, 'Black Jack' Randall would become Jamie Fraser's most feared enemy. He has a thing for lavender oil and for Jamie. Having been raped and tortured by him, Jamie had come to terms with and, indeed, 'cut out' the memory of his vile deeds, only for 'Black Jack' to appear again at Versailles in Paris in Season Two. Now, amidst the Culloden battlefield (Episode One, Season Three), covered in blood and sweat, Jamie spies his enemy amongst the

violence. He smiles, knowing that his fate is to die on the battlefield
with the rest of the Scots, but at least he will get the chance to take
vengeance on the sadistic British officer (played by the brilliant
Tobias Menzies), or die trying.

We rehearsed the final showdown for weeks. Everyone was
excited to shoot the famous battle, made all the more poignant that
it was the last time I would work with Tobias. He is a softly spoken,
charming and generous actor. His natural features, with deep
creases down his face, serve like scars from a previous battle and, in
spite of being such a nice guy, he plays the most excellent villain.
Before a take, I'd see Tobias raise his shoulders and snort like a wild
boar, as he channelled his predatory, vicious energy. His torture of
Jamie is methodical and emotionless – he is a psychopath in every
sense, unable to empathise with or understand his victims. He is
fascinated by Jamie's sense of honour and passion for Claire because
he doesn't understand loyalty or love.

We shot the battle sequence over two weeks during the Scottish
summer of 2016. Every day hundreds of extras would gallantly line
up and run across the battlefield, take after take. It was quite a workout, I remember going to shoot after an intense session at gym and
my legs were like lead. I recall the extras sweating, exhausted and
laughing whilst recounting their scuffles with the Redcoats. One had
even broken his leg whilst running toward the enemy line. To thank
them for their hard work, I ordered a bunch of pizzas one night (but
really it was to slow them down so I didn't have to run as fast!).

The battle was chaotic. Everyone knew their place amongst the
larger battle but there were several groups who had set actions that
could be moved around. The showdown between Tobias and me
was to be in the midst of the madness. Cannons roared and 'squibs'
(small explosions) were set off as I ran past – it was absolutely terrifying because you couldn't see where they were in the chaos, until
one blew up in your face!

The fight between Tobias and me was strange and poetic. We
were to die in each other's arms in an embrace – the two characters
tied in blood and fate, their stories interconnected. During the fight,
our characters lose themselves and enter a dreamlike world. A
nightmare, surrounded by fire and death, they have been fighting so

long they are hallucinating. Eventually, the lethal blows are struck, 'Black Jack' severs my femoral artery and then falls onto my sword. In his last moments he calls to Jamie and I believe you can almost hear him whisper, 'Claire?'

Having sent Claire, pregnant with his child, safely back through the stones, Jamie is released to die with his men on the battlefield. Earlier we had shot a sequence when Murtagh (Duncan Lacroix) appears and saves Jamie during a fight. I had been suffocating a man in the mud, beating his brains out with a rock, the violence messy and animalistic. Murtagh is prepared to die by Jamie's side and Jamie is thankful he's there.

We shot the night-time sequence with all the bodies on the field, the aftermath and mass destruction of the Jacobite army. Tobias was replaced by a stuntman and then a dummy, as we had to lie there most of the night. Jamie bleeds out and approaches death. Wendy appears; she's been having a blast the last few days. 'A bloody hot mess' is how she describes the Jamie look. Muddy, bloody, but always looking his best. There's a photo of me, holding a coffee, week two, dazed, tired and covered in sticky fake blood. The blood is so sweet, it attracts the summer wasps and you have to be very careful when you sit down that one hasn't gone up your blood-stained kilt!

Jamie was finally about to die and it was strange because I had sweated off all the make-up and now looked extremely clean. Wendy wanted Jamie to look porcelain, deathly white and cold. The post production team thought this strange so we had to reshoot much of the sequence, which was a shame as in the original shoot I'd virtually lost my voice from screaming, so my breathing was laboured and raspy. It added a real death-rattle to the whole dreamlike sequence. Just as Jamie is about to take his last breath, Claire appears in a dream and he realises he wants to live. Jamie is rescued by a few Highlanders and carried to safety off the battlefield; however there is one last surprise that our showrunner Ron Moore wanted to shoot. Back on the battlefield, the corpse of 'Black Jack' Jonathan Randall, deathly pale with bloodstained lips, opens his eyes and takes a large breath. The producers wanted to keep their options open on whether to bring him back. But, of course, they didn't.

It was here we said goodbye to many popular characters and, of course, the Highland way of life. Jamie survives, however many of the original cast do not. Shooting the last scenes, especially the execution of Rupert and other Highlander crew, was deeply moving and really sad as we had become a tight band of performers who had all been through a lot together. Grant gets on with the business of dying honourably giving a note-perfect final performance and Jamie survives, but as a shadow of himself. Not wanting to live without Claire, he at first is catatonic, lost, then feral and alone. Claire's ghost haunts him and he lives within the memory of her, unable to engage properly in the real world. Finally, he finds some peace at Hellwater in England, resigning himself to being a servant and groomsman for the rest of his life. As an actor, Season Three for me was the most rewarding to shoot. The story was so strong for Jamie and all the guises he has to assume to survive – Dunbonnet, MacDubh, Mac the Groomsman and eventually, Alexander Malcolm, the printmaker. He goes on to rebuild himself and his life, without his true love. It was so sad and bittersweet to go to work each day, playing a man who is only half of himself. However, eventually, Claire returns to him (through the stones once again) and they find themselves on a journey to Jamaica and the New World so the production travels to South Africa, to shoot on the boats and sets outside of Cape Town. I found myself there years later, shooting *Bloodshot* with Vin Diesel, desperate to see the tall ships we used still sitting in the desert, driven around on four wheels like they were sailing.

The Battle of Culloden marks the decimation of the Highland clans and their way of life and is a pivotal moment for Scotland. Only four years later (1750–1860), a silent revolution began in the Highlands (and later the Lowlands) as the 'cottars', who lived in cottages and farmed small lots of land, and tenant farmers were forcibly evicted to make way for sheep. Undoubtedly a part of the Agricultural and Industrial Revolutions happening across Europe, many historians feel it was also a form ethnic cleansing of the pugnacious Highlanders who had been a thorn in the side to all invaders or powers who tried to quell or subjugate them.

John Prebble in *Glencoe* writes, 'The Highland people were once the majority of Scotland's population, a military society that had largely helped to establish and maintain her monarchy. This society, tribal and feudal, could not change itself to meet a changing world, nor did it wish to.'

During the 'Clearances' it's estimated that 70,000 people left the Western Highlands and Isles between 1760 and 1803, although no one can be sure as many left no record of their departure. Overcrowding and repeated famines hit the 'crofters' (formerly farmers) left behind who were unable to work the land that had been communally shared for generations; the land was now owned by landlords and lairds running estates as businesses, which were expected to turn a profit. Around the time of the Scottish Potato Famine (1846–56) the Highlands lost *one third* of their population to emigration.

Just nine years after Culloden it's estimated that just over 50% of the Scottish population lived in the Highlands; by 1981 it was 21%, much of the heritage and traditions lost forever. However, some of the culture lived on in the Scots communities who settled in the 'New World', particularly in North America, which is possibly why *Outlander* has captured the imagination of so many Canadian and American fans today.

In the direct aftermath of Culloden all weapons were banned, plaid and Highland dress was outlawed and the bagpipes were declared by the government as a 'weapon of war', only to be played by certain people, such as the Highland regiments of the British army. Gathering in large groups was also off the list which, given we have been writing this book during the coronavirus lockdown of 2020, we all know how tough it is not seeing family, friends or clansmen.

Contrary to popular belief, Gaelic wasn't banned after Culloden (as it has been in 1616). Instead, there was a continual creeping death caused by British educational policy (making English the first language) and a unity between (unequal) trading partners who needed to conduct business in the international language of trade: English.

Catriona explains the only way the Highlanders could start to get certain freedoms back was to assimilate or join the British army in order to protect what was left of their culture. So that's exactly what happened and it explains why General James Woolf, aged nineteen, was fighting the Highlanders on the British side at Culloden, but only twelve years later was to fall mortally wounded into the arms of a Fraser Highlander on the Heights of Abraham after taking Quebec. A regiment of 1,500 Fraser Highlanders (the 78th Regiment) had been raised by the clan and sent to America to fight alongside the British, helping to win Canada for George II.

GRAHAM

For me the Jacobite story is but one chapter in the rich history of Scotland. One of the things that got me involved in the study of history generally is that it always reveals there were no easy answers. Scotland is no exception to this. Hence why I studied Glencoe so thoroughly – I wanted to see beyond the binary version of events. Good/bad, heroes/villains, black/white. As with Glencoe, the Jacobite Risings are a fantastic example of how history can be perverted. There *are* some incontrovertible facts. It *did* mark the end of Highland culture. Atrocities against the local populace *were* committed by the Crown. But beyond that, it becomes a matter of perspective. The love of the underdog, particularly in Scottish culture (just look at our football team!), leads to a romantic view of Jacobitism. The handsome prince trying to reclaim his homeland. The skirl of the pipes, brave Highlanders plunging to their deaths. But perhaps we should ask, what would Britain have been like if Charlie boy *had* won at Culloden?

Britain would have fallen under the control of Catholicism and, by extension, Rome.

Many, many people were *very* afraid of that outcome.

The lot for the average Scottish Highlander would not necessarily have improved (although admittedly they would have been spared having their crofts burnt down). Would the Highland Clearances have happened? Probably. As we have shown, clan chiefs were not necessarily known for their love of the common man. Many, however, had a great love for wealth. *Outlander* is, at its core, romantic fiction. Enjoyable and popular, but dramatic fiction nevertheless, and as such it needs villains and heroes; it can't necessarily afford the nuance or close examination of history that reflects what actually happened.

Arguably, one of the most interesting conflicts in the series was the one between Colum and Dougal. Dougal, the headstrong romantic Jacobite; Colum the leader who had to make *hard* choices. He was a character who reflected how real clan chiefs had to think, as instanced by the different branches of the same clan covering both sides, Jacobite and Crown, in order to survive.

SAM

So what became of the Bonnie Prince? Well, this part really does play out like something from the pages of romantic fiction – he hides out in the moors and mountains, evading capture with the assistance of many clans, none of them betraying him despite the £30,000 bounty on his head (which in today's money is around £5.5 million!). And he is famously helped by Flora MacDonald, who takes him in a small boat to the Isle of Skye, disguised as her Irish maid, 'Betty Burke'. Charles returns to Paris, and later Rome, continuing to live a louche life of wine, women and song (as portrayed by Andrew Gower in Season Two), conducting many affairs, one even with his first cousin (what are the upper classes like?) before dying in obscurity in 1788.

After a bracing day on the moor Graham gives me a hug. 'Thank you for today and for helping make this trip happen.' I hug him back. A man so passionate about Scotland and so well versed in its history, it is my pleasure to share the journey with him.

We raise our hip flasks to all those souls who perished on that cold April day on Culloden moor. Graham makes a toast to his ancestors and to John Tovey, a private in Munro's 367th regiment of foot, who was fifty-nine years of age (Graham's age) when his jaw was shot away that day in April 1746.

We are running out of light and once again darkness is claiming the battlefield. Yet we have one more surprise to honour the fallen. Piobaireachd, literally meaning 'pipe playing', is the classical music of the Great Highland Bagpipe. After the banning of bagpipes they created mouth-music, a way to continue to pass on the music

through word of mouth, and Ian, a young clan chief and master
piper, plays us a slow lament.

It's the hauntingly beautiful 'Moladh air Piob-Mhor Mhic
Cruimein' ('In Praise of MacCrimmons Pipes') by Clanranald poet
Alasdair mac Mhaighstir Alasdair (*c.*1695–1770).

> *Thy chanter's shout gives pleasure,*
> *Sighing thy bold variations.*
> *Through every lively measure;*
> *The war note intent on rending,*
> *White fingers deft are pounding,*
> *To hack both marrow and muscles,*
> *With thy shrill cry resounding . . .*
> *You shamed the harp,*
> *Like untuned fiddle's tone,*
> *Dull strains for maids,*
> *And men grown old and done:*
> *Better thy shrill blast,*
> *From gamut brave and gay,*
> *Rousing up men to the destructive fray.*

CHAPTER FOURTEEN

The Great Escape

*Life's journey is not to arrive at the grave safely in a well-preserved
body, but rather to skid in sideways, totally worn out shouting
'Holy Shit, what a ride!'*
**Hunter S. Thompson, The Proud Highway: Saga of a
Desperate Southern Gentleman**

SAM

Graham is surprisingly chipper this morning and hasn't complained
once about my driving or his knees being wedged against the dashboard. He is entertaining me with squeaky impressions of the tiny
Highland coo dangling by the neck from our rear-view mirror. I
think he might have actually *relaxed*. He even said he'll *think* about
getting on a motorbike later today.

That's not just progress, it's a bloody *miracle* given the hissy fit he
threw over kayaking. Oh, let's not forget the tandem!

I take a bend faster than I should, throwing Merlin off the sofa bed into the toilet – argh! Sorry! Graham doesn't flinch, now deep in conversation with the coo and doing his best Arnold Schwarzenegger impression.

Arnie: You are zo strong, dareleeng coo. Mighty and hairy. You remind me off me.

Coo (falsetto voice): Oh, Mr Schwarzenegger you're such a tease!

Arnie: And ve are both vegan.

Coo: You're no from around here are ye, pal?

We have a full itinerary ahead of us with some strongman lifting of stones and a visit to Rob Roy MacGregor's grave, as played by Liam Neeson in the film *Rob Roy* and, of course, captured in the eponymous novel by Sir Walter Scott. To be honest, Finlarig Castle was a bit of an afterthought – we liked the look of it because it was a ruin and connected to the famous MacGregors, many of whose heads ended up in a pit here, as we were about to find out. After a short journey we park up in a farmyard near the ruins next to some rusting farm machinery. Expecting a farmer or someone in overalls and jeans to welcome us in this rural setting, we are instead confronted by a small private army dressed in combat fatigues, wielding walkie-talkies. Graham is taken aback and, at that moment, I tell him that, according to Clan MacGregor and the current owner, Mons Bolin, Finlarig Castle has the 'darkest history in Scotland'.

'Welcome to Finlarig,' says one of the monotone military men, while the other, more unnervingly, starts to serenade us with a sombre piece on a guitar and mouth organ (which he has pulled from nowhere). It's like a scene from James Bond when the evil henchmen beguile the 'goodies' with displays of bizarre behaviour just before the fight scene breaks out. We stand and watch 'Duncan' play awkwardly; the other silently monitors us with cold eyes and a 1,000-mile stare. I shudder to think what they make of us two namby-pamby actors, arriving in an oversized fridge, wearing woolly tweed and what could be described as a dress, my kilt all limp and wrinkled after Graham got it soggy at Culloden yesterday. Graham has come as a gamekeeper in a 'shooting coat' and tweed cap on top but then he's teamed it with skinny jeans and Shoreditch brogues on the bottom half, revealing his true lovey credentials. We feel weak and unmacho.

Across the farmyard, there's an armoured personnel carrier parked by an outbuilding, presumably out of action, as another private mercenary is bent over the hood inspecting the engine. *Maybe he could give our camper the once-over, install an extra bit of horse-power and saw off the exhaust,* I muse. Suddenly Finlarig Castle-owner, Mons Bolin *[Graham: Which sounds a bit like a sailing knot. 'Secure your boat with a Mons Bolin . . .']* is striding towards us, sporting a beret and holding a stick under his arm like a commanding officer. Duncan stops playing and the mechanic stands to attention. I stand up straight, shoulders back and puff out my chest. Graham also stands bolt upright, looking like he's about to give a salute. He looks at me with wide eyes as if saying, 'Where *are* we?' and, 'Do we get to live in the end?'

Mons is standing in front of us, looking us up and down like he's inspecting his new recruits. He has a firm handshake. And, as we covertly nurse our crippled hands, he announces loudly to Graham, myself and all the nearby huddled crew that, yes, the insignia on his beret is, indeed, Swedish Special Forces. We all nod our heads pretending that he has answered the exact question on all our minds.

But what if Mons really *is* Swedish Special Forces? He looks about seventy, so it could be unlikely, but then again . . . I start thinking about all the multiple disciplines he could have trained in and suddenly hear myself asking him . . . no, grilling him . . . about it. 'I mostly specialised in covert water assault,' he informs me with unblinking eyes. I believe him. And so does Graham, who shifts uneasily in his gamekeeper get-up, betraying nerves by fiddling with his tweed cap. 'Have you ever killed a man with your bare hands?' asks Graham. I look at him in shock. I can see he is a man under stress and genuinely needs to know . . . but *really?* You want to ask that *now?* Of a man guarded by a small militia with a cache of military hardware? Mons shrugs and says, 'Follow me, gentlemen.'

'I see your APC [armoured personnel carrier] isn't working,' I say, trying to make small talk. I make it worse by telling him I've just shot an SAS movie with Andy McNab – as if this might give me a 'way in', or at least a small hope that the mute mercenaries won't make us die too slowly.

'Oh don't worry, it will be fixed shortly and we have plenty of toys around the grounds to deter the enemy,' he says. He marches off apace, his cane under his right arm, and Graham and I fall in behind him, mirroring his military style with our umbrellas. Not quite the crack unit of storm troopers that Mons is used to; I think Graham may even have a slight limp. Perhaps creating a war wound narrative to inspire clemency later? Duncan, the tall, dark, silent one, has put away his one-man band and disappears into the undergrowth. Possibly in a flanking manoeuvre . . .

The rain was beginning to come down as we made our way through the dripping trees. There, hidden from the road, was an eerie sight. A small, grey, square castle, impenetrable from most sides, with a gaping black pit in front. It was silent in the wood, no wildlife, as if the birds had seen our approach, or maybe there was no life at all. 'Dreich,' Mons said, his pseudo clipped military accent dropped for a Scottish burr. 'Aye, Finlarig in Gaelic means Holy Pass,' Mons told us, rolling his Rs. 'Once the home of the MacGregors, it came into the Campbells' hands though they never vanquished it, they purchased it.' The Campbells. Always some sort of shady history, always on the winning side. I'm sure they used their cunning to acquire the castle without too much bloodshed. I pulled my collar up, the chill and damp getting into my bones; the black history or dark atmosphere of the castle was beginning to reveal itself. The rain clouds seemed to frame the building, lying low to prevent us from seeing it whole. The trees behind us rustled and I knew we were not alone. Silent Duncan, or one of the men employed to always keep us in their sights. I moved the conversation forward. Or tried to. Mons was well prepared, like he'd done this before, rehearsed the narrative with military precision. He told us about the history of the dark castle.

GRAHAM

I've always preferred ruins to well-maintained castles. Like a good book, they allow you to use your imagination to fill in the gaps. You also find fewer people (no tacky gift shops selling Highland cow toys, maps of *Outlander* locations or Sassenach products!). You are really able to connect with the building, touch it, wander at your leisure and conjure up the living history around you. What

I hadn't expected was our guide to be the Swedish version of John Rambo.

Firstly, to history. Finlarig is, yes, you've guessed it, another Campbell castle. While other clans struggled on with one, maybe two castles if they were lucky, the Campbells always thought big. And one of the biggest thinkers was the guy who refurbished this ghostly gaff in 1609, none other than good old 'Black Duncan'. I mean, this fella never stopped. If he wasn't busy building Balcardine Castle, or renovating and expanding Kilchurn, he was laying the foundations for Achallader Castle and Lochdochart. Sometimes you feel like B.D. was some kind of seventeenth-century property developer/architect/badass. As his name 'Black Duncan of the Seven Castles' implies, he owned seven castles by the time he was sixty. I don't know what's more impressive, the number of castles or that he was still alive at sixty.

By the time he died at the staggering age of eighty-one, he owned 438,000 acres of lands stretching over 100 miles. His appetite for land led to the rumour that he tried to murder our old friend Campbell of Cawdor, as well as seeking to have the whole Clan MacGregor outlawed so he could add to his gargantuan property portfolio. You can't help thinking that he spent every waking moment planning how to just get *more* land, and that when he lay on his deathbed breathing his last, he regretted not building eight castles and owning a further 400,000 acres. That's the thing about chaps like Black Duncan, plenty is never quite enough. I can see him at Finlarig stroking a white cat on his lap, planning world domination. [Sam: I can see Mons doing that too.]

Just like Kilchurn Castle, this one was home to government troops during the Jacobite rebellions of 1715 and 1745. As a mark of royal favour, Black Duncan had James I (VI of Scotland) and Queen Anne of Denmark's royal coat of arms over the entrance dated 1609. This acted as a gigantic 'Fuck you' to anyone unwise enough to think of taking it over. Here lived a man (with six other holiday castles) with connections.

But to Mons . . . Michelle had already told us he was a character. But, as with so much of this trip, nothing could have prepared us for the reality. We arrive in our caravan followed by our motley crew, park up and wander into a cobbled yard next to a farm outbuilding with open sides and a roof *[Sam: aka a barn!]*. Inside is the usual detritus of farm life: tarpaulins, bales of hay, hoes, and shovels. But one thing dominates the barn: an armoured personnel carrier, complete with a .50 calibre mounted Browning machine gun. Obviously farming is done differently around here. Perhaps the sheep respond well to being chased across open fields by an armoured vehicle spraying bullets.

'Do you see that?' I ask Sam.

'Yes, unusual,' he says, stating the bleeding obvious.

I am still digesting this troubling sight when I see a figure approaching from the farmhouse. He is wearing a soft green beret, tweed jacket, plus fours, long socks, stout shoes and is carrying a stick with the head of a ram carved into the top. This must be Mons. Simultaneously, two other gentlemen arrive from the other direction. We all make our introductions, Mons speaking with an unusual cadence that makes me immediately sure he's 'not from round these parts'. And I'm spot on because it turns out he's Swedish, and not just any common-or-garden Swedish, no, Swedish Special Forces Swedish, his beret sporting a golden trident.

His two friends, Duncan and Johnny, are both ex-Black Watch regiment. Johnny shakes hands and sits on a ruined sofa in the barn, possibly about to sharpen bayonets, or field-strip a Bren Gun blindfolded. Duncan is a giant – six foot five at least. He is trying to give us his gentlest handshake but it still resembles being caught in a mangle. I think I can see tears springing from Sam's eyes as he is gripped by the paw of Duncan.

After these introductions, I address the proverbial elephant in the room. 'Erm . . . Mons. Why do you have an armoured personnel carrier in your barn?'

And these are his exact words: 'Ah yes, you see Duncan and Johnny are like, well, my home guard. We have a number of "toys" on the property. It helps to keep away unwelcome visitors. No one fucks with us here.'

A heavy silence descends and I gently soil myself. Sam is smiling and nodding, as though an armed encampment in the Highlands run by ex-soldiers is the most normal thing in the world, but inside

I suspect his mind is racing as fast as mine. The crew looks on aghast, but then that has become their default expression for this entire trip.

I look around, as if seeing things for the first time. Duncan and Johnny, lounging on the sofa, are looking at us without expression. Mons is dressed like a nineteenth-century laird, one who sports an ex-Special Forces beret. I scan the horizons to see if there is an enormous Wicker Man waiting for us in a field. All clear on that front, and then the penny drops.

Black Watch, Special Forces, Scottish/Swedish, these are guys who had met 'on operations'. Ex-mercenaries?! I gulp. And suddenly I realise who Mons looks like: a sixty-year-old Rutger Hauer. After that epiphany I expect him to whisper: 'Time to die . . . Graham.'

Time to look at the castle.

Mons is relishing his role as tour guide and he is actually rather fantastic at it. He gives us the rundown on the history and leads us to a 3.5m x 2m hole that resembles a mass grave. It turns out to be wittily known as the 'beheading pit'. In one corner lies a rusted chain that was used to manacle prisoners overnight because, as it turns out, the Campbells were very big on trials. Invariably short trials and ones that did not end well for the defence, especially if your last name was MacGregor.

Conducted at 'Judgement Hill' in a densely wooded area, set back from the castle, the laird would sit at the top of a mound with steps cut into the earth, rough stone slabs set into them, and convey his judgement. Perhaps Black Duncan sat on this very hill, I'm willing to bet dressed in black. Sam climbs the steps like a mountain goat and I carefully pick my way up to receive my judgement.

Now, I should pause here to emphasise that Finlarig Castle is a seriously creepy place. And, not just because of the armoured car, or the giant Jock with hands like a Kodiak bear, or Mons's disturbing habit of grinning conspiratorially at every other moment. The place 'feels' evil. I'm not one for dramatics [Sam: ha ha!], or ghosts, or haunted houses, but Finlarig definitely has a dark feel to it.

I climb the worn stone steps and think of all those who have (literally) gone before. No trial, just judgement. If you were a common man and found guilty, you were instantly hanged. If you were noble you were invited to spend the night chained up in the beheading pit and then you would have your swede nobly removed from your shoulders in the morning. [Graham: Swede, like what you did there!] Well, more likely the next evening at a Black (Duncan) Tie event. They would have drinks and dinner in the castle banqueting hall overlooking the pit and then pop out for a little after-dinner entertainment, watching a few prisoners' heads tumble. Followed by a little dancing and more refreshments, it would be a hell of a night.

The tree used for hanging was eventually cut down sometime in the twentieth century. The 'dangling' bough apparently had a deep groove cut into it from the volume of hangings. As Sam and I let these morbid musings crowd our thoughts, Duncan is now going hard on the bagpipes, sending mournful notes filled with foreboding into the trees. I can't help wondering if Mons is actually going to let us leave. And, come to think of it, we haven't seen Wendy for a while . . . !

We casually saunter back to our vehicles (but inside I want to leg it). I can hand on heart say I have never been so pleased to see the Fiat Fiasco in all my life. We drive away at speed and I look back in the wing mirror and see the three figures of Duncan, Johnny, and Mons standing shoulder to shoulder, arms folded, watching intently as we leave the grounds, before slowly returning to their toys, somehow disappointed, but not before I spot a large fluffy white cat joining them.

SAM

'Always have a beheading pit when building a castle,' says Mons. I see he's not joking and order Graham to get in with the tip of my umbrella. Not wanting to look soft in front of our hardened guide, Graham eases himself down into the muddy pit, slipping on the wet grass and landing heavily. What better way to test Lady McTavish's mettle, than to order him to his doom? The prisoners – many MacGregors – were left there for twenty-four hours before having their heads removed in front of a morbid crowd. I wondered if Graham would want to recreate that. As Mons and I wander away pretending to leave him there, I tell Mons more about my Andy McNab film.

It's nearing lunchtime and I can hear Graham's belly grumble from inside the headless pit. 'Time to crack on,' Mons orders and we beat a retreat back to the camper van (and clapped-out armoured car). We have to make it to Balquhidder by the afternoon as we have a date with a rock and Rob Roy.

Graham scrambles out of the pit, calling after us. 'We must see the judgement stairs!' he cries, puffing from the exertion. Not wanting to disappoint McHangry, we walk up to the ancient hill, hidden deep inside the quiet forest. There, covered in moss, broken and forgotten, are a set of uneven steps leading up to the ancient mound. Once the site of an ancient hill fort or 'Dun', it was where the clan chief would sit and give out ruling and justice to each prisoner or protestor.

I walk slowly up the very same steps that many men and women had climbed before, possibly their last steps, before being sent to the aforementioned pit. As Graham nears the top of ten short but heavy steps, he gasps for air. 'You're nimbler than I am!' We both stop. The ghosts of those before us, their lives condemned, fill the heavy air, sucking out the oxygen. Even Duncan, hidden in the bushes, holds his breath. 'Imagine,' Graham says, 'those steps could be your last and you're off to the pit . . . but thankfully, we're off to the pub!' Apologising to the spirits watching us (as well as Duncan), we race down the steps, looking for soup and sandwiches.

***

After a quick pit stop we are back on our way to Rob Roy's grave at Balquhidder. I should be looking forward to it but I have a sinking feeling knowing we are facing a possible 'argy' on arrival between our two guides: Donald MacLaren, chief of the MacLarens and Peter Lawrie, Vice-chairman of the Clan Gregor Society. Arch-enemies, or at least not known to see eye to eye, Michelle and I had decided to keep them apart, agreeing to meet Donald MacLaren at Balquhidder kirk and Peter at the site of the Puterach Stone – the plan being to avoid any arguments or uncomfortable stand-offs.

What's the saying about best-laid plans . . . ? But first a little back-story: I first met Sir Malcom MacGregor, 24th chief of Clan Gregor, when I received my (second) honorary doctorate in Dumfries, part of the Glasgow University campus, one of the oldest universities in the world. [Graham: *Was this the same day Ronald McDonald got his honorary degree for services to world cuisine?*] The main reason I accepted this great (unworked-for) honour was I knew it'd piss off McTavish twice as much. [Graham: *I stupidly chose to get my degree on merit.*]

Chief MacGregor was whispering to me during the Dumfries ceremony about the fascinating history of the MacGregor clan and notorious outlaw and folk hero Rob Roy MacGregor. What really struck me, whilst waiting to receive my scroll and initiation into the cloisters of the University, was that the MacGregor clan were actually *all* outlawed. Named 'Children of the Mist', for nearly two centuries the clan members were persecuted. Male members were not allowed to use their surname, own property or even possess a wife. Women could be branded and their children given away. Stripped bare, whipped and possibly sold into slavery, their heads could be sold to the government to attain pardon for various misdemeanours. A currency, so to speak. The site of a mass execution of MacGregors in Edinburgh at the St Giles Kirk still holds the Heart of Midlothian, a mosaic that it is still customary to spit on as you pass, much to the bemusement of passing tourists. They had no land and were practically living ghosts. I knew we had to have the chief in the show and discuss the notoriety of their most famous member, however, sadly, Malcolm MacGregor wasn't available so we were offered the services of highly knowledgeable Clan Vice-chairman Peter Lawrie. And, as if by sheer luck, the Clan Chief MacLaren was also available and agreed to join us too . . . !

And then we received the following emails:

Hi Michelle

One other thing. Sir Malcolm's message to me that you would have 'a second clan chief'.

Not Donald MacLaren by any chance?

If so, may I mention in advance that Donald MacLaren is upset by the hordes of tourists who visit Balquhidder to visit Rob Roy's grave. As a result he has put it about that Rob Roy is not buried at Balquhidder but over at Glengyle. He has personally produced and erected information boards at the entrance to the kirk proclaiming this.

Yours, Peter Lawrie (Clan MacGregor)

Follow-up email from Peter:

I'm just letting you know what Donald MacLaren's (incorrect) view is concerning the location of Rob Roy's burial and his long-standing complaints about hordes of tourists visiting Balquhidder being only interested in Rob Roy.

We were clearly going to get ourselves into some hot water. TV GOLD!

On 18th September 2019, at 16:17, Graham McTavish wrote:

But MacLaren doesn't believe it is the grave, correct?

Sam Heughan replied:

Correct. According to Peter. Controversy is good.

On 20th September 2019, at 20:08, Graham McTavish wrote:

You're very naughty.

We arrived at the Parish to set up and Donald MacLaren was already there, dressed in his finery, flask of whisky and mini dram cups hidden in his sporran. Soon Peter Lawrie arrives, also early and not at the kirk and, before we have even reached the grave, they are arguing! Respectfully and always maintaining a thin veneer of cordiality, but with passionate steadfast beliefs as to whether this was or was not the burial place of Rob Roy MacGregor. We walk through the chapel to the foundations of the 'little chapel' and circle around the grave in question. Donald MacLaren measures out a dram of his (personal labelled) MacLaren whisky, handing us all a dram. Peter's is definitely the smallest! We take a sip, Peter grimacing and trying not to swallow. Graham and I stand awkwardly as Donald begins to list the reasons as to why he believes this is the outlaw's place of rest. It's Peter's turn and he debunks Donald's theories, stating why the grave could not possibly be Rob Roy's. The day is fading, the arguments are wearing, the whisky is muddling and the days on the road are beginning to take their toll.

The gentlemen eventually agreed to disagree. Trying to appease the clan chiefs and find a diplomatic exit from the eternal debate, I started to plan a way of separating the gentlemen and finishing our day on a high. 'Let's film the last sequence at the Puterach Lifting Stone,' I say. 'And then you're welcome to join us for some food in the barn, down the road.' Expecting the men to politely decline, not wanting to spend a minute longer in each other's company, they look at each other for a beat, and agree to come in unison. What? That was not the outcome I was expecting! Clearly the historic argument can be put aside for soup and a sandwich.

Graham: And a bottle of fine wine!

GRAHAM

In the MacGregor corner is Peter, a *very* passionate representative of Rob Roy and his grave, and in the MacLaren corner is the very droll Donald who vehemently disputes the location of Rob Roy's remains. The graveyard at Balquhidder is picture-postcard beautiful: ruined church at the end of a picturesque glen. Placed before the entrance to the church is the grave of Rob Roy MacGregor, his wife, Helen Mary, and their sons, Coll and Rob. It has a guard rail around it and the words 'MacGregor despite them' engraved upon it. The 'despite them' could have referred to Mr MacLaren standing next to me. He definitely thinks the grave is a complete fraud, and that Mr MacGregor is buried somewhere else entirely.

What follows is a compelling discussion/polite argument between the two men over the location of the body. I need to set the scene. The MacGregor is dressed in a wonderfully eccentric Highland outfit – a lot of yellow, a kilt well above the knees, and a bonnet placed jauntily on his head. He also has magnificent facial hair and sounds like he's a member of the Mancunian band Oasis, which is very surprising!

Donald MacLaren is equally resplendent in full Highland

chieftain kit, right down to the eagle feather in his bonnet. He offers Sam and me whisky immediately from his flask, which makes me like him straight away. He also speaks with an English accent but a very posh one, as if he's just stepped out of Eton, which, indeed, he probably has done. They then proceed to argue the case for the prosecution and defence concerning where Rob Roy had ended up. MacLaren argues that when Rob Roy died his so-called resting place was on MacLaren ground and it's highly unlikely Rob Roy, enemy of the MacLarens and notorious cattle-thieving bandit, would have been allowed to be buried here at Balquhidder kirk. It's compelling stuff but I need to give you the lowdown on who exactly this Highland character was:

He was a tall man, Rob, but his height was, apparently, dwarfed by the enormous width of his shoulders. Some even said he looked deformed, so wide and massive was his torso, so barrel-like his chest above comparatively slender hips and very slightly bowed legs. This frankly disturbing physical appearance was only increased by the extraordinary length of his arms. Arms so long he could tie the garters of his Highland hose without stooping. (That's something even Jamie Fraser can't do.)

So basically Rob Roy resembled an African silverback gorilla dressed in tartan.

He was a prodigious cattle thief, or 'reiver' as they were known. He offered 'protection' for cattle and sheep passing through the territory of the Glengyle Highland Watch (just another name for the MacGregor clan). If you didn't pay, well, the cattle or sheep mysteriously failed to make it to their destination. John Menzies of Shian (no doubt related to the present-day booksellers) was once unwise enough to call Rob Roy 'Sheep Robbie'. Word got back to Rob and that very night Shian's entire herd disappeared. Sometimes as many as 350 head of cattle would disappear.

Rob kept his politics and religion under his bonnet. He was a Jacobite and probably a Catholic but the MacGregors had already learned the hard way about being on the losing side of things. Most of their lands had been taken from them, notably by Clan Campbell (no doubt good old Duncan of the Seven Castles was busy with this). Much of this appropriation was done through legal

manoeuvres rather than with steel. The Campbells had long understood the power of paper to prove ownership, rather than relying
on the sword. (In fact most legal charters were written on sheepskin
back in the day, which makes it ironic that the notorious sheep-
rustling clan should lose so much because of what was scratched on
the skin of such an animal.)

Lord Murray (the Secretary of State) took a particular dislike to
our orangutan-like Highlander. He sent men to arrest him but Rob,
knowing the country better than his dragoon escort, succeeded in
escaping – feigning exhaustion, he hung his head low, the picture of
a defeated prisoner, bouncing around in the saddle like Duncan
Lacroix, only to spring into life, catching hold of a passing tree using
his ape-like arms and pulling himself to safety before the dragoons
could do anything about it.

A few years later, Murray and Rob buried the proverbial hatchet
and even co-signed a document promising to be friends. What
caused this volte-face is not known; however it's interesting to note
that one of the witnesses to the signing in 1695 was none other than
the Old Fox himself, Simon Fraser Lord Lovat! Along with Alexander
MacDonnell of Glengarry and Alexander (brother of MacIain) of
Glencoe. The clans of the latter two men came out for the Bonnie
Prince, as did Lovat. It is highly likely that Murray (whose own son
went on to be Charlie's chief military adviser) was a secret Jacobite.
Rob, knowing this, and also knowing how to blackmail people
(having pretty much invented it single-handedly), used this knowledge to his advantage.

Hence the agreement.

Rob might have been a gorilla masquerading as a man, but he
was a canny gorilla. He was also a legendary swordsman, so much
so that MacNeil of Barra, no slouch with the sword, left his tiny
Hebridean home to travel to Loch Lomond, to Killearn Market to
challenge him to a duel in a pub, thereby fulfilling every Scotsman's
birthright of a free pint followed by a punch-up. MacNeil was no
match for Rob and his prodigious reach. MacNeil stayed a few
weeks convalescing from his injuries before returning to Barra with
his kilt tucked firmly between his legs.

Rob never made it to the second Jacobite rebellion – he died the year before – but he did find himself involved in the 1715 Rising. Controversy surrounds his involvement; some (including Sir Walter Scott) say he deliberately avoided the battle of Sheriffmuir in November 1715. However, it looks like Rob was ordered to wait at Flanders Moss for reinforcements and then cross the treacherous Forth to attack the government troops in the rear. The area near Stirling was Gregorach territory for hundreds of years and they knew every inch of the dangerous land. Stirling was a strategic crossing point to the Highlands, as Robert the Bruce proved at Bannockburn when he led Edward's army into the marshes. Rob expected a group of Highlanders to join his 250 MacGregors. None came. Meanwhile, the Jacobite forces elected to go ahead without him. When our redheaded friend heard, he marched his men to the battle, but by then he was too late. Some have accused Rob of treachery but it looks more like incompetence on the part of the Jacobite leadership, something that was to be repeated in 1746.

Rob's death, as with so much of his life, is shrouded in mystery. He is said to have died in his bed (not something a lot of Highland warriors could claim). Some, like our MacGregor friend at Balquhidder, say he was wounded in a duel and, as he lay dying, he sent for a priest to take his confession. The priest insisted he recount his sins and also forgive his enemies. Rob did but with the exception of John MacLaren. The priest insisted that MacLaren must also be forgiven. Panting, Rob said, 'I forgive my enemies, especially John MacLaren.' But then whispered a few indiscernible words to his son nearby. Rob then called for his piper to play, 'I Return No More' and died before the dirge was finished.

A few months later Rob's son, Robin Og MacGregor, calmly walked up to John MacLaren in his field and shot him dead while he ploughed the land MacLaren had stolen from his father.

Dougal MacKenzie would have approved.

SAM

A huge fan of weightlifting and watching strongman competitions, I've learnt about the numerous ancient stones around Scotland used for centuries as an initiation for young clansmen to become men or as a way to train them to be fearsome warriors. Not only a Scottish sport, stones can be found in Iceland, the Basque country and even as far as Japan. The ancient skill is still seen in 'Atlas Stone' lifting during strongman competitions. There are many stones still located around Scotland, but most have been lost, used in local masonry and construction. The Dinnie stones, named after a man who carried them both across a bridge in Aberdeen, weigh around 332.49kg, or 733lbs, an incredible weight.

However, I know that the Puterach Lifting Stone is supposed to be around 100kg, which is basically the weight of Mr McTavish after one of his extraordinary culinary feasts! The Puterach, older than the country of Scotland itself, stands defiantly in front of us. Traces of chalk from previous lifts colour its smooth surface. We have no chalk and Graham's hipster jeans are too tight (and too young!) for him, or that's his excuse. He pretends to try to lift it, but his new favourite hat nearly falls off so he bows out.

So now it's my turn and the pressure is on. I don't want to disappoint Peter, who has generously driven 200 miles to meet us. I reach down and try to get a grip. Wearing my kilt for extra flexibility – strongmen swear by it – I ease myself into a squat and hope I'll be able to stand up again. My heart's racing from lack of sleep, caffeine and the lunchtime libation. The stone rocks and I move it a few inches off the ground. 'He's lifted it!' Peter cries, claiming a victory.

Conjuring up the ancient warriors of old and hoping to prove my manhood, or at least break my back in doing so, the cuffs on my jacket help me get more grip on the stone's featureless surface. Remembering my *Outlander* personal trainer's advice, I thrust my heels into the ground, using my legs to lift and hoist the stone onto my knees. And up it goes! But I can't get it up any further and with one last shove I place it on the ancient plinth and step back, fighting hard not to pass out. Graham looks surprised and suspicious. Similar to his stone-lifting at the campsite, I think he thought it was a fake stone from the *Outlander* set. Peter cheers and Donald looks on from the gateway clapping. (We'd had to separate the experts again!)

GRAHAM

We basically go through someone's garden to lift the stone. I expect the owner to appear any moment screaming, 'There's another one here for that fucking rock!' But no one emerges. The stone is perched on top of an ancient stone plinth. This particular rock is a recent replacement. The original had dated back hundreds of years but some bitter Presbyterian type had decided that it was some kind of pagan ritual so had it removed to God only knows where.

Who was going to lift the stone? We push the rock off the plinth. I bend down to put my hands around it and realise very quickly that all that lies in my future if I try lifting it is a double hernia, and possibly some kind of rectal prolapse. I demur.

This serves only to inflame Heughan's desire to lift it even more and it also helps that after Episode Sixteen of Season One, he is no stranger to rectal prolapse.

He squats in his kilt and grips the rock and I watch him heave and grimace. I find myself idly wondering what would happen if he either a) slips a disc, b) drops it on his foot or c) both.

He can't lift it and I'm ashamed to say I'm pathetically pleased by this, but Sam catches a glimpse of my smug face and decides to try again. More heaving and straining, like Lacroix on the toilet the morning after, this time Heughan has got hold of it! He rolls it into his lap and slowly uses his legs to push himself upright. Yes! The bastard is standing up! Carrying a 200lb rock. He staggers to the plinth and rolls it on to the top.

He's done it! And I find myself genuinely delighted, cheering and slapping his back. I feel strangely proud. My boy! Peter the expert looks on admiringly and the crew are in raptures.

SAM

Graham is in excellent spirits so I decide to pounce. 'So how's about the motorbike ride, big man? You'll be in the sidecar, down a private road, nothing silly, get the footage, then have dinner at the award-winning restaurant at Monachyle Mhor and back to your hotel suite.'

I knew top-notch nosh in the bargain was the only way I could seal the deal.

Graham: Okay. All right. I'll do it. [PAUSE] And you do actually know how to ride a motorbike?

Sam: Been riding them for years.

Except I hadn't. I'd only *just* learnt to ride a motorbike and a sidecar was going to be a challenge . . . Not that I was going to tell Graham any of that. We'd found the classic motorbike on eBay, 'Needs some work' read the advertisement, but for a decent price and a handshake we got to borrow the bike for the evening. We had planned to take the bike for a spin along the banks of Loch Voil, the drone capturing the setting sun on our last day of shooting. With the prospect of fine wine and haute cuisine edging ever closer, Graham threw on his 1940s goggles and helmet, and then it started to rain.

GRAHAM

There's an expression in film-making called 'losing the light'. It's when you need that one more shot of the day, the sun is falling fast, everyone is scrambling to get it done. I remember on *Rambo* I had to do a sequence during the climactic battle where I had to tourniquet my own leg, roll down a hill, headbutt a soldier to death, take his AK-47, climb a hill with explosions and bullets going off around me, get behind a tree stump and start killing 'bad guys'. All in one take. I rehearsed it in my head. And then I heard the dreaded words, 'We're losing the light, we've only got time for one take.'

In my shocked silence that greeted this announcement I heard Stallone's voice booming from the video village, 'Hey, Graham?'

'Yes, Sly,' said I, thinking I was about to get invaluable advice from one of the great action stars of recent years.

'Don't fuck it up!'

'Action.'

If my trousers weren't brown already, they were now.

So when Michelle Methven said we were losing the light on our final day, I knew we didn't have long at all. Especially as the next day I was due to be picked up at 7am from the hotel to start a new job. This was going to be our only chance. The problem was, it involved Sam driving a motorbike and sidecar with me as the passenger.

We had arrived back at our lovely hotel, the Monachyle Mhor near Balquhidder, famed for its cuisine. My stomach was already rumbling. It already seemed to be getting dark when we arrived but this was not going to be a deterrent. I fantasised about carrying my bags to my room and relaxing with a pre-dinner drink. Perhaps watching the sun going down over the mountains. Enjoying the smell of a wood fire in the bar.

But no.

There it was.

A machine that looked like it had last seen action at D-Day.

Standing next to it was a huge bearded Ginger Glaswegian called 'Big Tam'.

'I don't think we have time for this, mate,' I said to Sam.

'It'll look so great, buddy, the road is completely deserted. We'll just do a couple of runs by the side of the loch with the camera car in front. Fifteen minutes tops,' he grinned.

Perhaps I had forgotten the last week. Perhaps I was drunk. Or perhaps I had actually grown to trust Sam. Actually I had. Even though he likes a laugh, he is not *actually* insane. In fact, I had grown close to him through all this, and realised what a capable and gener-ous guy he was.

So I nodded, and smiled.

'Sure,' I said, 'sounds good.'

Looking back, this is akin to a man nodding at the hangman as he slips a noose around his neck and saying, 'It's a lot more comfy than I expected it to be.'

SAM

Graham is moaning and grumbling about getting cold and wet so a waterproof poncho is produced which keeps him happy for a few minutes. We have a quick run-through of the controls – I'd never used a kick-start motor but then all bikes are basically the same. I jump on and start to rev her up. McTavish is cursing like a bawdy wench as he tries to fold himself into the sidecar. I hope he can unfold later!

'Oh, one thing you should probably ken,' says Big Tam smiling maniacally. 'Make sure ya keep it above 30mph, or it'll cut oot. An' good luck!' he says jumping on the kick-start a few times, smashing his ankle as his foot slips off the pedal.

Finally the bike coughs into gear, sounding like it's stuck in the 1940s.

'Go!' I yell above the noise, the other hotel guests probably cursing us for destroying their tranquil evening. The two clan experts (yup, they're still here!) wave us off.

GRAHAM

Much of what I will describe of this last sequence of shooting is a little blurry but there are several things that stand out. I don't really remember how it was decided that I should be in the sidecar and that Sam would drive the motorbike. I assumed it was because I'd never driven a motorbike and sidecar before. It would, therefore, be sensible to have the guy with experience doing the driving. It was, however, only when I was crammed in the sidecar that it turned out Sam had zero experience as well. Like me, he had seen war movies with motorbikes and sidecars: *The Great Escape, Where Eagles Dare,* but watching a movie as a teenager of someone else driving one of these things and actually driving it yourself is *very* different! As I was about to find out.

But first, the all-important costume change. The articulated lorry full of Sam's clothes arrived and Sam eventually decided upon a tight-fitting leather jacket, and a pair of impressive gauntlets. I was so low down in the sidecar it was difficult for me to see any other changes in his person. He might have been wearing arse-less chaps, and a pair of slingbacks for all I know. My costume change comprised a waterproof poncho. Same outfit. Just covered by a giant cape.

Getting into the sidecar was an interesting experience. A little like watching an illusionist being crammed into a trunk from which it seemed impossible to escape. It was a teeny bit of a tight fit. Once in, there was no getting out in a hurry.

It was from this position, a be-caped cork in a metal coffin, that I watched Sam being taught how to drive a motorbike and sidecar. Big Tam climbed aboard and demonstrated how to start the bike. It was not an electronic ignition (this being, as I said, a relic from

Dad's Army), it was an old-fashioned kick-start. The big bearded Glaswegian laboured away, once, twice, three times.

Eventually he gunned the beast into life. He showed Sam the clutch, the throttle (how apt a word this became) and the brakes. Fortunately, Sam could already grasp where to sit, otherwise we would still be there now. I think I was actually too shocked to speak. But this is what was going through my head: 'I'm in a sidecar driven by a man who has never been on one of these things before in his life. The bike itself is probably held together with duct tape, and I'm wearing a cape.'

It was then that Big Tam mentioned the petrol. 'Ah, yes. Youse wanna watch oot. The tank is leaking. That's what the smell is. But it shouldn'ae be a problem. It might stall going uphill so keep the throttle open.'

Everyone nodded, as if this was the most natural thing in the world. 'Here is your hire car, sir. We've checked it over. Apart from the leaking petrol tank and a tendency to stall going up any gradient bigger than an ant hill, it's in perfect condition. Please return it with a full tank. Bye!'

I looked on aghast. Surely we would abandon this folly?

'Isn't that a little dangerous?' I ventured.

'Naw. She's fine. Just give it plenty of gas on the hills. Full tank. Nae problem.'

'We're losing the light!' shouted Michelle.

Sam climbed aboard. Pounded on the starter pedal. The engine caught. He disengaged the clutch and . . . we stalled. Everyone laughed heartily. Everyone except me. I began composing my will. Big Tam stepped forward and got it going again.

Clutch, throttle, and we were off. Juddering forward like Duncan Lacroix on a Friday night. We drove around the car park. We turned around to come back. And stalled.

Big Tam jogged over, amiable as ever. I asked for a set of worry beads and a copy of the Bible.

'We've got to get a move on, people!' bellowed Michelle. The camera crew drove past into position. Big Tam smashed down on the starter pedal, once, twice, three times. Sam got aboard. The Lord's Prayer suddenly seemed a good option. Off we went.

'This is great!' shouted Sam as he wrestled with the handlebars.

'The weight pulls us to the left, though,' I howled. The 'weight' being me in the sidecar, and the 'left' being the loch that was flashing by next to me.

We began to gently fight against gravity, as we encountered the smallest of hills, and the bike sputtered and died. The car disappeared.

SAM

'Go faster!' I scream at the camera car in front crawling along. I need to go much quicker to keep this bike alive. As I pull on the throttle the bike stays alive, straining to be let go, as it veers to one side. I'm fighting to keep it straight but let the bike go faster, the rush of the cold air on my exposed face. 'So fun!' I shout, my words lost on my co-star sitting in his baby carriage, his hat, goggles and blanket covering him from view.

We race into the falling dusk up a country lane. Peering back over the loch into the increasing gloom, I can just make out the hotel, and further west, Balquhidder, the graveyard now silent. The bike gives up and decides it wants to nap by the side of the road. I come to a standstill. Warm petrol is pouring out the side of the bike onto the tarmac.

GRAHAM

I produced the walkie-talkie from inside the sidecar and spoke to the crew. 'We've stalled again.'

'We're losing the light!' said Michelle. Tam raced from the hotel.

He turned the bike around and, still with me crammed into the sidecar, rolled the bike downhill and attempted a jump-start. Once, twice, three times. Yes! It worked.

Back on level ground, Sam jogged over and climbed aboard. I think I may have had a mixed expression of surprise, hysteria, and a rictus grin. Off we went again. Sam gave it some welly, and we got up the 'hill'. We had now travelled at least 100 yards.

We slewed around the bends. As we picked up speed I actually allowed myself a moment of enjoyment. We hadn't crashed. Sam was getting the hang of this. Whisky was only minutes away. Then we stalled again.

Big Tam to the rescue. Back downhill. Jump-start. One, two, three. Sam is back on board. Off we go again. The light is fading. Soon there will be not enough light for the camera. Here comes a hill. Sam hits the throttle hard. I am willing it forwards, rocking like a mental patient.

Stalled.

SAM

'Probably best to call it a day,' my sensible producer's voice echoes out over the loch. 'We need to get it started again, though, so we can get back to base,' I say. Big Tam comes running up and I jump off to let him get a good kick at the temperamental motorbike. He kicks and kicks but the bike refuses to start. They start to roll forward, the gradient giving them momentum. *Maybe a jump start,* I think and turn to get in the camera van.

GRAHAM

This was a bigger hill in fairness. Reasonably steep. This is when several things happened in quick succession. Merlin, our sound man, jogs over to adjust my microphone. To do this he has to reach under my voluminous cape. He makes the adjustment and rushes away. Tam climbs aboard and starts to roll the bike down the hill. He hammers down on the starter pedal.

Nothing. We are picking up speed. Again he tries to jump start. Nothing.

Third time lucky?

No. It fails again. Perhaps we'd run out of petrol from the leaking tank. He prepares to try for the fourth time. The machine is rolling downhill nicely.

It was at this moment that I realised that my cape had not been put back inside the sidecar. It was flapping . . . outside. Just as my amygdala registered this, the flapping cape wound itself around the spinning wheel of the sidecar. In a fraction of a second the axle gathered up the material like a hungry monster. Then physics took over. One end of the cape was attached to a spinning axle and the other end attached to my neck! It was then that the word 'throttle' took on a whole new meaning.

Tam was poised to power down with his foot to start the engine.

My head was whipped so hard left towards the axle that I saw stars. It happened so quickly I couldn't understand what was happening.

In these moments the world truly does slow down. I remember shouting 'STOP! STOP! STOP!' as my head was being dragged towards the axle at speed.

Tam stopped, foot poised.

I was half out of the sidecar as if I was trying to kiss the offside wheel.

As Tam so succinctly put it moments later, 'That could've been quite nasty.'

Sam raced over. The camera car stopped. If Tam had got the engine started on that fourth attempt . . . ?

You may know the story of Isadora Duncan, the famous dancer and choreographer, who died when the enormous red silk scarf she was wearing in an open-top sports car got entangled in the rear wheel. She was pulled from the car, dying instantly. The word is, it pulled her head off.

SAM

I run up to my old friend, who is doubled over, his head perilously close to the front wheel, the poncho secured around his neck *and* now the axle. The crumpled mass of clothes isn't moving.

'Graham?' I shout, 'Graham! Are you all right?!'

Nothing.

The crew are on the scene and Big Tam is struggling to hold the bike upright.

Graham?!

He once saved my life from a runaway lighting rig on the set of *Outlander* and now I'd taken his (or at least dented it). Stay with me . . .

Suddenly, from the depths of the ditch *[Graham: what ditch?!]* and beneath a layer of wax rain gear came a familiar bellowing voice.

'Bloody hell, I could have died!'

Sam: He's alive!

GRAHAM

For all our joking and mock theatrics around danger and the teasing and the banter, when I look at Sam he is genuinely shocked at what has just happened. Or nearly happened. In that moment he showed me who he really is: a true friend.

'Are you okay to do one more, without the cape?' asks Michelle. 'We're losing the light.'

Sam: No, let's call it a day. It's a wrap, people!

SAM

The Grey Dog is okay, more than okay, just his pride and ego damaged. I breathe a sigh of relief and realise I'm really quite attached to the old git; he's a great friend and there's no one I'd rather share these incredible tales with.

It's going to cost me a lot in hotel bills, however.

GRAHAM

Back at the impromptu 'wrap' party (and it really could have been a 'wake' for me), the MacLaren chief wanders over; he's just learnt what just happened and wants to know if I'm okay. It's such a lovely spontaneous gesture from someone who barely knows me, I nearly weep.

SAM

Back at the hotel bar, the clan chiefs are sitting amicably together sharing Graham's bottle of expensive French wine and the crew begin to attack their supper of artisan sandwiches. I pour us all a dram and raise a toast one last time, 'To you all for your hard work, commitment and faith in us, we didn't know if we would be able to do it.' Everyone smiles, exhausted and glad of the warmth and strong liquor. 'And to good friends,' Graham says, through a mouthful of salmon tartare and dill, raising a glass of Montrachet. Even though he was nearly throttled, morale has soared with fine food and wine.

'To good friends,' I reply. We share a smile and a sigh of relief.

We had done it and Graham had lived!

I suggest a little music and song to lighten the mood and celebrate our journey. And, by chance, I have just the perfect ditty.

Ahem. Cue strangled cat impression . . .

> *Oh! Mactavish is dead*
> *And his brother don't know it.*
> *His brother is dead*
> *And Mactavish don't know it.*
>
> *They're both of them dead*
> *And they're in the same bed,*
> *And neither one knows*
> *That the other is dead!*
> **(Song by M. Ryan Taylor)**

CHAPTER FIFTEEN

The Journey Ahead

*Try and be nice to people, avoid eating fat, read a good book every
now and then, get some walking in, and try and live together in
peace and harmony with people of all creeds and nations.*
Monty Python's *The Meaning of Life*

GRAHAM

As we finally take time to reflect upon the incredible trip across
our homeland, what comes to the fore is that this mighty people,
the Highlanders, with their rich and complex tribal culture of
warfare, unforgiving landscape, stories, superstitions, whisky and
song, are the real Outlanders (outsiders) in a changing world. A
warrior people who had resisted Roman rule, Viking rule and, for
many centuries, British rule, refusing to be conquered and vanquished.

There's no denying that it's something that resonates with many
people today. We all respond to the notion of 'the underdog', the

put-upon, the oppressed and marginalised. In our globalised society we all secretly celebrate the struggle against cultural homogenisation, while appreciating the cultural traditions of individual societies. The resurgence of Gaelic in Scotland is just one reason for that celebration.

However, I am as guilty as the most ardent *Outlander* fan of romanticising Highland life. Very few people were, in fact, warriors, most scratching out a living with a stick, dealing with high rates of infant mortality, and a pre-industrialised society. The Highlands before 1746 were, in many ways, a society frozen in time, with more in common with the Middle Ages than with the Age of Enlightenment. But I believe a Highlander travelling through the stones today would be shocked. He would see a weakening in our society, both individually and collectively (this is after all a culture that despised a man for making a pillow from ice). The clan system had many faults but older members of the community were respected, honour was a real thing, as was personal responsibility. The clan chiefs *did* lead their men into the mouths of those cannon at Culloden. This is not something I can imagine any leader doing now. They also understood history. Oral history, but history nonetheless. They revered their past and used it to educate and inspire themselves. In many ways, despite high levels of illiteracy, they were more 'educated' than we are today. They knew their world intimately and understood the value of what was before their eyes, without the need to covet other lands – except of course the Campbells! Indeed the Campbells represented the new Scotland, the outward-looking country, a land of commerce and of the 'law' – two areas Scotland has always excelled in. If they represented one direction for Scotland, Jacobitism represented another. Who is to say which is better? Sadly we will never know.

SAM

The Highlanders had a simpler way of life but it was packed with jeopardy around every corner. I'd love to know the life expectancy . . . *[Graham: Allow me, it was approximately thirty-five years of age for a male in the 1700s.]* They were hardy men and women, coming from huge families that worked hard just to survive every brutal winter, every impending famine, every battle with another clan usually over the scarcity of resources in an unforgiving landscape. By contrast we are *far* more comfortable now, especially in the developed world where we turn on a tap for water, have heating, fridges, washing machines, cars . . . But in gaining all of the technology have we disconnected ourselves from the natural world and thereby lost our understanding of it? In spite of all our gadgets, medicine and amazing scientific advancement, many of us have no real sense of dualchas (of belonging to a landscape) and seem farther away from feeling part of the world in which we live. The trees and animals are *of* the world but somehow we are not. *[Graham: Hence our ever-increasing existential angst?]*

Even to this day we see nations internally divided by extreme politics, which leads to clashes just as it did in the Highlands, but would I like to go back in time and live during the Jacobite Uprising instead? Hell no. However, I live in hope we can make amends with each other and start to treat our planet with respect, learning from our forefathers who worked with nature, not at odds with it.

Graham has a good understanding of history and his ancestry but it's only whilst producing this book that I've begun to dig into my own and ask questions I felt I couldn't before. It's led me to discover my own extensive family tree, having always believed I'd come from a small family. Being confronted with the past has brought up some complex emotions and questions, but ones that I know will be rewarding in years to come. And I'm intrigued to see what else I will find as I delve into my own family history.

As actors we are always searching inside ourselves or within others for inspiration and this journey has given me so much material to help me understand the renowned characters of Highland history (and the many forgotten ones), putting flesh on their bones and allowing me to share their stories all over again alongside my follically challenged friend.

During the process of creating *Men in Kilts*, I've learnt a lot about myself as an actor, producer and hopefully as a friend. I tend to race ahead with projects, head down and charging at work like my determined star sign, Taurus the Bull. And I am not very good at sharing responsibility, relying on myself too much. I have always operated at breakneck speed and have multiple projects on the go, which is something to do with the feast and famine of the acting life. You have to 'make hay while the sun shines' because opportunities may not present themselves again. But what I've learnt – particularly from Graham – is that I need to slow down (slightly) to consider the finer details at times. There were several details I overlooked whilst making the initial production, which I just didn't have time to notice.

Before the COVID-19 pandemic, I was exhausted and yet I couldn't stop. At the beginning of the year, despite finishing filming, I had a three-month illness, nothing more than a bad chest infection (COVID?) and yet couldn't or wouldn't find the time to stop. I've been forced to slow down a little. Graham has taught me it's okay to sit in fourth gear (if you can find it) and enjoy the scenery. The journey up the mountain by chairlift can be equally rewarding as the one hurtling down it.

GRAHAM

Actually even third gear is fine. Sometimes even parked up in a layby for a nap. I've always prided myself on my energy and ambition, and eagerness to take on new challenges, but Sam takes it to a new level. I'm hugely admiring of his entrepreneurship (even if I mercilessly take the pish). It really is inspiring and does him enormous credit. He's also a champion of Scotland, and of its crafts and textiles, and he definitely puts his money where his mouth is. I knew from the moment I met Sam in that sauna-like audition in Soho that this was a guy I would get on with.

Something else I admire Sam for is his sense of decency and his privacy. In an age where people are too willing to splurge every iota of their lives for 'all the world to see', Sam has a healthy sense of holding back on that. He is admirably protective of his family, which speaks of a deep love and respect.

SAM

During lockdown I've had the time to dedicate myself to the finer pursuits of life, as enjoyed by Lady McTavish – writing, sleeping and drinking fine wine. And I have also been talking to friends and family far more, yet another benefit of this strange situation. I've learnt that writing is something I enjoy, although a great deal of practice is needed and it must be done regularly to retain the skill. I have great respect and admiration for our wonderful co-writer Charlotte, who can not only draw on multiple narratives and sources but also juggle being a mother and even manages to deal with two demanding actors who fancy themselves as prolific novelists.

GRAHAM

I am definitely familiar with the candle burning at both ends and I was travelling *way* too much before the virus situation. It has forced me to rediscover simple joys and connections. Spending more time with my children, and of course, writing this book. Sam's right, I honestly don't know how we would have managed if we hadn't had to stay at home. We were too embedded in a lifestyle that meant we were *always* moving. Sometimes it really is good just to stand still.

I'm sure this restless energy comes, for both of us, from a deep understanding that as an actor you have to make your own opportunities. I have always relied upon myself (sometimes too much), and this experience with Sam has made me enjoy the pleasure of cooperation and shared triumphs again.

One thing is for sure though, embarking on the *Clanlands* journey together has really felt at times as though we have been standing on one side of the standing stones in *Outlander* and stepped through into the world of our ancestry. Sam and I dived in, blissfully unaware of what this would involve, which, in my experience, is the best way to have an adventure. And this was definitely an adventure; one that I will never ever forget.

Would I do it again? We've barely scratched the surface. The clans have many more stories to tell and the history of this wonderful bruised land is teeming with characters, anecdotes, tragedies, romance, and triumphs.

So bring it on! But next time, I'll drive.

CHAPTER SIXTEEN

Men in Kilts – *The TV Show*

SAM

After working on an edit of *Clanlands* we pitched the show to Sony and Starz, the day after the Los Angeles red carpet premiere of *Outlander*, Season Five, held at the Hollywood Palladium on 13th February 2020.

I threw myself into an Uber, just moments away from the Starz offices, scrabbling on my phone, frantically trying to get the photos of Graham and me into the pitch 'deck' for our formal presentation. I had lost sight of Graham the night before on the red carpet, ahead of the celebrations. I recall him wearing a snazzy suit and well-manicured beard. I was feeling elated; it felt like a strong season with many surprises, Graham's return (as another character with long dark hair!) being one of them, and he played along to the assembled press. We had to pretend he was just there for support but managed to mention the up-and-coming *Clanlands* show. We were in talks at this point with Sony and Starz and I hoped the fans would be thrilled to hear we were potentially going to be filling the Droughtlander with our buddy road trip.

That night at the after-party in a local restaurant and bar, I saw Graham and Duncan upstairs, standing next to a bemused waitress as they emptied her tray of *Outlander*-themed cocktails. I was desperate to get involved in the action and intrigued to hear how Duncan had fared on his first trip to the City of Angels. Two nights before, as an unofficial premiere party warm-up, we had met in his hotel bungalow and quickly emptied the minibar. I introduced him to some expensive tequila, which no doubt stung as he settled the final bill the day after. Each time I squeezed my way through the crowd towards the two bearded hellraisers, I would be stopped by a journalist or friendly fan. As the night wore on, the combination of jet lag, free liquor and selfie requests took their toll. I was exhausted and ready to crash, plus we had an important meeting the next morning.

Walking into the freshly painted Starz offices, I spied the surprisingly chipper Lady McTavish standing in reception. The receptionist looked flustered and asked for his ID once again. 'If you could just fill in your details on the iPad,' she asked. Graham placed his now tepid latte on the desk and leaned forward to stare her straight in the eye. 'I'm in the show and no, I don't want to give you my email address.'

GRAHAM

Complete and utter fabrication! The email bit is, however, probably true. I have never understood why people give out their email addresses at the drop of a hat. I once bought toothpaste and was asked if I'd like to put my email address in their database. 'Why would I do that?' I asked, genuinely bemused.

'Some people like to hear from us about offers, or get-togethers,' came the response.

'Do you honestly mean there are people who buy toothpaste and then give their email address in the hope of being invited to a gathering of other toothpaste buyers who are complete strangers?'

'Yes,' says the robot masquerading as a human being.

'I'll pass, thanks.' But I would *never* tell someone I was 'in the show'. I suspect this is a mantra that is repeated inside Sam's own head, and sometimes he thinks it's actually someone else speaking.

I did, however, notice that Sam was trying to flog his whisky at reception. It appears he carries around a small handcart containing bottles, complete with his own credit card machine . . .

SAM

'Graham!' I called, intervening in what could potentially be a tricky situation. I could tell the bearded technophobe was about to tell the receptionist *exactly* what he thought of their online procedure. 'I've got it, let me fill these in,' I said, hurriedly completing the check-in process for both of us. As I filled in my email for us both, the large screen behind the reception jumped into action, displaying the latest trailer for *Outlander*, and I couldn't help but smile as an aged Jamie Fraser glared back at me, from the mountains of North Carolina. In a quick exchange, Graham and I finalised the talking points and then were led upstairs to conduct our meeting.

As we walked into the third-floor offices, the far wall was covered in pictures from various Starz shows. I had now got to know many of the actors on other productions and it was nice to see our extended family up there. 'Wait, how many pictures are there of me?' Graham paused. I looked again. He was right, there were at least four pictures of him (one with his top off and strategically placed mud contouring his abs). 'Hmmm, not so many of you. Oh dear,' he whispered gleefully. *[Graham: Obviously I had called ahead and insisted that all pictures of the grinning ginger were removed.]*

I nudged him into the meeting room and we took our seats at the head of the table. I was relieved to see the deck had been uploaded into a projector, my last-minute Uber construction had worked and it now presented a large photo, both of us sitting tweed-clad and proud on our bicycles, in front of Cawdor Castle. Jeff Hirsch (the new head of Starz) strode into the room with the wonderful Karen Bailey, big smiles and no sign of a post-premiere hangover. The meeting commenced and we eagerly relayed our pitch. Graham described the journey, complete with hand gestures and dramatic sound effects. Dare I say it but we worked in great unity, symbiosis even. All that time spent in the RV in close proximity, the whisky shared and the mountains climbed, had strengthened our bond. We knew how each other worked, finishing each other's sentences and setting up jokes for the other to deliver the punchlines. Either that or we were still drunk.

We were a team, a double act, not quite father and son, more Laurel and Hardy than Butch Cassidy and the Sundance Kid. We rounded up the concept of what we thought the show could be and leaned back in unison against the plush swivel chairs. Expecting a tough negotiation and hard sell, out of the corner of my eye I caught Graham taking a breath and I crossed my fingers. We had spent a great deal of time and commitment on this project; if they didn't like it, our journey would likely end here. No more road trips, no more adventures in the Fearsome Fiat Camper.

Silence.

Karen nods and looks to the head honcho Jeff, who paused for what felt like an eternity.

'We'll take it,' he said, breaking his strong poker face.

'What, really?' I blustered. Graham almost fell back in his chair.

Karen looked surprised and followed up, 'Yes, we will. We've never done this in the room before, agreed to take something outright, but we really want it.'

GRAHAM

In the moments after Jeff made his pronouncement I suddenly felt very proud of the two of us, Sam and me. We'd taken a semi-drunken conversational idea over the phone and actually gone out and made it, and now *sold* it to a major TV network. It was very frustrating that we couldn't immediately go and get slaughtered in the nearest bar to celebrate.

SAM

Graham and I were elated, maybe more so than when we marched across Culloden battlefield in the rain with an accompanying pipe band. We had done it. Our very own TV show! We shook hands and agreed to start the process of creating the new *Clanlands* show, soon to be named *Men in Kilts*. As we hurried out of the building into the LA sunshine, now sporting our newly appointed executive producer titles, we made our way to Graham's favourite coffee shop for a celebratory latte, saving the whisky for later.

Executive Producer Graham McTavish orders at the counter whilst chatting away to the owner and another customer excitedly.

Soon the waitress follows him over to our table with several trays of milky caffeine, pastries, muffins and croissants, his grey beard quivering in anticipation.

Graham: Surely we can add this to the budget?

Some things never change.

'Lord, ye gave me a rare friend,
and God! I love the old sod well.'
Sam Heughan on behalf of Diana Gabaldon,
Dragonfly in Amber

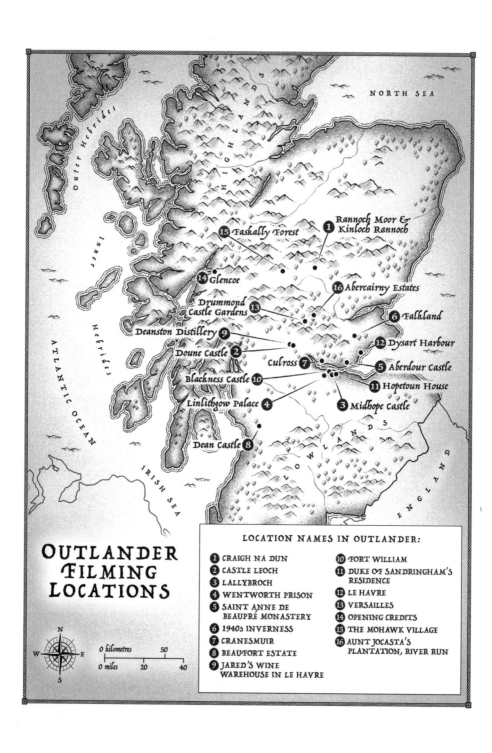

OUTLANDER FILMING LOCATIONS

NORTH SEA

HIGHLANDS

Outer Hebrides

Inner

Hebrides

ATLANTIC OCEAN

IRISH SEA

LOWLANDS

ENGLAND

① Rannoch Moor & Kinloch Rannoch
⑮ Faskally Forest
⑭ Glencoe
⑯ Abercairny Estates
Drummond Castle Gardens ⑬
⑥ Falkland
Deanston Distillery ⑨
⑫ Dysart Harbour
Doune Castle ②
Culross ⑦
⑤ Aberdour Castle
Blackness Castle ⑩
⑪ Hopetoun House
Linlithgow Palace ④
③ Midhope Castle
Dean Castle ⑧

0 kilometres   50
0 miles   20   40

LOCATION NAMES IN OUTLANDER:

① CRAIGH NA DUN
② CASTLE LEOCH
③ LALLYBROCH
④ WENTWORTH PRISON
⑤ SAINT ANNE DE BEAUPRÉ MONASTERY
⑥ 1940s INVERNESS
⑦ CRANESMUIR
⑧ BEAUFORT ESTATE
⑨ JARED'S WINE WAREHOUSE IN LE HAVRE
⑩ FORT WILLIAM
⑪ DUKE OF SANDRINGHAM'S RESIDENCE
⑫ LE HAVRE
⑬ VERSAILLES
⑭ OPENING CREDITS
⑮ THE MOHAWK VILLAGE
⑯ AUNT JOCASTA'S PLANTATION, RIVER RUN

Acknowledgements

Sam

Chrissie – who gave me every opportunity, an idyllic childhood and ensured Scotland was my home.

To my wonderful agent Ruth who has guided me through a fun, roller-coaster career, Thea and Zoe at UA plus my fantastic American team at UTA: Theresa, Mike and Chris.

Alex, my patient/inspired business partner and all at Great Glen Company/MPC who work so hard to inspire our Peakers (thank you Peakers!) and support our brilliant charity partners.

Diana Gabaldon for creating the character that has changed my life, adding her words to this book, and for being a good friend.

Viewpoint, Hodder – Briony and our passionate, dedicated, hard-working co-writer Charlie who has the same sense of humour as us!

My *Outlander* crew, co-stars and ginger friends – what a family, love you all! Caitriona, I owe you.

The MIK/Clanlands crew, our fantastic guests, Sony (cheers Chris!) and Starz (Karen, for your guidance and great cooking!) for supporting us on this journey.

And of course, my bearded – at times, reliably grumpy – travel companion McTavish.

Sláinte

Graham

In writing this book a twelve-year-old boy has seen his dream come true. I have too many people to thank, and I'm sure I will forget to include some of them. To those people I beg forgiveness.

For my parents, and family. My wonderful kids and my wonderful love, Garance Doré. For Des Margetson for insisting I be in a school play, for Nigel Alexander for making my university life so rich in experience. For my late friend, Martin Graham-Scott who always believed in me, I wish you were here mate. For Alistair MacLean and Willard Price for helping me fall in love with reading. And for my teacher Mrs Pamela Grew who always encouraged me

For Richard Baron for directing me in some of the best theatre experiences of my life.

For Andrew Hinds for giving me a chance to fly solo on stage, and for Nick Pace for travelling around the world with our play about Vincent and Theo Van Gogh.

To Duncan LaCroix, Paul Kavanagh, Claire Edwards, Emma and Andy Quinn, Jason Connery, Nolan North, TJ Ramini, Aaron Rabin, Brian Benben, Chris Egan, Mark Hayford, Tessa Souter, Garth Ennis, Dougy Rao, Michael Glenn Murphy, Brian Blessed, Gwen Isaac, Stuart Robertson, and far too many others for being there and for laughing at my jokes. And to my trainers Nicky Holender and Tee Richards who have stopped me from falling apart physically.

For, among many others, Jack Shepherd, David Winning, Robin Hardy, Sylvester Stallone, Peter Jackson, Richard Wilson, the marvellous, late, Terry Jones, and Brian Cox for taking a chance on me.

And, of course, to the wonderful Charlotte Reather, and our stellar editor, Briony Gowlett, Zoe Ross at United Agents, and Cheri Barner my manager for being the best team anyone could hope for in making this book possible. I sincerely thank each one.

For all the above, truly, this has been written thanks to your love, guidance, patience and humour.

And finally, for Sam Heughan for calling me that day, for quite simply being the best companion on this journey (if not always the best driver) and for dragging this grumpy bloke out of his comfort zone. Here's to the next time.

Picture Acknowledgments

The authors and publishers would like to thank the following copyright-holders for permission to reproduce images in this book:

Northcote Theatre; Alamy/Collection Christophel; Bridgeman images/Everett Collection; Getty Images/ David M. Benett / Contributor; Getty Images/ Mark Sagliocco / Contributor; AMCNetworks.com; Getty Images/ Jesse Grant / Stringer; Royal Lyceum Theatre, Edinburgh; Traverse Theatre/Richard Campbell; Photostage/Donald Cooper; Alamy/dpa/Britta Pedersen; Alamy/Allstar Picture Library Ltd/ Sony Pictures Television; Alamy/Lionsgate/courtesy Everett Collection/Ron Harvey; PA Archive/PAImages/ Lucy Christie; Shutterstock/Jeff Holmes; PA Archive/PAImages/ Andrew Milligan; Shutterstock/Matt Baron; Shutterstock/Kristina Bumphrey/StarPix; Shutterstock/Starz/Koba; Getty Images/Jean Baptiste Lacroix / Stringer; Shutterstock/Eric Charbonneau; Shutterstock/Sony/Columbia/Kobal

Men In Kilts photography by Peter Sandground. Men In Kilts © 2020 Sony Pictures Television Inc. All rights reserved. Artwork © Starz Entertainment, LLC. Starz and related service marks are the property of Starz Entertainment, LLC.

All other images are care of the authors' personal collections.

The authors and publishers have made all reasonable efforts to contact copyright-holders for permission and apologise for any omissions or errors in the form of credits given. Corrections may be made to future printings.

Author bios

Sam Heughan is an award-winning actor and philanthropist, best known for his starring role as Jamie Fraser in the hit TV show *Outlander*. From his early days at the Royal Court Theatre to his most recent role in the hit action film *Bloodshot*, Sam has enjoyed a career in theatre, television and film spanning almost two decades. With his growing success and fame, Sam has also lent his voice and platform to raise funds and awareness for many notable charities, including Marie Curie UK and Blood Cancer UK. In recent years he has raised over $5 million for blood cancer research, hospice care and testicular cancer awareness education. Due to his outstanding contribution to charitable endeavours and artistic success he was bestowed by the University of Glasgow and the University of Stirling with an honorary doctorate in 2019.

Graham McTavish has been acting for over 35 years in theatre, film and television. On film and TV he is best known for his roles as Dougal MacKenzie in *Outlander*, the fierce Dwarf Dwalin in *The Hobbit* trilogy, and AMC's cult show *Preacher* as the Saint of Killers. He has performed in theatre all over the world from the Royal Court Theatre in London to the Metropolitan Museum of Art in New York. He is delighted that the dream of his 12-year-old self to be a published author has finally come true!

Charlotte Reather is a *Sunday Times* No.1 bestselling co-writer, Charlotte is a leading country lifestyle journalist, humorous columnist, comedy writer and mother of two fabulous, feisty daughters.

charlottereather.com / @charlottereather

We hope you enjoyed our boys' adventures in *Clanlands*. For this and even more of their Scottish odyssey, join them for their new original series only on STARZ.

MEN IN KILTS: A ROADTRIP WITH SAM AND GRAHAM.

Don't forget your whisky of choice!

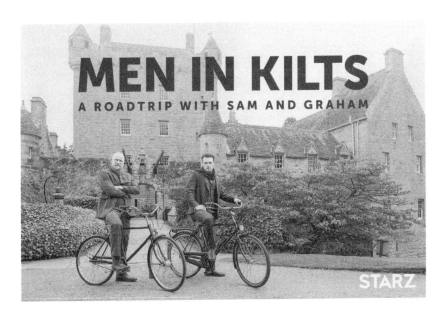

An invitation from the publisher

Join us at www.hodder.co.uk, or follow us
on Twitter @hodderbooks to be a part of
our community of people who love the very
best in books and reading.

Whether you want to discover more about a book
or an author, watch trailers and interviews, have the
chance to win early limited editions, or simply browse
our expert readers' selection of the very best books,
we think you'll find what you're looking for.

And if you don't, that's the place to tell us what's missing.

We love what we do, and we'd love you to be a part of it.

www.hodder.co.uk

@hodderbooks

HodderBooks

HodderBooks